ARMAGH

Armagh

The Irish Revolution, 1912–23

Donal Hall & Eoin Magennis

FOUR COURTS PRESS

Typeset in 10.5 pt on 12.5 pt Ehrhardt by
Carrigboy Typesetting Services for
FOUR COURTS PRESS LTD
7 Malpas Street, Dublin 8, Ireland
www.fourcourtspress.ie
and in North America for
FOUR COURTS PRESS
c/o IPG, 814 N. Franklin St, Chicago, IL 60610.

A catalogue record for this title
is available from the British Library.

ISBN 978–1–80151–080–6

Printed in England
by CPI Antony Rowe, Chippenham, Wilts.

Contents

Illustrations

Credits

1, 19, 20: private collection; 2: NLI, Lawrence Collection; 3, 4, 5, 6: Armagh County Museum (ARMCM.2.158, ARMCM.82.2012.340, ARMCM.82.2012. 483, ARMCM.82.2012.466); 7, 12, 13: Éamon Donnelly Collection, courtesy of NMD Museums (Newry and Mourne Museum Collection); 8: Jim McCorry; 9: UCD Archives; 10, 11: Horse Power: The Museum of the King's Royal Hussars; 14: PRONI Lawrence Collection; 15: Louth County Archives Service; 16: Newry and Mourne Museum; 17, 18: NLI, Hogg Collection.

Abbreviations

ACM	Armagh County Museum
AG	*Armagh Guardian*
AOH	Ancient Order of Hibernians (Board of Erin)
BMH	Bureau of Military History
BNL	*Belfast News-Letter*
CAB	Cabinet Office
Cd.	Command paper
CI	County Inspector, Royal Irish/Ulster Constabulary
CO	Colonial Office
CÓFLA	Cardinal Tomás Ó Fiaich Library and Archive, Armagh
CSB	Crime Special Branch
CSORP	Chief Secretary's Office Registered Papers
DATI	Department of Agriculture & Technical Instruction
DD	*Dundalk Democrat*
DÉ	Dáil Éireann
DI	District Inspector, Royal Irish/Ulster Constabulary
DIB	*Dictionary of Irish biography*
FJ	*Freeman's Journal*
FS	*Frontier Sentinel*
GAA	Gaelic Athletic Association
GHQ	General Headquarters
IAA	Irish American Alliance
IFS	Irish Free State
IG	Inspector General, Royal Irish/Ulster Constabulary
II	*Irish Independent*
IMA	Irish Military Archives
IN	*Irish News*
INF	Irish National Foresters
IPP	Irish Parliamentary Party
IRA	Irish Republican Army
IRB	Irish Republican Brotherhood
IT	*Irish Times*
ITGWU	Irish Transport & General Workers' Union
IWSF	Irish Women's Suffrage Federation
JP	Justice of the Peace
LGB	Local Government Board
LM	*Lurgan Mail*
LT	*Lurgan Times*

MP	Member of Parliament
MS	Manuscript
MSPC	Military Service Pensions Collection
NAI	National Archives of Ireland
ND	Northern Division of the IRA
NEBB	North-East Boundary Bureau
NLI	National Library of Ireland
NR	*Newry Reporter*
NW	*Northern Whig*
O/C	Officer Commanding
PN	*Portadown News*
PRONI	Public Record Office of Northern Ireland
PT	*Portadown Times*
RDC	Rural District Council
RIC	Royal Irish Constabulary
RIF	Royal Irish Fusiliers
RUC	Royal Ulster Constabulary
TCD	Trinity College Dublin
TD	Teachta Dála
TNA	National Archives, London
UCDA	University College Dublin Archives
UDC	Urban District Council
UG	*Ulster Gazette*
UIL	United Irish League
USC	Ulster Special Constabulary
UUC	Ulster Unionist Council
UVF	Ulster Volunteer Force
UWUC	Ulster Women's Unionist Council
WO	War Office
WS	Witness statement to Bureau of Military History

Acknowledgments

One of the aims of the *Irish Revolution* series is to bring to life the local experience of these turbulent years in different counties across the country by bringing together the rich archival material made more available in recent years with an interpretative narrative of the events of the 1912–23 period. The opportunity to produce a single volume narrative for County Armagh was welcomed by the authors but was not without its challenges. As we shall show, the organization and theatre of operation of the 4th Northern Division of the IRA, formed in early 1921 under the command of Armagh man Frank Aiken, extended into three counties – Armagh, Down and Louth. By the summer of 1922, the Division was to a large extent operating from headquarters and camps outside Armagh and inevitably became embroiled in the Civil War in the new Irish Free State. At that point the story divides – one for Louth, covered in another volume in this series, and another for Armagh. This book explores the experiences of Armagh men and women during the Civil War, alongside the violence and uncertainties that accompanied partition and the administration of a new government in Belfast.

The authors acknowledge the assistance and encouragement of Frank Aiken and Dr Rory O'Hanlon. We are indebted to the friendly and efficient staffs of many libraries and archives, including the Cardinal Tomás Ó Fiaich Memorial Library and Archive, Armagh; Armagh County Museum, Armagh; Newry & Mourne Museum, Newry; Irish Military Archives, Dublin; Kilmainham Gaol Archives, Dublin; Louth County Archive Service, Dundalk; Museum of the King's Royal Hussars, Winchester; National Archives of Ireland, Dublin; National Archives, London; National Library of Ireland, Dublin; Public Record Office of Northern Ireland, Belfast; and UCD Archives, Dublin.

The authors are indebted to the series editors Professor Mary Ann Lyons and Dr Daithí Ó Corráin. While we acknowledge the patience and skill of the editors in helping to shape this book, the contents, discussion and any errors contained herein are ours and ours alone. Our thanks also to Dr Mike Brennan for drawing the maps in this volume.

Donal Hall would like to acknowledge the continued support of Kevin Hall, Sheila O'Donoghue, Brendan McAvinue, Lorraine McCann and Jean Young. Special thanks are due to the continued inspirational friendship of Professor Terence Dooley, Maynooth University. None of this would amount to much were it not for the unstinting support of my wife Patricia in relation to whom carefully drafted words of thanks are woefully inadequate. And of course, my children Róisín, Éilís and Ciarán are a constant source of surprise and joy. The arrival of a new generation, James Lyons, Alice Lyons, Hazel Lyons,

Lily McHugh and Óisín McHugh is sobering in the realization that *their* grandchildren will commemorate the bicentenary of the events described in this book, hopefully in an Ireland at peace with itself and its past.

Eoin Magennis would like to thank the extended Magennis, Murphy and Aiken families for the generosity with which they have shared their knowledge over the years, for a project long in the making. In particular, my parents Yvonne and Feidhlimidh (RIP) have been treasure troves for the past of Newry and Armagh, and, I hope, have influenced an empathetic view towards what happened and why. Acknowledgments are also due to a fine group of local historians who I have had the pleasure of working with: Dr Allan Blackstock (RIP), Sean Barden, Joe Canning (RIP), Dr Dónal McAnallen, Dr Neil McGleenon, Kevin McMahon (RIP), Mary McVeigh, Mgr Réamonn Ó Muirí and Damian Woods. One person who has been with me every step of the way on this project, has read drafts and brought the wood out of the trees, is Dr Lesa Ní Mhunghaile, a wonderful scholar in her own right and, luckily for me, my wife. The book is for her and the next generation: Conor and Anna Clifford, and Doireann and Lily Ní Fhathaigh, the most recent arrival.

The Irish Revolution, 1912–23 series

Since the turn of the century, a growing number of scholars have been actively researching this seminal period in modern Irish history. More recently, propelled by the increasing availability of new archival material, this endeavour has intensified. This series brings together for the first time the various strands of this exciting and fresh scholarship within a nuanced interpretative framework, making available concise, accessible, scholarly studies of the Irish Revolution experience at a local level to a wide audience.

The approach adopted is both thematic and chronological, addressing the key developments and major issues that occurred at a county level during the tumultuous 1912–23 period. Beginning with an overview of the social, economic and political milieu in the county in 1912, each volume assesses the strength of the home rule movement and unionism, as well as levels of labour and feminist activism. The genesis and organization of paramilitarism from 1913 are traced; responses to the outbreak of the First World War and its impact on politics at a county level are explored; and the significance of the 1916 Rising is assessed. The varying fortunes of constitutional and separatist nationalism are examined. The local experience of the War of Independence, reaction to the truce and Anglo-Irish Treaty and the course and consequences of the Civil War are subject to detailed examination and analysis. The result is a compelling account of life in Ireland in this formative era.

Mary Ann Lyons
Department of History
Maynooth University

Daithí Ó Corráin
School of History & Geography
Dublin City University

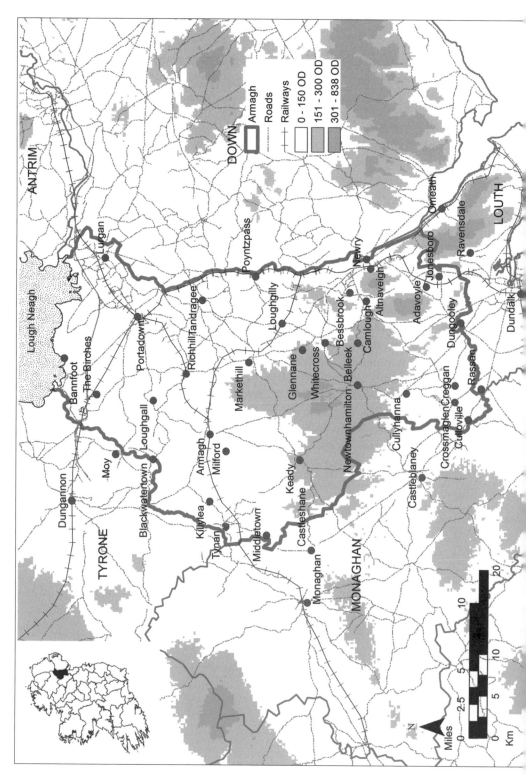

1 Places mentioned in the text

1 Armagh in 1912

Armagh is a small inland county of 327,902 statute acres, bounded to the north by Lough Neagh, to the west by Counties Tyrone and Monaghan, to the east by County Down, and to the south by County Louth (see map 1). The region which came to be delineated as County Armagh took its name from Ard Mhacha (or height of Macha, an ancient Celtic goddess) and it is significant in the Ulster Cycle, part of which centred on the massive earthworks of the still surviving Eamain Macha (Navan Fort). The religious importance associated with Eamain Macha offered the see of Armagh a basis on which to build an ecclesiastical primacy after the fifth-century arrival of Christianity.[1] By the time of the Norman invasion of 1169, the region was deep within the territory of the O'Neill kingship and into the sixteenth century the parishes of the northern part of the diocese of Armagh (modern County Armagh) were described as *inter Hibernicos*.[2] They would remain part of the Gaelic world even as the Ulster plantation divided Armagh's lands between English undertakers (dominant in the north), Scots undertakers (in the east), the Church of Ireland and Trinity College Dublin (in the west) and the Irish (in the south and more marginal lands).[3] Dispossession and possession of land, economic conflict over the emerging linen industry in all parts of the county, and deep political divisions between and within religious denominations produced regular outbursts of violence from the seventeenth century onwards. Successive communal organizations, including the Hearts of Oak, Peep of Day Boys, Defenders, and the Orange Order, all originated or drew their initial strength from Armagh in the eighteenth century. Into the next century, Ribbonism, Fenians and the Irish Republican Brotherhood (IRB) continued the tradition of nationalist secret societies. Sectarian rivalry was, by far, the more important and remarked upon division within Armagh. In 1911 Protestants comprised 39,000 members of the Church of Ireland, 18,900 Presbyterians, 5,000 Methodists and 2,700 other denominations; they had a majority over Catholics who totalled 54,500.[4]

The county of Armagh was characterized by high population density, next only to County Dublin, following the eighteenth-century arrival of the linen industry, but was also marked by population decline since the Great Famine. The population of Armagh virtually halved from 225,190 in 1841 to 117,783 in 1911, though the decline slowed from 1871, probably linked to the strength of Belfast's economy. The 1911 census recorded an overall 4.3 per cent population decline since 1901. Only Portadown and Lurgan, with their respective populations of 12,553 and 11,727, showed an increase. In the areas around the shore of Lough Neagh and in the south of the county, the population decreased by almost one-fifth.[5] A third of the county's population lived in the ten largest towns, but apart from Lurgan and Portadown, they were losing people, including Armagh city (7,356), Bessbrook (2,888), Keady (1,434) and Tandragee (1,409). The other four population centres – Crossmaglen, Markethill, Milford and Newtownhamilton – were effectively large villages, each with a population of less than 1,000.[6] With mechanization and urbanization, Lurgan became a centre for weaving (three of its firms being among the ten largest in the UK), and Portadown became important in the spinning industry.[7] Armagh city's decline had been a long one, beginning in the later eighteenth century, after which 'it lost much of the dynamism it once had had'.[8] As Alvin Jackson has pointed out, Lurgan and Portadown had 'siphoned trade and population from the middle of the county', and 'though there was no perceptible lull in political and sectarian rivalry, the Nationalists and Unionists [in Armagh city] occasionally expressed a common sense of vulnerability in the face of a northern economic threat'.[9]

As with most Irish counties, agriculture was central to society and the economy. Of those in work in 1911, 42 per cent (22,600) were employed in agriculture, either as farmers, the sons of farmers or agricultural labourers and farm servants.[10] In Armagh, approximately 275,000 acres (or 84 per cent of the total) were farmed, shared almost equally between grasslands and crops (including the orchards for which the county had a strong reputation).[11] In 1876 the top thirty-five landowners in Armagh had more than 177,000 acres between them.[12] It is no surprise, therefore, that landownership had long been contested between different groups which, in turn, led to widespread nineteenth-century agrarian violence in the county. Over time, this developed from local ad-hoc acts of violence on behalf of kin groups or community interests to an era of actions organized at the behest of national movements such as the Land League and the United Irish League (UIL).[13] The land question had also been politically divisive among unionists. John Lonsdale, then a new MP for Mid Armagh, was in favour of the 1903 land purchase legislation but Colonel Edward Saunderson, the Cavan landlord and North Armagh MP, reflected an older conservative landlordism in describing the idea as 'pure and unadulterated robbery'.[14] Nevertheless, implementation of the 1903 Land Act prompted a decline in agrarian violence and the purchase of holdings from large landowners. From 1903 to 1921, 215 Armagh estates were sold (the vast majority of these by 1912) to more than 12,000 purchasers. The county had the third-greatest number of purchasers behind the large counties of Cork and Galway, reflecting the level of land hunger in Armagh, irrespective of political or religious affiliation.[15] By 1912, the land question was believed to be largely settled. There were almost no evictions and relations between tenants and landlords, with the exception of town tenants, were reported as generally good by the Royal Irish Constabulary (RIC).[16]

According to the 1911 census, 23,400 or 43 per cent of those in employment were working in industry. Unusually for the time, this was greater than those working in agriculture. As mentioned above, the linen industry was dominant with more than 12,000 workers, two-thirds of them women. It was located mainly in Lurgan and Portadown, but also in smaller centres in Armagh, Keady and Darkley. Villages like Milford and Bessbrook were founded by paternalistic industrialists specifically for mill work. Bessbrook, where 40 per cent of those employed worked in the mills, was created as a model temperance village by John Richardson, a Quaker. His family oversaw the development of the village which had a mixed-denomination population, a school, dispensary and good-quality housing with individual allotments for growing vegetables.[17] There were other large industrial employers, including the food industry, construction and stonework/quarrying, but only a few hundred worked in either engineering or metal work. About 2,230 women found employment in domestic service, a reflection of the burgeoning middle class, while a small number of men, less than 300, worked in the legal or other professions, or as teachers. Several hundred worked on the railways and in transportation; government employment was made up of almost 300 in the army and 600 working either in central or local government. The balance consisted of almost 1,500 working in retail, financial and religious occupations.[18]

While the role of the state expanded in the early twentieth century into areas of welfare and pensions, government institutions continued to focus on crime, punishment and education. Control of crime was the responsibility of the RIC. On 31 December 1913 the force had a strength of 204 in Armagh, one to every 589 persons, a similar police/population ratio to Monaghan (1:580), but a higher ratio than Down (1:732).[19] There were four RIC districts in Armagh, each under the command of a district inspector (DI), centred on Armagh, Lurgan, Newtownhamilton and Portadown. The number of stations fluctuated slightly over the years but in 1914 there were twenty-nine in operation.[20] Courtney C. Oulton, a Tyrone native, was the county inspector (CI) during much of the revolutionary period until his retirement in June 1920. He made monthly reports on the condition of the county, recording the strength of various political groups, serious crime and outrages, and the state of the harvest. Oulton was succeeded by Alexander Dobbyn, who assumed responsibility for Counties Armagh and Monaghan.

The British army also had a significant presence in Armagh. The barracks in Armagh city was the depot of the Royal Irish Fusiliers (RIF), which had two full-time regiments, and two part-time (formerly militia) reserve battalions. In 1881 British army regiments were re-constituted in order that they would be more readily associated with geographic localities in Britain and Ireland. The 87th (Prince of Wales Irish) and the 89th (Princess Victoria's) foot regiments became the 1st and 2nd Battalions of the Princess Victoria's RIF respectively, with their headquarters in Armagh city and the depot area covering Counties Armagh, Cavan and Monaghan. Part-time militia reserve battalions (the 3rd, 4th and 5th) from these counties were linked to the new regular army battalions in the hope that the militia would develop into feeder units for the full-time battalions. The Monaghan militia was disbanded in 1908, following post-Boer War reforms, and Louth (previously in the Belfast depot area and whose militia battalion was also disbanded) was brought into the RIF depot area. Thus in 1914, the depot area of the RIF covered Counties Armagh, Monaghan, Cavan and Louth, with two full-time battalions, the 1st and 2nd battalions, and two part-time reserve battalions, the 3rd and 4th. The 1911 census recorded 176 soldiers from the 3rd (County Armagh) reserve battalion in Armagh barracks, of whom 143 were born in Ireland (of these 58 were born in Armagh), 77 were Roman Catholic (44 per cent) with 52 Church of England, 34 Church of Ireland and 13 Presbyterians. The average age of those reservists was twenty-seven, many were single men and their occupations included a significant number of labourers and weavers. Of the 176, only one was listed as a farmer.[21]

The presence of an army barracks in Armagh brought with it obvious economic benefits, as a customer of locally produced supplies, house rentals and soldiers' pay. The average wage of an unskilled civilian labourer was 15s. a week and this could be supplemented by army wages payable at enrolment in the reserve battalions and at annual training during summer months. However, the reserve battalions were of dubious military ability, which was brought into sharp relief when the Armagh militia was mobilized for the first time in almost fifty years in 1900 some months after the outbreak of the Boer War. It was reported that they displayed a distinct lack of warlike enthusiasm and that as their troop train left the Armagh railway station, they shouted support for the Boer leaders and sang 'God Save Ireland' and 'The Boys of Wexford'.[22] Some months earlier, the militia units from neighbouring County Louth displayed an equal level of disloyalty at Dundalk, and caused a sensation when they refused to volunteer to serve in South Africa as a unit.[23] In common with the rest of the country, many nationalists in Armagh opposed the war. An effigy of Michael Davitt, one of the main opponents of the war, was burnt in 1900 by foundry workers in Portadown, as they paraded with cannons that they had made for the British army.[24] Two years later, Davitt unveiled a memorial statue in Armagh city cemetery to Hugh Carberry, a local GAA stalwart who had died fighting for the Boers in the battle of Rietfontein. The unveiling allegedly featured seditious speeches, including one by John McGlone, then in charge of the memorial committee and later of the UIL.[25]

Armagh city also hosted one of the larger regional prisons after Mountjoy, Dublin; Crumlin Road, Belfast; and Cork city. Built to accommodate a total of 125 males and females, during 1911, 635 males and 231 females were committed or remanded to Armagh gaol. With an annual cost in 1911 of £1,059 (or £13 4s. 10d. per prisoner), Armagh gaol was one of the more expensive of Ireland's eighteen prisons to maintain. Prison work was compulsory and harsh; males made jute bags for mail and yeast, carried out construction work within the prison, stone-breaking and 'picking or teasing oakum', while female prisoners engaged in knitting, needlework and washing.[26] Male prisoners could be punished either for violence or 'idleness', presumably refusing to do prison work. After April 1918 the gaol incarcerated females only.[27]

Armagh had 265 national schools, all bar five under religious control. The denominational breakdown was as follows: 103 Catholic, 88 Church of Ireland, 48 Presbyterian, 15 Methodist and 6 Quaker. Most schools had an average daily attendance of less than 50 pupils with only a small number in the larger towns having over 100 pupils on average per day.[28] In 1912 the schools inspector for the county, a Mr Carroll, reported that most accommodation was passable and improving over time. However, he lamented that there were too many small schools because each denomination wanted their own, and the proficiency in literacy and numeracy in some one- and two-teacher schools was criticized. The quality of teachers was praised, if not their application at times: 'I fear too many of them act on the principle that very little work should be done after three o'clock on five days of the week and certainly nothing on Saturday'. Attendance was often poor – between four-fifths in the town and less than half in the country schools – and this was blamed on parents. Finally, Carroll noted that Irish was taught in many Catholic schools, with classes generally organized by individuals not associated with the schools, and he could 'offer no opinion from personal knowledge as to the success of the teaching'.[29]

The 1911 census recorded that 83 per cent of the population over the age of 9 years old could read and write, a further 6 per cent being able to read only. Literacy levels had increased throughout the nineteenth century and consequently a local newspaper industry had emerged alongside the dominant Dublin and Belfast dailies. In Armagh, in 1912, there were eight well-established weekly or twice-weekly local papers: the *Armagh Guardian* (started in 1844), *Portadown News* (1859), *Lurgan Times* (1879), *Lurgan Mail* (1890), *Ulster Gazette* (1844), *Newry Reporter* (1867), *Frontier Sentinel* (1904) and the *Dundalk Democrat* (1849). The first six were unionist in leaning, while the last two were nationalist and served the southern end of the county from Newry and Dundalk. Some of the editors were important figures in their own right. Delmege Trimble purchased the liberal unionist *Armagh Guardian* in 1893; his family also owned the *Impartial Reporter* in Enniskillen. Trimble fundraised for prisoners of war during the Boer War, supported the local Ulster Volunteer Force (UVF) company in 1913 and founded a cycle corps, before fundraising for prisoners during both World Wars.[30] In Newry, Joseph Connellan was apprenticed to the new *Frontier Sentinel* when he was fifteen and became editor in 1920, consolidating its conversion to the cause of Sinn Féin (SF) before later buying the newspaper. He was devoted to the memory of the Newry native John Mitchel and became prominent in separatist and Irish-Ireland circles from the mid-1900s, leading outings to Slieve Gullion and promoting the work of the Gaelic League and the Gaelic Athletic Association (GAA).[31]

As the nineteenth century progressed, use of the Irish language declined in Armagh for the familiar reasons of famine, internal migration and emigration. Inter-denominational rivalry also had a major impact on the decline of the Irish language and culture. The Catholic Church became fearful of the effects of proselytizing by Irish-speaking Protestant missionaries. It grew hostile to the language and culture to such a degree that by the turn of the twentieth century, many native Irish speakers believed propagating their language and culture to outsiders threatened their Catholic faith.[32] In the 1901 census, 4,485 people were recorded as having English and Irish, and there were two people who spoke Irish only. By 1911, the census recorded that 2,792 were able to speak Irish and English, and no one spoke Irish alone. The largest decrease since 1901 in the population who claimed to be proficient in Irish occurred in the 30–60 age group, most likely attributable to migration and a sense of utility or otherwise.[33] The *Armagh Guardian* took issue with what it called 'illusory' figures and, revealing the politics of the issue, argued that few had any proficiency in Irish: 'A person who can talk a dozen words in the language may have returned himself as being able to speak Irish, and probably has done so.'[34] There were efforts at language revival with the Gaelic League having a small presence in the county in 1912 with four branches in Camlough, Whitecross, Armagh city and Lurgan. Although periodically boosted by social occasions such as the anniversary of the Battle of Benburb (marked in June 1912), sports events and céilithe, the revival struggled in Armagh. Consistent membership of the League or attendance at classes proved elusive.[35]

The GAA put down roots in Armagh during the late 1880s, recording nine active clubs, and a county board met for the first time in March 1889 under the secretaryship of John Vallely of Armagh Harps. In 1912 CI Oulton reported that there were seventeen clubs, fourteen affiliated and three non-affiliated.[36] Police reports regularly linked GAA matches or social events and the attendance of Irish Republican Brotherhood (IRB) members. The surviving evidence points to a broader spectrum of involvement. In Armagh city, for instance, the Harps club had as its secretary the town clerk, James Lennon, as well as two UIL councillors, John Conway and Patrick Hughes. The club and the local Catholic Reading Room, which had Cardinal Michael Logue, Roman Catholic primate of All Ireland, as its patron, overlapped in its leadership. The local press, especially the *Frontier Sentinel*, recorded regular club and county football matches, though there was less evidence of hurling or camogie at this point.[37] Soccer appears to have been a more popular, or better reported, sport in these years in Armagh. Senior clubs existed in Lurgan (Glenavon and Lurgan Celtic) and Portadown, which played in the Irish League, as well as junior clubs playing in the Mid Ulster League and leagues across mid and north Armagh. On a typical Saturday in November 1912, fans in Lurgan could have watched a senior game at Mourneview, or Lurgan Celtic in Celtic Park, though the largest crowd of several thousand travelled by train to a Mid Ulster cup tie at Dungannon to watch Glenavon Reserves.[38] Milford FC, founded by the local mill-owner and sports enthusiast William McCrum, took part in the Mid Ulster league and was probably most famous for its founder's innovation: the penalty kick.[39]

Other sports and recreations were more exclusive in terms of membership. A number of golf, lawn tennis and even archery clubs were established during the 1890s, reflecting the spread of greater numbers engaged in commercial and professional occupations.[40] In 1893–4 three golf clubs, which are still in existence, were founded in Armagh city, Lurgan and then Portadown. The Lurgan club's initial meeting was an all-male event, and involved a bank manager, two solicitors, the local headmaster and three linen manufacturers. The first captain was Harry MacGeagh, later a Unionist delegate to the Irish Convention in 1917, and by 1915 the membership comprised 138 men, 'ladies' and juveniles with twenty-two members enlisted in the army.[41] Cricket, too, emerged as a sport in both larger towns and smaller villages across the north of the county in the 1860s, first associated with the elite and the military before gaining a wider membership and permanent homes, not least on The Mall in the middle of Armagh city.[42] Sport and recreation were important parts of associational life more generally as men, women and younger people clubbed together to build or express their common identity or, just as simply, to pursue the 'leisure of Saturday night and Sunday morning'.[43] County Armagh had the full range of clubs and societies in 1912, from cooperative societies in Keady, Armagh and Portadown; chambers of commerce in the larger towns; through to Boys' Brigade troops, farmers clubs, and various church-based organizations. Many of these, bar the Boys' Brigade, were open to all religions but most reflected the social dominance of Protestant society, especially in the northern half of the county. The Armagh Musical Society's 1912 committee of fourteen men and one woman (Mrs Belford) can be identified in the 1911 census. All were members of the Church of Ireland, with the exception of the president, R.G. McCrum, an 81-year-old Presbyterian linen manufacturer.[44] In Portadown, the Boat Club had a smaller committee of ten men and a broader spread of denominations between Methodists, Church of Ireland, and Presbyterians, but only one Catholic, J.J. O'Hanlon, who won Irish titles in rowing and chess in 1913 and was an emerging businessman in the town.[45]

Politics centred on competition for Westminster seats and representation in local government. The electoral system was transformed by the 1884 Representation of the People Act, which extended the franchise from 7,500 in 1880 to 24,000, though the vote remained restricted to male heads of households. The 1885 Redistribution Act abolished the county and borough Westminster seats and replaced these with three single-seat constituencies, North, Mid and

South Armagh.[46] Despite these changes, parliamentary electoral contests were rare after 1886, with the exception of South Armagh where contests took place on five occasions out of a potential seven. In the constituency of Mid Armagh, out of the six general elections and three by-elections, only one was contested in 1900. Of a potential seven contests in North Armagh, only the general election in 1900 and a by-election in 1906 were contested.[47] In 1912 the representation in Westminster was along predictable lines. Dr Charles O'Neill of the Irish Parliamentary Party (IPP) represented South Armagh, having been first elected in 1909. O'Neill was nearly 70, resident in Scotland for many years, successful in business and described as perhaps the 'greatest example of [IPP] upward mobility'.[48] Sir John Lonsdale, who was elected MP for Mid Armagh in 1900, was born near the city in 1850, and ran the family food exporting business from its Manchester headquarters. He was chief whip of Irish Unionist MPs in Westminster from 1903 and, only occasionally visiting Armagh, he relied on his brother James and Joshua Peel to keep him close to developments in the constituency.[49] William Moore succeeded Sir Edward Saunderson as MP for North Armagh in 1907, having lost a seat in North Antrim the year before. By laying great stress on his Orange Order connections, Moore was secure in his constituency seat in 1912.[50]

The reform of local government in 1898 created a county council, five urban district councils (UDCs), Armagh, Lurgan, Portadown, Tandragee and later Keady (created in 1903 from a previous rural council), and five rural district councils (RDCs) – Armagh, Crossmaglen, Lurgan, Newry No. 2 (taking in south Armagh and, from 1921, Crossmaglen) and Tandragee (see map 2).[51] In 1912 unionists held a majority in Armagh County Council, Armagh RDC, Lurgan UDC, Lurgan RDC, Portadown UDC, Tandragee UDC and Tandragee RDC. Nationalists controlled Armagh UDC, Crossmaglen RDC, Newry No. 2 RDC and Keady UDC. The local government elections in 1911 passed off with little comment or contest as no council changed hands. Only in two places did the elections spark much interest. Armagh UDC returned a small nationalist majority amid much celebration, including the carrying of a coffin labelled 'death to unionism'. This turned into attacks on property, including the house of the unionist election agent, Joshua Peel, and the windows of unionist-owned shops. Cardinal Logue denounced the violence, describing the behaviour as 'like that of Red Indians', in particular the 'unchristian' use of a coffin.[52] The Portadown UDC election saw six councillors from the newly founded Tenants' Defence Association, led by several sitting councillors, campaign for more public housing in the town. Though they were not Labour candidates, the appeal to build hundreds of houses in public ownership had mobilized cooperative leaders to support the association and two were elected to the council.[53] In Lurgan the poll was topped by John Lunn, described as the 'mouthpiece' of the Weavers' Union and Labour politics, though he was backed by the local unionist political machine to keep UIL candidates out.[54]

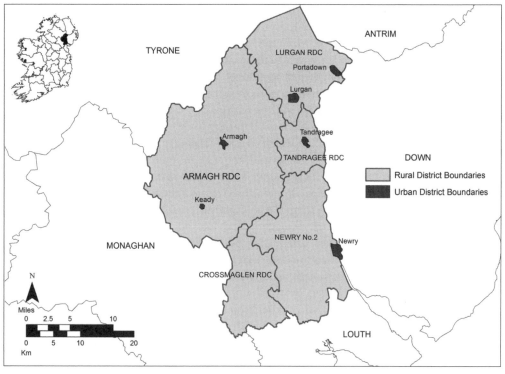

2 Local government divisions

The appearance of this association in Portadown and Lunn's candidacy in Lurgan are a reminder that the unionist and nationalist political machines were dominant, but not completely so. Political ascendancy depended to some degree on what Alvin Jackson has described, in relation to unionism in Mid Armagh, as a mutually reinforcing relationship with other organizations. For unionism these included the Boys' Brigade, the Little Builders of the Empire (revived in 1912), temperance bodies and the Orange Order.[55] The Orange Order was the largest and most famous of these bodies, founded in Armagh in 1795 and the county provided many of its leaders. The latest of these was Sir James Stronge of Tynan Abbey, grand master of both Ireland and the county. By 1912 the Order had approximately 5,800 brethren in Armagh (or 26 per cent of adult Protestant males), spread across 165 lodges in eleven districts. The strength of Orangeism, in terms of membership and numbers of lodges, lay in an arc from Portadown and Lurgan through Loughgall to Tandragee with the middle parts having smaller districts (around Armagh city) and then lodges with smaller numbers in the south of the county.[56] In nationalist circles, the Orange Order was probably best known for conflict with Catholics and nationalists; police reports regularly described violence associated with parades through nationalist areas, or attempts to persuade the Order to take other routes.[57] Nationalist newspapers usually associated Orangeism with 'rowdyism' or 'scoundrelism' in their headlines, even if the events had little to do with the Order.[58] However, the Orange Order and its network of halls also acted as a 'binding agent within Irish Protestantism' and an association which strengthened communal solidarity through marching, social gatherings, lectures and even bagatelle competitions.[59]

A similar role was played within nationalism by the Ancient Order of Hibernians (AOH), the Irish National Foresters (INF), and the aforementioned Gaelic League and GAA, all of which stressed Irishness and all things linked to that identity. The AOH was the strongest organization and key to nationalist mobilization in Ulster during the home rule crisis of 1912–14. It had fifty-three divisions (including six ladies' divisions) in Armagh, and acted as a vibrant, and when occasion required it, strong-armed political machine led by Joe Devlin, IPP MP for Belfast, and the Armagh native, John D. Nugent, in Dublin. The AOH also offered a regular calendar of public demonstrations (including St Patrick's Day and the 15th of August), that brought its members on to the streets in colourful displays of strength that matched those of the Orange Order.[60] The AOH was strongly disliked by Cardinal Logue, who denounced it in two pastorals in 1909 as a 'pest and a cruel tyranny' and 'organised blackguardism', but its continued growth, with eight new divisions established in the three years that followed, was abetted when it took on the role of administering sickness and unemployment benefits for members after the passing of the National Insurance Act of 1911.[61] Politics was a factor in Logue's denunciation but so was the perceived danger of entertainment centring on drink and dancing that often followed local addresses.[62] The pastorals were music to the ears of both the AOH's unionist enemies and those nationalists who disliked the Hibernians. This dislike would strengthen as the AOH later provided significant opposition to the burgeoning republican movement. John McCoy's recollection was typical, that the AOH was the 'Catholic edition of the Orange Order'. However, recent scholarship has taken a different view, where the Hibernians have been described as 'catering to constitutional separatists'.[63] John Nugent was certainly an ardent supporter of Irish-Ireland causes, including the Gaelic League, and told audiences in 1909 and 1910 that AOH support for the IPP was conditional on it achieving political success.[64] Neither were Hibernians deferential to the Catholic clergy, clashing in Cullyhanna in 1911 over permission to march in regalia to Mass, which resulted in members refusing to pay church dues for a time.[65]

Although the political contest over the third home rule bill was between nationalists and unionists, there were divisions within the two blocs. Within unionism, opposition to home rule from the 1870s onward focused on securing the place of Ireland within the Union and the British Empire. This was accompanied by efforts to create a cross-class and cross-denominational unionist bloc.[66] Alvin Jackson's excellent studies of North and Mid Armagh in the 1900s provide detail on earlier divisions as well as the success of the Ulster Unionist Council (UUC) and local leaders in extinguishing these. Until the UUC was formed in 1906, unionist constituency organizations were often dormant and vulnerable to attack from both the Sloanite working-class movement and the Russellite land reform one, the latter appealing to Presbyterian tenant farmers in particular. Jackson shows how Lonsdale treated a land reform challenge in Mid Armagh in 1906 as something to learn from, as he became the 'farmers friend'.[67] Lonsdale worked with local election agents to ensure that registration and patronage were taken care of and that potential dissenters, among them Presbyterian farmers and businessmen, were included in a broad church. This cross-class consensus was stressed by the *Ulster Gazette* when reporting on a meeting in January 1912. It claimed that unionist opposition to home rule was not based on 'a few wealthy landlords or capitalists', but on small farmers, linen workers and labourers.[68]

There was also a harder edge to unionist politics that preceded what looked like radicalism in the home rule crisis.[69] Jackson has referred to this as part of a continuous policy whereby the UUC's strength 'lay in its effective rejection of parliament and its return to political and sectarian basics'.[70] Even before Lonsdale and William Moore were elected in 1906 and 1907, a new type of leader came to the fore. In North and Mid Armagh, W.J. Allen and Harry MacGeagh in Lurgan; Dr George Dougan, John Collen and James Johnston in Portadown; and H.B. Armstrong and the Peels in Armagh city were local businessmen or professionals who were often unapologetically linked to the Orange Order. These leaders were also determined to aggregate local government power and patronage in unionist hands. They were central to the mobilization of the Unionist Clubs after 1911 and then the UVF. Part of this work was to revive local party machinery based on the three parliamentary constituencies. Associations met several times a year to hear from their MPs, to elect officers and delegates to the UUC, and to discuss policy.[71] Even in South Armagh, where unionism was much weaker, the local association saw to it that Richard Best contested an election in 1910, delegates were sent to the UUC, and unionists added to the electoral register.[72] These associations sat atop a dense network of organizations that were unionist in outlook and identity, from church bodies through to the Orange Order.[73] The same names mentioned above were often involved in many of their committees, alongside representatives of the landed gentry, such as the Copes and Stronges, who continued to have their part to play 'but it was no longer a part considered theirs by right'.[74] The UUC also incorporated both liberal unionists, who were suspicious of landlords and the Orange tradition, and commercial leaders, more open to the exclusion of Ulster from home rule than those unionists close to the landed and all-Ireland unionist interest.[75] The idea of exclusion and 'Ulster' came from a creation of an Ulster identity or mythology, which sought to emphasize the separateness of the north-east from the rest of the island.[76] The local unionist press in Armagh could be found referring to a common Scots lineage, the success of plantation, and adherence to lawfulness and industrial development.[77] Most importantly, all of this meant that in 1912 unionism in Armagh was largely united around the diktat of the UUC.

The local world of nationalist politics was much more febrile as the IPP struggled to put past divisions behind it and to deal with other threats from separatists.[78] In Armagh, the enemy of the IPP who generated most antipathy was Tim Healy. He had held the North Louth constituency since the 1890s, receiving the strong support of Cardinal Logue and some of the Catholic clergy, and was a thorn in the side of the Redmondite leadership.[79] After a decade of splits, divisions and conflict over candidate selection in the South Armagh constituency, it appeared the battle was finally over with the result of the election of December 1910. The sitting MP, Charles O'Neill, was opposed by Stephen Hugh Moynagh of the Healy/O'Brien All-for-Ireland League while Healy contested North Louth. Logue declined, for the first time, to endorse Healy, who lost his seat, while O'Neill won easily with a majority of more than 1,800 votes.[80] Despite these victories, Joe Devlin reported to the UIL directory in January 1911 that the battle to run 'factionists' out of Ulster continued.[81]

As in east Tyrone, the battle waged by the AOH and UIL leaders was also against supporters of the IRB, though the threat was weaker in Armagh.[82] The IRB had a presence in the county, with possibly twenty-five circles in Armagh in 1911. Its members had provided the backbone of the 1798 centenary celebrations, supplied some local government representatives (John Trainor in Armagh city), and supported the radical political parties, including Cumann na nGaedheal and SF in the 1900s.[83] By 1912, the IRB was concentrated in parts of the north of the county (tied to a Belfast/east Tyrone arc) and in and around the Newry district.[84] In June 1915 the CI suggested that although 'there are old members of this organisation in the county, I do not think that there are any working circles'.[85] As we shall see, some of these individuals became involved in the Irish Volunteers in 1913–14 and would later provide a 'paternal' interest around which separatist politics could align and the Volunteers revive in 1917.[86]

The labour movement in County Armagh was also concentrated in the northern half of the county and around Newry, where the IRB were influential on the Trades Council. The textile industries in towns such as Lurgan, Portadown, Armagh and Bessbrook had produced labour activism and later trades union organization from the 1870s and especially in the 'new unionism' wave of 1889–90. In Lurgan, for example, women textile workers organized the Lurgan Hemmer and Veiners' Trades Union in 1886 and went on strike on several occasions in the handkerchief factories before fading away in the 1890s. It revived once more in the 1900s, organized a strike of women hemstitchers in 1907 and led to a more general Ulster Weavers' and Winders' Trades Union being established in the same year.[87] Another factor of note was the local support from some employers (including textile manufacturers such as John Compton in Armagh city and Thomas Shillington in Portadown) for better conditions for particular groups of workers. This found an echo among other middle-class elements, such as William White, editor of the *Lurgan Times* and town councillor. However, the county did not see either the rise of general industrial trades unions associated with Larkinism after 1907 or the arrival of local trades councils that were a prerequisite of a strong labour movement, as we can see in Derry in this period.[88]

The role played by women workers in the labour movement in Lurgan raises a question about the extent to which women were able to play a political role in Armagh by 1912. The suffrage movement, which had its beginnings in Ulster in the 1870s and then revived strongly in 1911 with the establishment of the Irish Women's Suffrage Federation (IWSF), was the first sign.[89] Branches of the IWSF appeared in Armagh city in 1912 and Portadown in early 1913 and, though we have no idea of their size, there may have been membership in the twenties. A further IWSF branch in Newry, with forty-eight members, may have catered for parts of south Armagh.[90] The *Irish Citizen* newspaper provides some detail of their activities in 1912. This included a meeting in Armagh city addressed by Charlotte Despard in September 1912 and another afternoon meeting at which Louie Bennett, a Dublin suffragette and trade unionist, spoke.[91] The key organizer in Armagh was Edith Cope of Drumilly House, near Loughgall, who lobbied Armagh Unionist politicians in Westminster to have women's suffrage included in the third home rule bill. She was hopeful of support from William Moore but he and Lonsdale abstained, while Charles O'Neill voted against the amendment.[92] Women were also involved in unionist politics in Armagh, through the North and Mid Armagh Women's Unionist Associations (established in 1911). Members organized propaganda campaigns in Britain and later, in 1912, the Women's Declaration signed alongside the Ulster Covenant.[93] The *Armagh Guardian* took a different view about the role of women, an editorial in January 1912 noting that the Mid Armagh Women's Unionist Association annual general meeting showed the intensity of opposition to home rule, 'given the domain of women is not in politics'. In July 1912, opening a church fête in Kildarton, near Armagh city, the local businessman William McCrum commented that 'women were coming to the fore, especially where the plate glass of windows is concerned', to which the organizing chairperson, Mrs Crozier, responded by criticizing suffragettes for their 'great mistake … to try to get too much'.[94] The fact that John Redmond's IPP did not attempt to mobilize female activists to any extent reveals much about the party's views in 1912.[95] The AOH had a Ladies Auxiliary after 1910 and Armagh had ten branches by 1923, while female separatist politics did not emerge in an organized fashion until 1917.[96]

The social, economic and political contexts that obtained in Armagh in 1912 had a crucial formative impact on events during the decade that followed. Armagh was one of those Ulster counties in which unionists were in a (small) majority, but not in every part. The differences between the southern, middle and northern parts of the county were reflected in the different community experiences of political changes in the 1912–23 period. This book examines these changes, beginning with the political crisis and paramilitary mobilizations associated with the third home rule crisis before treating the First World War and its impact on the county in chapter 4. That chapter also examines the Easter Rising and its aftermath, specifically the growing prospect of partition and the battle for the hearts and minds of Armagh's nationalists. The violence of the years 1919 and 1920 clearly revealed the strength of unionist armed resilience, with or without the support of the British government, and the limitations of the IRA campaign when compared to other parts of Ireland. The final chapters deal with the manner in which the intense violence of 1922 was met by the growing power of the new Northern Ireland government and how, when combined with the spillover from the outbreak of the Civil War, this confluence marked the end of the revolution in Armagh. The Boundary Commission fiasco that followed was hardly needed to reinforce the feelings of bitterness and isolation among Armagh nationalists.

2 Enemies and adherents of home rule in 1912

Opposition to the third home rule bill came in two guises, military and political. They were not distinct; unionist political and business leaders encouraged the growth of paramilitarism with the avowed intention of violently opposing home rule should it be introduced. The demonstrations surrounding 'Ulster Day' and the impressively large number of men and women who signed the Solemn League and Covenant, vowing to oppose home rule by any means, served notice of warning on nationalist confidence that self-government was only a matter of months away. Nationalists initially treated the threat with bemusement and derision. This chapter explores how the ending of the veto of the House of Lords and the first attempt to pass a home rule bill in 1912 gave impetus to political and military mobilization in Armagh.

The result of the January 1910 general election meant that the Liberal government was now reliant on the IPP for a majority in the House of Commons. A second general election in December 1910 and legislation in 1911 to curtail the House of Lords' veto put home rule firmly on the political agenda for the first time since the 1890s.[1] In response, there were calls for unionists once again to be watchful, prepared and ready to resist any changes to the union. However, the unionist mobilization of 1912 – the revival of Unionist Clubs, drilling, demonstrations, and the signing of the Ulster Covenant – created an entirely new political dynamic in Armagh. This mobilization, in turn, sparked a response – albeit a more cautious and muted one – among nationalists. Dr Charles O'Neill, MP for South Armagh, derided the unionist mobilization as 'bunkum and bluff'.[2] However, they also needed to maintain a difficult balancing act of ensuring the voice of nationalism in Armagh was heard, but without provoking a backlash from the unionist majority in the county. For nationalists, Ulster could not be ceded to Edward Carson and his unionist followers, either in propaganda terms or in any form of exclusion from a home rule settlement. Unionist mobilization in 1912 was both proactive and strategic, while the nationalist response was more passive and reactive.

Thomas Bartlett has described the home rule bill as a 'legislative mouse', given the limited powers allowed to the new parliament, a resident viceroy whose function was to approve or veto legislation and that other powers (on policing, tax collection or pensions) would only be delegated at a later date. Despite Bartlett's view that 'in essence Home Rule was always more about image than substance', most nationalists, outside the ranks of 'advanced' circles or parliamentary opponents of the IPP, adopted a positive view of the third home rule bill and what it would mean for Ireland.[3] The grounds for debate were laid down in March 1912 when Tom Kettle, IPP MP for East Tyrone, addressed a large crowd in the Foresters' hall in Armagh. He portrayed the forthcoming bill as one that 'would be of such as a character as to be acceptable to the dignity of the Irish nation'. People should pay attention to the individual clauses, he said, especially the measure of control over taxation and the promise of 'conscience money' or 'restitution for past over-taxation'. Kettle also believed that the new parliament's powers for customs and excise could be exercised to provide for government without causing a tariff war with Britain.[4] Given its opposition to home rule, the unionist *Armagh Guardian* unsurprisingly criticized the economic arguments in the speech and, in particular, attacked Kettle for his denial of any evidence of religious intolerance shown by nationalists.[5] This articulated Armagh unionists' views of what self-government in Ireland would mean locally and nationally and the dangers for Britain and her empire.[6] Their arguments combined the negative (the threat of 'Rome rule' and intolerance by the AOH) and the positive (pride in the British Empire and in an Ulster identity).[7]

Unionist mobilization in Armagh was well underway by the start of 1912. The CI reported in January 1912 that ladies Unionist Clubs were being formed in Lurgan to resist home rule. However, while resolutions were passed in Orange Order lodges urging the formation of more Unionist Clubs, which would before long become the initial vehicle for militaristic displays, 'little practical effort has been made up to the present'.[8] Thereafter, most monthly reports recorded the formation of clubs, initially at places such as Portadown, Poyntzpass, Mountnorris and Lurgan. There was circumspection in the police commentary. CI Oulton wondered if the Orange Order, by its very existence, was a brake on this new movement.[9] This seems unlikely given the support already shown by two Orange Order leaders in the county: William Moore, MP for North Armagh, and W.J. Allen, deputy county grand master, in 1911. When establishing a Unionist Club in Lurgan in May 1911, Moore and Allen not only spoke uncompromisingly against home rule but also focused on the idea that Ulster's resistance could result in its exclusion from any settlement made for the rest of the island. Allen spoke of the north-east being different to other parts of Ireland and that it would not yield but would resist to protect the 'glorious heritage' of Ulster that loyalists across the empire would recognize. Moore spoke of the need to organize clubs and drilling across Ulster and that Monaghan or Clones would draw comfort from what Lurgan did.[10] As Patrick Maume put it, their support expressed 'populist particularism … in asserting local self-determination against the nationalist claim to represent a single-island unit'.[11]

When opening a new Orange hall in August 1911 at Milford (outside Armagh city), the Anglican rector of Keady, Revd Moses B. Hogg, defended armed resistance to the government. At the same meeting, W.J. Allen delivered a rousing 'No Surrender' speech against home rule which, he said, promised rule by Rome and the lawlessness of 'Mollie Maguires'.[12] The demonstration at Craigavon, James Craig's house outside Belfast, in September 1911 acted as a rallying point for mass mobilization. A contingent of around 100 men from Armagh city, who were reported to be drilled by an ex-army sergeant, had marched 'in form' to and from the town's train station and the aim was to have 1,000 men drilling in the county by Easter 1912. The huge crowds at Craigavon included men from the Unionist Clubs and Orange lodges in Armagh and Tyrone who marched in the procession from Belfast city centre 'as men who had been drilled'.[13] By December 1911 it was claimed that Orange lodges in the county were making plans to buy arms from Birmingham to assist in their drills.[14]

Given the imminence of a home rule bill, the RIC inspector general (IG) compiled a report for Dublin and London in February 1912, entitled 'Drilling in Ulster'.[15] It suggested that 12,000 men were already drilling at 119 different places in seven counties of Ulster (excluding Monaghan and Donegal). Armagh had 761 men drilling in twenty-two different places across the north and middle parts of the county. The local infrastructure provided by the Orange Order was crucial to the geographical spread, as nineteen of the twenty-two venues were Orange halls. The instructors were generally ex-soldiers, some local leaders of the Boys' Brigade and, in Ballinary and Derryadd, the local rector, Revd W.B. Allinar. In terms of a timeline, CI Oulton reported that in some places, notably around Lurgan, Portadown and Charlemont, drilling had only recently begun, but that in other places (further south in Armagh) it began a year earlier, then declined, but was expected to revive for the next large anti-home rule demonstration to be held in Belfast at Easter.[16]

In 1912 the efforts to promote Unionist Clubs and drilling across the county intensified. The number of clubs rose from 22 in February 1912 to 34 by January 1913, with Lurgan and Portadown, the largest towns, more prominent than previously. Membership passed the 1,000 mark by the end of 1912.[17] The police regularly reported on the drilling activity and emphasized its legality as it had been sanctioned by two Justices of the Peace (JP) as the law permitted. Activity ebbed and flowed with the time of year, the needs of work and the political temperature. However, CI Oulton argued that any lull in activity was temporary and partial, with some places remaining active when others were not. No arms were being used and the drills consisted of marching in fours, 'squad movements', and processions to local meetings. One meeting at Portadown, on 20 February, saw clubs from Corcrain and Summerisland march; in the same month clubs from Glennane and Tyrone's Ditches marched to Mountnorris in south Armagh, accompanied by a band from Loughgilly, and were addressed by a local unionist organizer.[18] Before the local club at Tynan in January 1912, the South Tyrone MP, William Coote, argued:

> [The] day might come when they would have to shoulder their rifles in defence of their homes, their children and their freedom. ... [Clubs] at three days' notice could mobilise 100,000 men ready and willing to do their part in defence of the rights they held so dear.[19]

Part of the attraction of drilling was, according to Oulton, to make a 'good show' at the large anti-home rule demonstrations.[20] In January 1912, at a demonstration in Omagh, it was noted by one speaker that a special train had arrived from Armagh 'from which 50 men marched up in military formation'. They were described in the *Irish Independent* as superbly well-drilled.[21] Local pride was again served in the case of Balmoral in April with three companies (Armagh, Allistragh and Milford) marching in the procession who were said to be better trained than many from larger towns with better facilities. Their colour party, carrying a Union Jack and Orange flag, included two elderly ex-soldiers 'who had seen service on many a foreign field and carried the tokens of their valour on their breasts'.[22] Others hoped that these demonstrations, if they passed off quietly, would lead to an ebb in activity with the RIC IG arguing after the Balmoral demonstration that the men 'who were tiring of drill' in Armagh 'will become slack'.[23]

Unionists drew on a strong sense of history in their mobilization efforts. Orange Order speakers, such as William Moore MP in a typical oration at Portadown in September 1912, claimed that loyalist persecution went back to the time of the Pharaohs and invoked the memory of the trinity of loyalist victories: Derry, Aughrim and the Boyne. Moore noted that his parliamentary predecessor Sir Edward Saunderson had led opposition to home rule in 1886 and 1892. Moore justified the use of drilling in the 1912 anti-home rule campaign by asserting that there was no legal sanction against it. He based his argument on an 1886 prosecution of six Richhill men which had collapsed.[24] Stronge, as an Orange grand master, drew on a belief of persecution as well as the resistance of Orangemen to this since their formation in 1795.[25]

Initially, at least, Armagh nationalists quietly regarded the unionist mobilization with a mixture of amusement and hope that it would disappear.[26] Typical of the attitude was a cartoon in the *Irish Independent* on 14 January 1911 dismissing the 'Ulster will Fight' rhetoric and the images of drilling that were coming from the North as a bluff.[27] When members of the '80 Club' of home rule-supporting Liberal MPs visited Armagh city at the same time as the unionist demonstration at Craigavon, they were welcomed by a reception committee of local nationalist councillors, led by P.J. McGarvey, town clerk James Lennon and by bands from the INF and the Irish War Pipes club. At an Armagh UDC reception, the chairman, Michael Short, told them that 'the Nationalists of Armagh were as strong in their demand for Home Rule as anywhere in Ireland'. The MPs then met Cardinal Logue, who claimed that if Ireland were as well treated as other colonies in the empire, then she would be as loyal as those places. Instead, Logue said, when the issue of Ireland came up in parliament, it was treated 'as in a game of pitchcock, everyone must have a throw at it'. The *Irish Times* report treated Short's claims of friendliness between the political factions in the city somewhat ironically and reported that a nationalist delegation from Lurgan had pointed to only one Catholic council employee there and told the Liberal MPs that the rule of the 'Ascendancy party' would end with home rule.[28]

By March 1912 there was growing nationalist annoyance at the government's toleration of unionist mobilization and their talk of plans to set up a provisional government for Ulster. An editorial in the *Frontier Sentinel* contrasted the treatment of trade unionists in Britain and unionists in Ulster, both of whom were appealing to the military not to act against them:

> The English Syndicalists were arrested and imprisoned because they were regarded as being sincere in earnest; the Ulster Provisional Government was allowed to shout 'treason' until it was hoarse because ... its 'sedition' was looked upon as so much bombast.[29]

A UIL meeting in Ballymacnab in May heard an exasperated McGarvey argue that the 'enemies of the Irish race' had to be combated. At the same event, the Bessbrook solicitor and later MP, Patrick Donnelly, said that he 'desired no quarrel with their Protestant friends ... [but] must make it plain to them that they would not be allowed to stand in the way of Ireland's progress'.[30] In Armagh city, another UIL meeting, chaired by the local leader John McGlone, denounced any suggestion that Ulster did not want home rule and McGlone proposed a resolution that while the city might be in J.B. Lonsdale's constituency, the people 'resent and entirely repudiate the suggestions that the County Armagh should be excluded from the operations of the Irish parliament'. The response of the local unionist newspaper was to dismiss such talk as 'nonsensical'.[31] However, when Thomas Agar-Robartes, a Liberal MP, proposed an amendment in June 1912 to exclude four Ulster counties (including Armagh), the Unionist MPs in Armagh were either supportive like Moore or silent like Lonsdale. Moore claimed not to 'support it as a wrecking amendment, but because he was an Ulsterman'. Backing his stance, the *Armagh Guardian* commented that Ulster needed to be excluded rather than being forced 'under the heel of intolerance and idleness of men who own a different rule and are a different people.'[32] It is clear that for some Ulster unionists the idea of exclusion or partition of all or part of Ulster had firmly taken hold by this point. In December 1912, Moore was more explicit in debates on the home rule bill, referring on several occasions to 'two nations' and claiming 'we are West Britons ... we regard the term Briton as the emblem of liberty'.[33]

Unionist leaders knew the risk of being portrayed in the British and Irish press as the aggressors and were, therefore, keen to stress the peaceful nature of the large demonstrations of 1911 and early 1912. The *Armagh Guardian* accused the *Freeman's Journal* of lying when the latter reported the abuse of bystanders at Armagh railway station after the Balmoral demonstration and the firing of shots from a special train going to Newry. The stationmaster was quoted in the

Guardian as saying that no fights had broken out and the shots had not been aimed at anyone.[34] However, both the police and the local press were well aware of the potential for trouble. A hopeful RIC report in June 1912 noted that although 'party feeling is in evidence at present, neither side seems disposed to attack the other.'[35]

The violent events elsewhere in Ulster during the summer of 1912 had local reverberations.[36] The events themselves – an attack on a Sunday school excursion at Castledawson by a crowd returning from an AOH demonstration at Maghera on 29 June and the subsequent violent attacks and expulsions of around 2,000 Catholic and Liberal Protestants from the Belfast shipyards and Sirocco works on 23 July – were bad enough. But the bitterness engendered by the failure for months afterwards to re-admit workers, by the jailing of Hibernians at Castledawson but not of loyalists in Belfast, followed by the release of Hibernians in early 1913, all provided fuel for the fires of animosity.[37] Locally, nationalist papers did not cover the Castledawson incident, choosing instead to concentrate on the Belfast troubles and the belief that the shipyard workers were 'dupes' for malign leaders.[38] The *Armagh Guardian* took a different view. Under a headline of 'AOH cowardly intolerance', a report portrayed drunken Hibernians scattering and terrifying women and children while stabbing one teacher in the hand and seizing and destroying Union Jacks. The Belfast events were relegated to a 'sequel', where one Hibernian in the shipyard of Workman & Clark was attacked, two others injured, and other Catholics left work.[39] J.B. Lonsdale was quickly into the fray with a letter on the 'Castledawson Outrage' carried prominently, as was his attack on Stephen Gwynn's 'untruths' on the same subject. Lonsdale believed that the Castledawson incident was a sectarian attack, while events in Belfast were due to shipyard workers attacking those who supported home rule. According to the MP, the fault lay with the Liberal government for 'awakening anew the passions of the ignorant and superstitious population of Ireland'.[40] The passions did not die there as the *Armagh Guardian* continued the 'whataboutery' into August. When Cardinal Logue was reported to have sent a subscription to aid the expelled nationalist workers and condemned the 'unguarded utterances of high placed politicians', he was reminded that a nationalist election victory in Armagh city in January 1910 had been followed by window-breaking in unionist areas.[41] His condemnation of these acts, covered in the previous chapter, was ignored. Later in August, William Redmond, brother of the IPP leader, was criticized for denying the Castledawson incidents were as bad as reported. He, too, was reminded that the same had happened in Armagh when a Sunday school excursion from Bessbrook was attacked and the ringleaders were jailed.[42]

The 'paper wars' were not the only reverberations in Armagh. The Twelfth demonstration had 'passed off quietly' and the county was generally peaceable, but the RIC IG noted in July that:

... though there does not seem any general desire to get into collisions with the opposite party things seem to point that in a good many places the Unionists are ready to fall into line with their leaders and support them in any project they may attempt to carry out.[43]

Parades and excursions were always potential flashpoints, the CI noting that 'party feeling runs high ... and at times when processions are forming it would be a very easy matter to create disturbance.'[44] When an excursion party was returning to Armagh city on 7 July from a Gaelic League feis in Maghery, on the shore of Lough Neagh, shots were fired at the group. Their route home had posed a dilemma as a returning party in 1909 had fired shots at a nearby rural Orange hall at Canary and tensions remained about that incident. Therefore, the police advised taking a different route and provided an escort. When the group passed Tullyroan, where a crowd had gathered at an Orange arch, shots were fired at a horse-drawn brake. A bullet passed through a headrest and then through the clothing of a member of the Armagh War Pipes Band. While the unionist press claimed that the excursionists had refused police advice, one nationalist paper emphasized the peaceful nature of the excursion party and that the feis had been held to raise funds for a chapel in Loughgall.[45] Other skirmishes also occurred when the police formed a barrier (and fired warning shots) between Orange bandsmen from Madden, who wanted to march through Keady on their way home from the Twelfth demonstration, and local nationalists out in the town on a fair day.[46] After the events in Castledawson and Belfast, Joe Devlin called off all AOH demonstrations for a period of eighteen months. This was denounced by William Moore as a cynical attempt to show the AOH's tolerant side.[47] Tensions were reduced, however. For example, a feis in the Clonmore area, not far from Loughgall, was cancelled after being criticized as 'a challenge to attack'.[48]

On 28 September 1912 just under half a million unionists signed either the Ulster Solemn League and Covenant or the women's declaration that was designed as an ancillary. The planning for Ulster Day was only briefly noted in the CI's report.[49] Enthusiasm was built through the Royal Black Preceptory demonstration in Lurgan on 31 August, addressed by William Moore and W.J. Allen, who urged the crowd to show their determination to resist home rule by signing the pledge.[50] Unionist Clubs were addressed on the need for the Covenant and drilling was intensified to prepare for a Portadown meeting on 25 September, one of the last stops on 'Carson's Trail'.[51] The large crowd that attended this meeting was addressed by British and Ulster unionists, witnessed Unionist Club members drill with wooden rifles, and saw a parade of 'Volunteer nurses'. The normally sympathetic *Pall Mall Gazette* concluded that there had been a 'slightly unreal atmosphere' at the event.[52] In the south of the county detailed logistical arrangements were communicated through Orange lodges for men to gather in Clarkesbridge and Newtownhamilton to march first to church services and then to sign in their regalia.[53] Finally, advertisements were taken out in the local press. These indicated the signing places, that the signing would take place over a few days, and that it was for all adults aged over sixteen years.[54]

On the 28th, everything appeared to go to plan. The *Irish Independent* and the *Irish Times* differed in their coverage with the former referring to the celebrations in Lurgan as 'a rather tame affair', while the latter highlighted the thousands of men and women who participated.[55] The *Armagh Guardian* carried much local detail and gave a sense of how unionists had come out very strongly on the Saturday having been urged by their religious ministers to do their duty. One correspondent reported about Armagh city: 'Never before was the primatial city stirred to a greater depth of enthusiasm – earnest and subdued – than on Saturday.' Businesses were closed for the afternoon to allow for church services and signing. The main services were held at St Mark's, where Lonsdale led the signing, the Church of Ireland cathedral, and First Presbyterian. In the latter Revd David Miller spoke of the need for the two different races in Ireland to stay together under the Union. After the signing finished for the evening, there were parades in town by the Church Lads' Brigade, the Boys' Brigade and the local Orange lodge (LOL No.109). In Lurgan and Portadown the same pattern of church services and signing was followed. In Lurgan women were encouraged to use the parochial hall to sign their declaration, while in Portadown, Carleton Orange hall was open for women to sign.[56]

The report in the *Ulster Gazette* captured the extent of the cross-Protestant alliance in places. At Killylea, Anglican, Presbyterian and Methodist ministers joined together in service, while in Newtownhamilton, Revd R.J. Ballard led a service in the Church of Ireland church and the congregation went afterwards to the hall beside the Presbyterian church to sign. A similar service took place in Tandragee, where Revd McEndoo of the Church of Ireland and the local Baptist minister, J. Murphy, led the service and people signed first in the graveyard, led by the duke of Manchester, and then the women went to the courthouse and the men to Manchester hall. In other places, the Orange Order took centre stage – particularly in Grange, Cladymore (where the Order had tables in the church yard), Clovenden (where they attended service in full regalia) and Druminnis. Finally, at Richhill, the ideological importance of the day was not forgotten as Richard Best and the Presbyterian minister, Revd A.W. Johnston, both spoke and said those gathered faced enemies in the AOH, the UIL and the Catholic hierarchy and the 'spirit of imperialism' witnessed during the Boer war in Ulster would see them through.[57]

The digitized records of the Ulster Covenant give a sense of the response to Ulster Day in Armagh.[58] David Fitzpatrick's work on the Covenant shows that 77 per cent of men in the Protestant adult population in Ulster signed and 72 per cent of women.[59] The Armagh total is 39,018 signatures, a figure which 'approached 90%' of the adult Protestant population, the highest in any Ulster county.[60] More than half of the total (52 per cent) signed the women's declaration, in line with the average in Ulster, although Portadown had a much higher share (66 per cent), perhaps reflecting the importance of the linen industry there.[61] There were 109 signing places in thirty-eight districts across the county (for details see appendix). Nineteen of the venues were Orange halls with churches, church halls and, in Lurgan and Portadown, town halls making up the balance. Each venue had an agent or secretary in charge of collecting the signatures and the organizers had forty-seven of these, most of whom were laymen associated with the constituency associations, Unionist Clubs, Orange Order or all three. However, there were also a number of prominent Anglican ministers involved in the Covenant as agents, including W.B. Allinar (Ballinary), F. Halahan (Drumcree), G.H. Daunt (Knocknamuckly) and E.A. Nelson (Drumbanagher). CI Oulton referred to 'very extensive signing' with 'scarcely any abstentions'. In Portadown, Lurgan and Armagh city, 'a very high percentage of Unionists over 16 years of age signed', while in rural areas 'the farmers and their families have been just as keen about signing.'[62]

Nationalists attempted to dismiss Ulster Day and the Covenant as another form of bluff or, as the *Frontier Sentinel* put it, a hollow and 'blasphemous farce'. In a series of articles that brought the newspaper before the courts for libel, it described the signatories as 'the hooligan, the bolt-thrower, the bottle-flinger, the revolver-man and the boycotter' and went on to claim that most did not attend any church, 'were coerced into preaching a doctrine they do not believe' and would soon come to their senses.[63] By and large, the Ulster Day events passed off peacefully, though there was, as one newspaper reported, some banter and abuse in both Armagh and Lurgan that resulted in fines for disorderly conduct before the petty sessions.[64] However, a cautionary note against this complacency about a unionist bluff was sounded by a correspondent from the London *Times*. He visited Armagh city in September and reported a conversation with local businessmen and unionist leaders ('the terms are almost synonymous in Ulster'):

> When I asked if the opposition to Home Rule was as strong here as elsewhere the reply was always given, with a grim smile, it was stronger. 'Our men', said a prominent Unionist employer to me, 'are only waiting for an opportunity to express themselves. They want an even plainer lead than has as yet been given them.'[65]

Others paid less attention to the unionist opposition, perhaps because they could not see any advantage in the home rule bill. SF was trying to breathe new life into the movement in the south of the county. In August 1912 Major John MacBride spoke at a rally in Jonesboro and the nearby Corrinshego branch was reorganized the following month. However, the CI believed that as an organization SF had little impact: 'if any influence is exercised, it is by individuals.'[66] Elsewhere, the Belfast solicitor, Gaelic League activist and antiquarian, F.J. Biggar, presented St Winnoc's temperance pipe band in Middletown with a new banner in the days before Ulster Day. He told them that 'he would rather see them clothed in orange made in Ireland, than in the most national colour made in Manchester.'[67]

As 1912 drew to a close, CI Oulton was hopeful of peaceful times ahead. The numbers drilling in the Unionist Clubs were falling and a bigger worry seemed to be emerging both over the bad harvest of potatoes and the threat of foot and mouth disease in cattle.[68] The UIL held meetings, including one in Lurgan addressed by Richard McGhee, to provide an update on 'doings in parliament' but, in general, the CI reported a 'great fall in politics at present'. Unionists appeared disappointed as the home rule bill moved towards the House of Lords and divisions over tariff reform in the Conservative Party caused concern about the opposition's future.[69] People in Armagh could have been forgiven for holding their breath, not sure what would come next and hoping that political tensions would abate.

3 'Prepared to begin the fight': the deepening home rule crisis, 1913–14

The Ulster crisis intensified in the eighteen months before Britain declared war on Germany on 4 August 1914. This period saw a series of political and military events that would reverberate in Armagh: the formation of two paramilitary forces along with the spread and consolidation (with arms) of paramilitary structures; the discussions over the exclusion of some or all of Ulster from home rule; the Curragh incident; the Larne gun-running; the Buckingham Palace conference, which was a last-ditch attempt to avoid civil war; the Howth gun-running and the shooting by the British army of civilians at Bachelors' Walk in Dublin. The cumulative impact of these events increased pressure on Unionist and Nationalist politicians and their followers to compromise over the north-east, and exacerbated local tensions in Armagh.

Throughout 1913 economic concerns were to the fore in Armagh. A 'home industries' exhibition was organized by the Armagh Chamber of Commerce, commencing Monday 27 January, to highlight the products of some 150 local firms and to show that many of these producers were selling into markets far from the county.[1] That week, a conference of local employers debated the future of industry. John Compton, a linen manufacturer and county councillor, worried that his industry provided work predominantly for women and wondered what employment could be offered to men.[2] Industrial strife broke out in Lurgan in January 1913 as a strike of weavers and winders began in four textile factories.[3] It lasted for a month and was reported to have been carried on in an 'orderly' fashion with police reinforcements sent home after a few days.[4] The employers refused the union's pay demand and initially closed the factories for two weeks after most of their 1,500 workers struck. Eventually, the factory owners made an offer and this resulted in a pay rise of between 3*d.* and 4*d.* a week, half of what had been demanded. There was a narrow majority in favour of acceptance and an increase in union membership among textile workers, many of whom had been non-union before the strike.[5]

Paternalist approaches to industrial relations remained common. As the Lurgan strike moved towards a resolution, a local Portadown UDC member, John Palmer, spoke to the Portadown Textile Operatives' Association on the need for better wages and union organization in their town to avoid similar trouble.[6] Likewise, the tone was polite in Bessbrook in February 1913, when an address and some silver was presented to the virtual magnate of the town, J.N. Richardson, and his wife. He spoke of the necessity of industrial peace and the *Armagh Guardian* was moved to record 'in these times of political and industrial strife in many places it is gratifying to record such harmonious proceedings' as the largely female millworkers of Bessbrook expressed their thanks for a new playground.[7] Despite such hopes, local strikes continued as the year went on, including one in April over employment of non-union workers in Thurston's mill in Lurgan and the threat of another in June.[8] Other efforts were made to obtain pay rises, including by road workers who sought an extra shilling a week from Armagh County Council, and also to organize general workers.[9] And later during the Dublin lockout, local trade unionists and members of the Irish-American Alliance (an offshoot of the AOH) and SF sent what the CI recorded as 'trifling sums' to the ITGWU.[10] On the other side, John D. Nugent opposed efforts to send children of locked-out workers to England where trade unionists could take care of them, though his AOH members were more ambivalent.[11]

Politics, however, continued largely along the same lines with a 'very strong and bitter undercurrent of feeling on the Home Rule question'.[12] CI Oulton's first report for 1913 had struck a positive tone: 'County quiet and people generally have kept themselves under restraint as regards political events.'[13] The RIC's report in terms of sectarian disturbances was prescient as 1913 was quieter than previous years. The celebrations by nationalists in Armagh city of the Derry by-election victory and the public burning of the home rule bill in Portadown were comparatively peaceful events.[14] Plans for parallel unionist and nationalist meetings in Armagh city on 30 January to mark recent political events were called off after an appeal by the police to 'influential persons'.[15] In June 1913 the AOH County Board for Armagh announced that the annual 15 August demonstration would be postponed for another year. When a number of bands and local divisions defied the ban near the Moy, they were disciplined with several expulsions from the order.[16] Even local provocations – another clash at Tullyroan in July and an Orange band marching through the nationalist Shambles area of Armagh city – were largely ignored. CI Oulton noted that 'the nationalists are under strict instructions to give no offence and I believe would almost go any length to avoid getting into a collision with the opposite party'.[17]

Tactically, nationalists in Armagh maintained discipline, stressed their loyalty to the IPP leadership and avoided sectarian clashes. The UIL branches came to life in the spring as their local organizer J.P. Convery and other leaders (John McGlone and Patrick Donnelly) spoke almost weekly at meetings across the south and middle of the county. The twin messages were that Redmond could be trusted on the Ulster question and that the goal of home rule was within reach.[18] In February 1913 the overwhelmingly nationalist Newry No. 2 RDC in the south of the county passed a motion thanking the IPP and Redmond for the passage of the bill. The councillors denounced the action of the House of Lords in rejecting the measure and criticized the suggestion made in debates that Irish people were more interested in rent abatement than home rule.[19] In April, as the home rule bill was rejected for a second time in the Lords, a 'very large and representative meeting' of UIL was held in the National hall, Mullaghbawn. It elected its committee for the coming year, promised a record parliamentary fund, and passed motions of support for Redmond and home rule. Convery stressed the need to combat unionist propaganda, especially the idea that a Catholic majority would persecute Protestants under home rule. Other speakers dismissed the majority in the Lords as now irrelevant 'gilded nonentities' who hated Ireland.[20]

Elsewhere, local nationalist politicians sought to consolidate the newly-won political control of Armagh UDC. In September 1913 new voters were presented for registration and both sides challenged those they believed were non-resident householders. The CI noted that unionists were disappointed with the final outcome and appealed to the court of King's Bench. However, the judge decided that there were no technical reasons to disbar these non-resident voters, the UDC's solicitor agreeing that 'there are "swallows" on both sides'.[21] The upshot was that there were no contests for the Armagh UDC in January 1914 and the nationalist majority continued.[22] As the Healyite threat passed, the UIL and IPP leadership regarded advanced nationalists as weak or factional. The RIC continued to monitor the influence of separatist or Irish-Ireland bodies such as the IRB, IAA, SF, the Gaelic League and the GAA, but were dismissive of them. SF members were reported as lending support to the ITGWU after the Dublin lockout, while a successful Gaelic League St Patrick's Day procession in Armagh city was noted.[23] Individuals and small groups attempted to keep radical politics alive, often through meetings and circulation of newspapers and anti-enlistment propaganda.[24] In 1913 these organizations offered an alternative political culture outside the UIL and AOH, attracting as members future revolutionaries like Charles McGleenan and Frank Aiken.

Unionists stepped up a gear as the home rule crisis deepened. An example of the radicalization of their mindset was provided when Unionist MPs were posed a question by the *Daily Mail* about whether they would accept home rule if endorsed by a general election. Most, including John Lonsdale, confined their answers to a simple 'no'. The MP for North Armagh, William Moore, added that 'he would give no such advice as long as he had 12 rifles in Ulster'.[25] His rhetoric escalated. In Birkenhead, in March 1913, he suggested that if home rule was 'carried over the heads of the people that its baptism in Ireland would be a baptism of blood'.[26] Moore was suspended on 26 March from the Commons for abusing the chair of the ways and means committee in a procedural row that had nothing to do with home rule.[27] At a public meeting in Portadown, Moore pointed out that the IPP, probably correctly, and at variance with their usual practice, supported the motion for his suspension because of their need to keep the government in power.[28] He was the guest of honour at the AGM of the North Armagh Women's Unionist Association and in his first public utterances after his suspension was lifted, he emphasized that there would be no compromise by Unionists, whose mantra was essentially 'Hands Off Ulster'. He stated that 'they stood where their fathers stood, in opposition to every proposal which would place them under the domination of a majority hostile to them, their ideals, their industries and their religion.' And if through 'the treachery and cowardice' of the present government civil war was threatened, unionists would 'pour forth at the call of duty in greater numbers and battle for the cause of freedom'.[29]

Rhetoric and defiance were important but the key element that turned this political drama into a deeper crisis was the emergence of armed paramilitary organizations in 1913–14. As political attitudes hardened and the room for compromise grew smaller, this militarization suggested that Ireland might be heading for civil war by the summer of 1914. The UUC decision on 13 January 1913 to establish the UVF was intended to impose some regularity on the various Unionist Clubs, Orange lodges and others who were already drilling across Ulster.[30] The development of the UVF was initially patchy and there was competition for members and officers between the different local drilling bodies. However, the spread of the UVF was more rapid after the tours by Edward Carson in June 1913 and especially the instructions to the Orange Order in September to enrol its members in the new force.[31] Armagh newspaper reports support the picture of a slow beginning in raising the UVF, at least until the summer of 1913. There are accounts in April and May of meetings in Kilmore and Portadown at which audiences were urged to enrol, but little detail of drilling, procurement of arms or regularization of the organization.[32] RIC reports present a disjointed story where new Unionist Clubs were being formed, including one in Markethill in January 1913, and they continued to function throughout the spring.[33] The IG reported that there were signs of the new UVF organizing in the north-west of the county, but that it was 'in its infancy' and would be a month 'before it gets properly started.'[34] The RIC initially believed that the UVF might be confined to the area around Killylea, Loughgall and Tynan, where Sir James Stronge was 'pushing on the movement', but soon there were reports of declaration forms being distributed and names taken in the larger towns, such as Portadown, Lurgan, Armagh and Bessbrook.[35] The towns were deemed critical for success. The 'Portadown Clubmen' were rumoured to be tired of drilling without arms and thus the organization of the UVF with its promise of arms held great attraction.[36] Enrolment in Lurgan may have been slower as nationalist and unionist workers found common cause in the series of industrial strikes.[37]

The first three of four models for UVF units, as described by Tim Bowman (feudal, civic, politicized societies and friendship), are certainly present in Armagh.[38] Stronge formed two companies where he was the local landlord and this provides an example of the 'feudal gentry-led' model. It was reported that members there 'would do anything they might be called on to carry out'.[39] The appeal to local or civic pride is seen in Armagh city and Portadown in March 1913, where J.B. Lonsdale and W.J. Allen respectively urged their audiences not to leave their towns lagging behind in enthusiasm for the UVF. Lonsdale's call prompted the editor of the *Armagh Guardian*, Delmege Trimble, to form a cyclist corps in the city.[40] The evidence of a politicized association appears with members of the Church Lads' Brigade marching in military formation on Ulster Day in Armagh city and then joining what was to become 'A' Company, 1st Battalion, Armagh UVF.[41] By July 1913, CI Oulton reported on the spread of the UVF in Portadown, Armagh city and, to a much lesser extent, the Bessbrook district. The strongholds of the new movement were in Killylea, along the Blackwater river to Portadown, and down to Tandragee and Poyntzpass. There was less enthusiasm in the areas around Armagh city, such as Richhill and Markethill, while Lurgan was also slower than expected to take up paramilitarism. Assessing the strength of feeling, the CI

> [did] not think that the people in general would have an idea of taking the field under arms, but they would join in making government under Home Rule auspices difficult if not impossible.

He believed businessmen, particularly in Armagh city, were temporarily holding back but would follow the UUC leadership. There were doubts about whether home rule would become law, given 'it has been hanging on so long', but the antipathy towards nationalists was still apparent.[42]

In his monthly report for July, Oulton added detail on UVF numbers, arms and its level of organization. He reported that 3,770 men were believed to have signed up to the UVF in Lurgan, Portadown and Armagh. Arms were allegedly available for drilling: 800 rifles in Portadown, 50 in Killylea, the same in Armagh city and more at Tandragee and Lurgan.[43] A further intelligence report from July 1913, based on information gathered by RIC Sergeant William Hall from UVF sources around Armagh city, detailed the operation of a UVF camp held at Stronge's house, Tynan Abbey, which had been visited by Carson. The highlight of the two-day event occurred when a despatch rider drove to the site of the battle of the Boyne near Drogheda, placed a Union Jack there and wrote on the bridge 'captured by the UVF'. It was reported that rifles were clearly visible at Tynan, as James Stronge Jr had apparently brought nine Lee Enfield rifles home from England. Another 50 Martini rifles had been taken to Killylea from Belfast on the Twelfth and arms had also come into Armagh city from Belfast and were hidden in the Palace Demesne.[44] Hall's detailed report was probably one of those dismissed as idle rumour by Dublin Castle officials and Liberal ministers keen to deny the seriousness of the situation.[45] A Castle memorandum in March 1913 stated, against all the local evidence, that 'in Armagh and Monaghan counties in which the Protestant population is notoriously Orange the enrolment of the "Volunteer Force" has not even commenced'. Sir James Dougherty, under-secretary for Ireland, claimed that he gathered his information from sifting the police reports coming into the Castle and ignoring those which 'serve up the gossip of the Orange Lodges' on issues such as arms and drilling. He even suggested that 'some DIs and CIs are lending themselves as willing instruments to a game of bluff'.[46] On 24 July, the day before the Tynan camp, Augustine Birrell, the Irish chief secretary, told King George V that the army would not be fighting in Ulster as 'there would be no one to fight with' and the provisional government 'would not last a week'.[47] Officials in Dublin Castle were clearly refusing to take unionist militant mobilization seriously.

Who were the local Armagh leaders of the UVF? The 1st Battalion of the Armagh UVF in 1913 covered the city and hinterland, and twenty-five of the twenty-six company and corps commanders can be identified using the 1911 census.[48] From the census returns only Sergeant Francis Murphy, commander at Summerisland, indicated that he had served in the army, while the only other person with some military background was Joseph Willerton who recorded his sergeant's rank. Two other UVF commanders – Robert Sleator and Richard Townshend – are known to have subsequently joined the RIF and both died in the war.[49] The most striking aspect of the UVF commanders is their variety. The eight companies in Armagh city were mostly commanded by men in professions or trades, while farmers, their sons or workers in the textile industry were in charge in rural areas. Three exceptions to this were Maynard Sinton, mill-owner; Ralph Cope, the son of the Loughgall landlord; and C.H. Ensor, linen merchant and landlord's son. In terms of religion, fifteen commanders were in the Church of Ireland (including two ministers), eight were Presbyterian, and one each were Methodist and Quaker. The average age of the commanders was just over 34 years old, but Revd Foy in Lisnadill was over 60. As Bowman has commented, the highest levels of the UVF 'comprised a strange combination of the very experienced and utterly amateur'.[50] In the summer of 1913 Carson and the UUC leaders moved to make the UVF under General Sir George Richardson the only effective unionist paramilitary organization. In August 1913 a circular letter to 'Fellow Covenanters' called on the Unionist Club members to enrol in the UVF. The provincial secretary of the Orange Order issued a similar instruction to local lodges that all drilling activity was to come under one entity.[51]

A planned meeting by Sir Edward Carson in Armagh city on 4 October also had an impact. CI Oulton reported in September that 'a good deal of recruiting [is] going on due to Sir Edward Carson's meeting, letters, etc and I believe it numbers over 6,000'.[52] The Carson meeting had some similarities to the events of 1912 in Portadown and across Armagh on Ulster Day. The detailed programme for the day included religious elements (John Crozier, Church of Ireland archbishop of Armagh, was to open with a hymn and then preach, though he chose not to do the latter), speeches from Unionist dignitaries, including Carson and F.E. Smith. J.B. Lonsdale was to chair the meeting, which would close with 'God save the King'.[53] However, Carson's main goal this time was to inspect and review a united UVF movement in Armagh. While the local Unionist Clubs had taken part in a procession and added colour to rallies in 1912, the paramilitary mobilization itself was the object of the exercise by 1913. According to Oulton's report of the day, almost 17,000 attended the demonstration and Carson reviewed 3,500 UVF members.[54] A correspondent from the *Irish Times* suggested larger numbers (20,000 and 4,700) and detailed the UVF parading along the Mall to Dean's Hill, where the rally took place. UVF companies from Portadown, Lurgan, Newry, Keady, Newtownhamilton, Bessbrook, Markethill, Tandragee, Killylea, Loughgall, Richhill and Armagh city all attended. There were also nursing volunteer corps from Milford, Armagh and Lurgan, who marched in their uniforms.[55] The nursing corps was highlighted by the unionist press, in the hope that the involvement of women might spur the less keen young men into action. There was also a cross-class emphasis in the press that 'the mill girl of Lurgan and Portadown is just as anxious to take a hand in the great work of preparation' as 'ladies with plenty of leisure time'.[56] The coverage of the speeches and claims of preparation for the provisional government and the debates over exclusion of some Ulster counties or not (which was rejected from the platform) was in second place to the paramilitary display.

The nationalist press reported the demonstration in a very different way. The 'revue' was derided as a tame affair with Orange songs, indifference and 'tawdry decorations' the order of the day.[57] The display was described as follows:

> Mainly the processionists were young men and boys … they were, generally speaking, a very plain, up-and-down, rather sad-looking lot and trudged along with solid placidity.[58]

Another paper focused on the 'violent scenes' at the train station where Lurgan and Portadown UVF members had allegedly frequently fired revolvers.[59] The Armagh city demonstration highlighted uncomfortable issues for local nationalists, not least the choice of the city, where nationalists had a small majority on the district council. It was claimed that the meeting 'was invaded by outsiders, in order to give the impression that Armagh is Covenanters' territory. Yet Armagh is certainly not homogeneous.'[60] Nationalists in Armagh had reason for concern. A month before the Armagh city demonstration, the former lord chancellor, Lord Loreburn, called for a conference to consider proposals for an accommodation, seriously prompting Carson to consider the exclusion of all or part of Ulster for the first time.[61] Despite all their denials to Redmond, the Liberal government was now open to compromise on the 'exclusion' issue. The home rule bill was expected to go through the Commons for a third time and there could be no Lords' veto, but there were questions over whether amendments might be accepted this time, specifically around exclusion or partition.[62]

The insistence that the unionist position was a bluff was now being openly questioned by some commentators, given planning for a provisional government was at an advanced stage, the large-scale support by the unionist public for the Covenant and the growth of the UVF.[63] Thus unionist leaders urged continued activism during the winter of 1913, including J.B. Lonsdale:

> I know a great deal about the position on this side [London], and I cannot impress upon you too strongly the utmost importance of the Volunteer Force during the next few months. Upon its vitality and energy everything depends. There should be frequent route marches, and as much publicity given to it as possible.

Lonsdale had been told by H.B. Armstrong that the business class in Armagh city was responding poorly to calls to support an indemnity fund. The MP advised a personal canvass among the businessmen and a drive to impress on local UVF leaders that subscriptions and drilling in the winter months could 'save their country from Nationalist domination'.[64] A January 1914 memo to the government from the Ulster-born former chief commissioner of the Dublin Metropolitan Police warned that 'things have now gone too far for the Covenanters to sit quiet, even if Carson and other leaders were to advise them to lay down their arms'.[65] And CI Oulton also reported a growing intensity of feeling in the county about home rule the following month.[66] By mid-February Lonsdale had reason to be more cheerful about the UVF in Armagh city. He attributed this to two key factors, the presence of drill sergeants, which he was paying for, and discipline:

> It is very good of Major Goring to have taken so much trouble in inspecting, etc., and I hope the result will be – as you say – to infuse more interest and spirit into the movement. May he soon return to continue his good work![67]

Whether due to Lonsdale's urgings or not, UVF activity exploded in the winter of 1913. The RIC reported that 114, 167 and 176 drills were carried out in the first three months of 1914, in 37, 54 and 59 places respectively.[68] Training camps were held at Drumilly House (home of the Copes of Loughgall), Carrickblacker (home of Colonel William Blacker) and Tynan Abbey again. Olwen Purdue has pointed to the importance of these and other landed families taking an active role in the UVF, not least for providing venues for drills, camps and, later, stores for arms and ammunition.[69] The unionist business classes, despite Lonsdale's earlier concern, were now providing funds for uniforms and camping equipment.[70] The training camps saw intensive attempts to professionalize the paramilitary corps, following a reorganization of the county into five battalion areas and a special service unit in late 1913.[71] Easter Monday (in April) was set aside for field manoeuvres across north and mid-Armagh at Lurgan, Portadown, Killyman, Ardress and Richhill.[72] At Richhill a 'war game' between two companies ended after a horse bolted and a young boy driving a cart was killed.[73] The week-long camp at Drumilly in June was reported on in detail in the *Armagh Guardian*. Almost 250 men of the 1st and 2nd Armagh battalions encamped for the whole week with a focus on night-time manoeuvres, including, on one night, an attempt by despatch riders from Belfast to break through perimeter guards.[74] The camp was intended to include all classes with 'poor men' having their wages covered by the Carson fund.[75] The newspaper reports also pointed to the fact that though 'very few men outside the camp were aware of the fact … every man had his rifle and bayonet and there were plenty of rifles to spare.'[76]

The reported surplus of arms in Drumilly House highlighted the success of the efforts to arm the UVF. By July 1914 a local commander in Richhill could order his men to go home and come back to drill and parade with their rifles.[77] Before the Larne gun-running there were repeated reports in 1913 and early 1914 of hundreds of rifles coming into the county, often in ones and twos and mainly from weapons imported into Belfast.[78] The RIC were aware that the houses of Colonel Fitzgerald in Clontilew, William Blacker at Carrickblacker, T.J. Atkinson, John Collen and Dr Dougan, all prominent Portadown unionists, were places where rifles were stored. A car belonging to Maynard Sinton was said to have been used in February to take guns to the episcopal palace in Armagh city and then on to Keady.[79] However, Larne was the key to increasing the availability of arms for the UVF with up to 20,000 rifles and 2 million rounds of ammunition landed on the night of 24 April 1914.[80] The UVF across north and mid-Armagh mobilized overnight to watch roads as rifles moved into mid and west Ulster.[81] Later newspaper reports in May concentrated on picaresque adventures like the distribution of rifles around Armagh on carts under heaps of manure and said that the RIC had stopped cars taking arms from Armagh into north Monaghan.[82] It was never clear how many UVF arms were in Armagh after Larne, though an audit in February 1917 gave a total of 4,180 rifles. This probably underestimates those held by individuals but given the estimates of around 7,000 UVF members in the county on the eve of the war, it suggests a significant total number.[83] Tim Bowman has concluded that, in the absence of army intervention, the UVF could have overwhelmed both the RIC and any nationalist resistance to establish a nine-county provisional government. However, he also makes the point that the worst rifles were sent beyond Antrim and Down and that there were difficulties with ammunition for those weapons.[84] In 1917 Armagh had no machine-guns and of the 4,180 rifles, 2,920 were the hated Italian rifles and only 397 were the highly desirable Lee-Enfield, the standard British army rifle.[85] Armagh might be a case study of Alvin

Jackson's contention that Larne changed the UVF from being largely unarmed to badly armed.[86] The quality of their arms makes it questionable how long the UVF in Armagh could have resisted a serious intervention by the British government.

The letter from the former Liberal lord chancellor, Lord Loreburn, in September 1913 which called for an accommodation on Ulster was said to have shaken nationalists out of their complacency about the 'Ulster bluff'.[87] If so, it did not happen immediately. The following month Charles O'Neill continued to claim that unionists were bluffing, while Redmond and other IPP leaders repeatedly denied any reports of changing government policy on Ulster.[88] However, this was the background to Eoin MacNeill's 'The North Began', a manifesto calling for action to preserve home rule for the whole of Ireland and for the formation of the Irish Volunteers in November 1913.[89] In Armagh there were two phases to the development of the Irish Volunteers, in December 1913 and May 1914.[90] In the first, given the hostility of the IPP leaders, the initial development was the work of radicals, either members of the IRB or close affiliates.[91] It began when Gaelic League instructors in Armagh city and Lurgan introduced companies of Na Fianna Éireann and drilling exercises in the towns.[92] They were probably inspired by the decision in July 1913 of the Fianna leadership, particularly Bulmer Hobson, to begin drilling.[93] In January 1914 an RIC report noted the circulation of leaflets in Armagh city by James Mallen (or Mallon), a 'local barber':

> The leaflets, it is said, were sent to Armagh by John Southwell of Newry, who is working to establish a branch of the Irish National Boy Scouts [Na Fianna] in Armagh but, so far, without success.[94]

IRB activists exploited nationalist anxiety that the absence of radical leadership was holding them back from drilling and arming at a time when the UVF was growing in strength.[95] By early 1914 an Irish Volunteer company was established in Blackwatertown, while other companies with small numbers invited Countess Markievicz to inspect their corps in Newry and adjoining areas in south Armagh.[96] These moves prompted debate within the AOH about whether nationalists in Armagh should follow the example of the UVF by setting up their own armed body, independent of the Irish Volunteers. By March 1914 the AOH in Lurgan were reportedly drilling with arms in their hall and other divisions were doing likewise, supposedly with the blessing of their local leaders and Joe Devlin. They were under strict instructions to 'be discreet and secretive in their actions so as not to give offence to their opponents'. CI Oulton believed that this activity was 'to keep out the I[rish] V[olunteers]', which had taken off in neighbouring east Tyrone.[97]

Events in March and April 1914 – especially the so-called Curragh mutiny, rumours in the south of the county about arms searches, fresh debate in the press about exclusion proposals and the Larne gun-running – prompted the second phase in the development of the Irish Volunteers in Armagh.[98] The usual loyal motions from UIL executives in north and south Armagh were accompanied by growing dissent. An angry letter from a 'South Armagh Nationalist' to the *Irish Independent* called for a demonstration against exclusion to be held in different places in Ulster simultaneously and lamented not having a Parnell-like leader:

> When the Parliament Act was passed we were told we would have complete Home Rule for Ireland. We swallowed the Budget and also the Insurance Act which nobody seemed to want, and now our reward is Home Rule for the other three provinces, which we could have had for the asking almost 20 years ago. I would like to hear the answer Parnell would have made if any British statesman had then proposed the exclusion of Ulster.[99]

On 9 May 1914 the AOH leadership directed its members to join the Volunteer movement to control its development.[100] The response of young nationalist men and women was instantaneous and enthusiastic. Within a fortnight companies enrolled recruits, initially across the middle and northern parts of Armagh. CI Oulton was quick to dismiss the movement as yet in its infancy – the 'better classes do not care much for it but are rather afraid not to do so' and the recruitment included 'corner boys' – but he noted that unionists did not like this development.[101] Catholic clergy were said to be either supporting or in sympathy with the Irish Volunteers, although 'as a body they have not given it any decided support'.[102] Press reports emphasized the enthusiasm of those flocking to the movement (with perhaps 5,000 enrolled by June in Armagh) and the determination to ensure they were properly instructed in their drills.[103]

Throughout June nightly drills took place in Armagh city, Lurgan, Keady, Cullyhanna and Middletown. This followed a number of public meetings held in Armagh's Flax Market, where upwards of 1,000 enrolled and a drilling ground and instructors were procured.[104] The named centres had other companies acting as satellites. For example, the Keady district had 800 men enrolled: 250 in the town, 150 in Darkley, 150 in Corran, 100 in Derrynoose, the same in Madden, and 50 in Tassagh. These numbers could swell to 3,000, when a larger gathering took in surrounding parts of County Monaghan and the Armagh city companies.[105] By the end of June there were thirty-two Volunteer branches or companies in Armagh and 140 drills had been held in twenty-eight different places during the month. While the AOH had suspended demonstrations, the Irish Volunteers emulated the route marches of the UVF in Armagh city (accompanied by the War Pipes Band) and Keady (with St Winnoc's Band, 'in full Gaelic regalia').[106] However, there was a paucity of arms as the IRB had little ability to provide many and Nugent's directive to AOH divisions to cooperate with the Volunteers could only promise that the provision of arms was 'getting close attention'.[107] Fundraising for the Volunteers began in June in Armagh city (supported by the clergy). Within a month more than £550 had been collected, including significant sums raised in the south of the county in Lislea, Crossmaglen and Lissumon.[108] The fundraising and the Howth gun-running raised hopes of arms for the Irish Volunteers. John McCoy recalled 'waiting up through a summer's night when I heard that rifles were actually on their way to us in the hope that if supply was limited that I at least would get one'.[109] It is not clear whether arms from the Howth haul ever came to Mullaghbawn, although an intelligence report claimed that the Hibernians in Armagh refused to send any of the £400 collected in the city to purchase arms 'unless to pay for arms first delivered to Armagh'. On 27 July 100 rifles and ammunition finally reached the city.[110] A 1917 audit counted 276 weapons in the hands of the Redmondite National Volunteers, a fraction of the amount needed to arm its own members and a twentieth of the arms available to the local UVF.[111]

The political allegiances of the Irish Volunteers were as complicated in Armagh as in many other places. In Armagh city and the area closer to Newry, radicals led the movement, at least initially, whereas in Lurgan the AOH dominated. Among the rank and file many had joined for protection from the UVF whom they viewed with 'considerable dread', though in some areas this was still seen as a 'bluff'.[112] In terms of the leaders, many of those who addressed meetings, such as Thomas McLaughlin and P.J. McGarvey, were well-established local UIL councillors. However, interestingly, in Armagh city and Keady the names of Edward (Éamon) Donnelly, Daniel Dumigan (the new chair of Keady UDC) and Peter Leenagh, all later involved with SF, began to emerge.[113] The June takeover of the movement by the followers of Redmond occurred relatively smoothly in Armagh, as in neighbouring Monaghan.[114] The South Armagh UIL executive met on 7 June, just days after Redmond's ultimatum to the Volunteer executive, and Charles O'Neill MP called on young men in South Armagh to join the Volunteers. He was followed by Canon John Quinn of Camlough who proposed a motion that 'we will recognise no other army save that directed and controlled by our Parliamentary leaders'.[115] Redmond's ultimatum was followed by a concerted campaign by the UIL and others in support. The North Armagh UIL executive in Lurgan praised Redmond's actions and were supported by Irish Volunteer meetings in Middletown, Keady and Armagh city.[116]

The home rule bill went through the House of Commons for the third time in late May and the CI's first concern was that celebrations in Keady and Armagh city should be cancelled to prevent clashes among 'rowdies'.[117] The position of Armagh under home rule was as yet unclear. The government's amending bill, introduced in the Lords on 23 June, suggested the exclusion of six counties (including Armagh) for a period of six years after which they could opt into home rule or opt out on a county-by-county basis. Unionists supported this but the amendments they added to it were unacceptable to the government.[118] Outside parliament the question of how far the IPP leaders were prepared to compromise on exclusion was raised. These leaders were certainly keen to have room to manoeuvre but resolutions against any further concessions were received from various places in Armagh. In Middletown, on 22 June, a large Irish Volunteers gathering, presided over by the local curate, unanimously adopted a resolution against any further concessions on exclusion.[119] A UIL meeting in Mullaghbawn the following day similarly passed unanimous resolutions against further concessions.

Notwithstanding nationalist opposition, it appeared clear to Liberal MPs in London that 'Carson has won and the sooner the public knew it the better'.[120] Locally, unionists were preparing for the moment the bill became law and that the provisional government would take power in Ulster. In early July CI Oulton reported that the UVF was drilling less frequently, believing themselves to be well prepared for what was anticipated, and had kept the 'lower class of Portadown in check' by preventing attacks on AOH excursionists returning to Warrenpoint from Dublin.[121] A large UVF gathering near the Moy, including men from Summerisland, paraded with full arms including bayonets and were counselled by their commanders, Edward Cowdy and Lieutenant-Colonel Fitzgerald, to be mindful of their preparations.[122] A Twelfth gathering at Tynan was addressed by Stronge. He asked those assembled to show loyalty and sympathy for the king who wanted to act the right way by Ulster, although his majesty's actions stood to be misinterpreted by 'unscrupulous politicians'.[123] Throughout July and the start of August, intelligence reports from Armagh noted that hundreds of rifles and rounds of ammunition were being issued out of stores to companies, especially those across the north of the county. All of this fed a belief among the senior ranks in the RIC that general orders had been given for mobilization to support a provisional government, which would occur six hours after the home rule bill was on the statute book.[124]

At this point, civil war in Ulster appeared more likely than world war. On Sunday 19 July Revd Henry Todd, from Bessbrook, preached at Donaghmore in County Down to UVF members and worried aloud that civil war posed a risk not just to them but to Britain and the empire. There was a risk of industrial strikes crippling Britain and foreign powers taking advantage of troops being sent to Ulster. He wondered whether unionists could not be left out of home rule initially and then perhaps persuaded in by its supporters in the future. He also presciently asked his congregants whether they were prepared to fight for the retention of Donegal.[125] Todd also spoke at an Orange demonstration in

Mullaghglass, near Newry, on the last Saturday in July and again shared his concerns that civil war might come, but stated that this had been forced on them by the current government and 'Ulster was prepared to fight her own battles'.[126] The events of the summer of 1914 tested nationalist confidence in the IPP. The proposal of the Liberal government, including the apparent exclusion of six counties without time limit, seemed to be accepted by John Redmond and his colleagues. After the Buckingham Palace conference collapsed without agreement towards the end of July, T.P. O'Connor stated that the IPP had given all they could, but were considering modifying the time limit. In Derry and Armagh, he said, 'we have begged our minority for the time being to submit to the vote of the majority'.[127] In Armagh city, Joe Devlin, speaking to Volunteer companies, pledged that home rule would be law within days and that volunteering had been an 'answer to the indefensible taunt that the Irish people do not care about Home Rule'. However, he did not address the potential exclusion of the county from home rule.[128] Although the bill was placed on the statute book on 18 September 1914, the shape of the settlement remained unresolved as far as it impacted on Armagh.

The deepening crises of 1913–14 saw home rule reach the statute book, a victory for nationalist politicians that had evaded the giants of Irish politics for a century, but with the threat of a seemingly inevitable civil war between unionists and nationalists. Both sides of the divide had armed or were in the process of arming, the unionists being far in advance in terms of military capability and organization, although not in the true sense capable of prolonged resistance if challenged by a professional army. They were, however, much more capable than the nationalist volunteers. Their expansion was sluggish as they too began to arm themselves, but with the historical irony of organizing to fight in support of the British government. They were barely underway when all plans relating to home rule were put on hold with the outbreak of war in Europe. The Irish Volunteers were hit by the consequent organizational split which effectively excluded County Armagh from any meaningful role in the Irish Revolution until 1919–20.

4 War and a distant rebellion, 1914–16

The outbreak of the First World War in August 1914 changed everything. The danger of civil war receded as unionists back-pedalled on the threat of declaring independence for Ulster, or part of it, and the Irish Volunteers split with the overwhelming majority supporting John Redmond. Known as the Irish National Volunteers, the Redmondite body quickly disappeared in Armagh while the radical Irish Volunteers, under the titular command of Eoin MacNeill, struggled to establish itself in the county. In the meantime, both nationalists and unionists responded sluggishly to enlistment appeals to join the British armed forces. The outbreak of the Easter Rising in 1916 allowed loyalists to claim justification for their suspicion of nationalists.

The collapse of the Buckingham Palace conference on 23 July 1914 was seen to be the final attempt to avoid the widely anticipated civil war in Ireland. Prime Minister Asquith later observed 'nothing could have been more amicable in tone or more desperately fruitless'.[1] Edward Carson returned to Belfast to make preparations for an illegal provisional government that would claim jurisdiction over all nine counties of Ulster, a move that was expected to unleash sectarian clashes, draw in sympathetic nationalists and unionists from other parts of Ireland, and force the deployment of the British army. For all the tension, CI Oulton reported that in July 1914 'not a single untoward incident has been reported' for reasons that went beyond parochial or national boundaries: 'the prospect of a European war and the United Kingdom becoming involved appears to have eclipsed everything else and the question of Home Rule has faded into the background.'[2] With European war imminent, the British government and opposition agreed to postpone further discussion of the home rule bill. On 1 August *The Times* reported that Carson had offered the use of the UVF for home defence or for deployment anywhere they might be required.[3] On 3 August 1914, in the House of Commons, Redmond pledged the services of the Irish Volunteers for the defence of Ireland and urged the British government to concentrate her army on attacking Germany. In a matter of weeks, the Home Rule Act would receive the royal assent, but the government also passed an act to postpone its implementation until 'not earlier than the end of the present war' and allowing for special provision to be made for Ulster. During the next eighteen months the dominant role that Ireland had played in the business of Westminster receded.

The general mobilization of all British armed forces meant the loss of men with military experience from both the UVF and Irish Volunteers. As a consequence, there was an immediate decline in drilling and route marches. There was, however, no surge in recruits with CI Oulton reporting at the end of August that 'the UVF as a body have not joined the army and are slow in making a move till the H[ome] R[ule] question is settled or postponed. The I[rish] V[olunteer] F[orce] seem to be acting similarly in this respect.'[4] Matters improved somewhat in September 1914 when it was reported that of 7,000 members of the UVF in Armagh, about 900, mainly from Lurgan, had enlisted and gone for training at Clandeboye.[5] Contemporary newspaper reports recorded an enthusiasm for enlistment, but recent research has pointed to low recruitment levels in Ulster, outside Belfast, and a slump after the 'rush' of September and October 1914.[6] In Armagh, the CI noted that unionists in rural districts were especially unenthusiastic due to the abundance of employment and the fact that, as a body, the farmers 'saw little beyond their immediate surroundings and they are besides not keen for fighting'. Irish Volunteers in the towns were expected to enlist but like their unionist counterparts, it was not anticipated that there would be much recruitment in the rural districts, 'particularly in south Armagh [where] they have little notion of fighting'.[7] Asquith placed the Home Rule Act on the statute book on 18 September alongside its postponement. Nationalist Ireland was triumphant and this was echoed locally in Armagh city when UVF recruits to the army, more accustomed to marching to the train station with the sound of effusive encouragement under loyalist street decorations, were jeered with home rule slogans as they passed through nationalist areas.[8] Unionists were hostile and stormed out of the House of Commons. In Armagh, they reacted with 'sullenness' when the home rule bill received the royal assent, and in one church the congregation left in protest when 'God Save the King' was sung.[9]

Nationalists reacted cautiously to appeals for their service. On 23 August William Redmond, who later joined the army and was killed in Flanders, and Joe Devlin addressed the Armagh city battalion of the Irish Volunteers. They praised the Volunteers' steadfastness for home rule and their martial spirit but no mention was made of enlistment.[10] At this juncture, the CI recorded that enthusiasm within the Volunteers for drilling had dropped off for fear of 'being thought efficient' and, as a consequence, forced into enlistment en masse.[11] John Redmond's Woodenbridge speech, on 20 September, in which he urged the Irish Volunteers to continue drilling and to go 'wherever the firing line extends', split the organization. A new IPP-led Irish National Volunteers was consequently formed on 30 September.[12] In October Oulton reported that while the Armagh National Volunteers 'nominally' supported Redmond 'for the most part', there was little enthusiasm for recruitment, with only 300 members out of a total of 4,500 enlisting. In the mirror image of their unionist counterparts, most nationalist recruits were from the Lurgan area, and there was a 'poor show' in the rest of the county.[13] Public support for Redmond was explained more as a reaction against factional strife and 'cranks' (or those in the Irish Volunteers), than as a positive reflection of support for the war effort.[14]

An interesting example of one nationalist's reaction to events is that of John McCoy, later adjutant 4th Northern Division, IRA. He was from Mullaghbawn, in south Armagh, and had been raised a traditional nationalist by a father who was a UIL branch officer with a dislike of secret societies. McCoy had joined the Irish Volunteers when a branch was established locally but had little regard for it as it had no arms and no one to train them properly. He initially had an ambivalent attitude towards the war, recalling that he was neither in favour nor against it, and felt no resentment towards acquaintances who joined up. During 1915 he attended recruitment rallies and, at the urging of a friend, applied for an officer's commission in the RIF. He was offered a commission in the Lancashire and Yorkshire Light Infantry, but as there were no vacancies in the Fusiliers McCoy turned the commission down and thus ended his attempted foray into the British army. Given the right circumstances, the army missed an opportunity to recruit a man who would prove to have significant military and organizational abilities.[15] He recalled the atmosphere of south Armagh at the time:

> all over south Armagh a spirit of at least tolerance of the British war effort was everywhere apparent. Dances and entertainments were frequently held for the British Red Cross and a lot of 'Nationalists' attended. Announcements were frequently made of locals killed in action or missing at the war fronts. There was generally a feeling of disinterestedness in every phase of political life at this time.[16]

In November 1914 CI Oulton ascribed the National Volunteers' aversion to enlisting more to a reluctance to getting killed than any strong anti-war sentiment.[17] Recruitment centred largely on the towns, in particular Lurgan and Portadown. The initial limited rush to the colours at the outbreak of the war was followed by a slump after November 1914 and, from as early as April 1915, recruitment had virtually died out, in spite of recruiting drives in the spring of 1915 by the locally-based RIF and further bolstered by men from the prestigious Irish Guards.[18] John Dillon's address to an AOH audience in Armagh in November 1915 encapsulated all of the ambivalent IPP thinking on the war. He maintained that in return for home rule, the IPP was honour-bound to support the British Empire's war against Germany, and while he pledged that conscription would never be introduced in Britain or Ireland due to the IPP's opposition, he believed the demand for 51,000 new Irish recruits was reasonable.[19] Conscription was introduced shortly afterwards in Britain but not in Ireland.

There are no exact figures of how many men from Armagh served in the British forces. A conservative estimate would put about 5,000 men from Armagh in the various branches of the armed forces during the war. An official report from 1916 estimated that 4,183 men from Armagh had enlisted in the army alone, with perhaps 200 in other services, making a total of 4,383 by that stage.[20] These figures do not reflect those who enlisted outside of their home county, and may not include men who were already serving in the armed forces. Another estimate can be made using the absent voters list, compiled in early 1918, comprising eligible servicemen who registered to vote in the forthcoming general election. The lists for all three Armagh constituencies are among the few that have survived in Ireland and show that 3,440 men with home addresses in Armagh were serving in all branches of the armed forces in May 1918.[21] In addition to those shown on the absent voters list, some simply did not register to vote, others from Armagh were living outside their native county and, of course, there were those who had been killed, which has been estimated at 1,381.[22] As to the religious/political make-up of the recruits, half of the 1,024 who joined the army between December 1914 and December 1915 were in the UVF, a quarter in the National Volunteers and another quarter had no known affiliation. It was also noted that 695 recruits were Protestant, and the balance of 329 were Catholic.[23] According to these indicators, unionist enlistment probably exceeded nationalist enlistment by a ratio of slightly more than two to one by the end of 1915 (and this may have increased over time). In that light, it is reasonable to estimate that out of a conservative total of 5,000 Armagh servicemen, about 3,350 were unionists and 1,650 were nationalists.[24]

In a review of 1916, CI Oulton reported that recruiting in Armagh was at that stage negligible, at about fifteen men per month. He was of the opinion that nationalist lack of interest in recruiting meetings could be attributed to the Easter rebellion and its aftermath (though enlistment had died out long before then), but offered no reason as to why unionists had also abandoned the cause.[25] Recruiting during 1917, if mentioned at all, continued to be 'very poor' and by December 1917 was 'practically dead'.[26] It was still 'very poor' in April 1918 but Oulton noted that more had joined up since the passing of the Military Service Act which extended conscription to Ireland (although it was never enforced). Oulton made a final point in June 1918 that those who desired to join up had already done so and that unionists were not keen to see 'slackers' conscripted, nor to join up themselves unless nationalists did so.[27] In comparison, the CI in Louth, which was also part of the RIF depot area, reported in August 1914 that although anti-German sentiment was intense, until the home rule bill was enacted there was not 'much prospect of Nationalists doing any fighting for the Empire outside their own country'. Recruiting in Louth remained poor in September 1914, picked up in October with improvements in soldiers' pay and allowances, but had died out by the autumn of 1915. It has been estimated that approximately 3,000 men from Louth served in the First World War, but like Armagh less than 300 were known to be members of the National Volunteers.[28] In both Armagh and Louth, the AOH held considerable sway and Redmond was politically popular among nationalists, but local and national IPP figures campaigned to improve recruitment figures with negligible effect.

Leaders of the main churches in Armagh may have influenced attitudes towards the war, but they too seem to have had little effect on enlistment. The Church of Ireland archbishop of Armagh, John Crozier, was a consistent, vociferous supporter of Britain's war effort, endowing it with the religious semblance of a medieval crusade against a Germany that was materialist or atheist in its views.[29] Crozier encouraged recruiting and, in contrast to the Catholic Church, great care was taken by the Church of Ireland to identify with the armed forces; a roll of honour became commonplace in many churches to record the names of parishioners who had enlisted.[30] Crozier visited the front in early 1916, along with Sir James Stronge, and took the opportunity to meet with troops from across the island and to praise their joint efforts.[31] Other Protestant clergymen also voiced their support for the war, stressing the importance of defending the empire and, in one case, arguing that the war was a contest between 'either Protestantism or the Papacy, either freedom or the serfdom of Kaiserism that they were pouring out their blood for'.[32] In contrast, Roman Catholic Cardinal Logue's view of the war has been described as 'for the empire, against the government'.[33] While he sympathized with the allied cause, Logue largely restricted himself to ensuring that the spiritual needs of Catholic soldiers were adequately provided for.[34] He refused to endorse recruitment drives and in April 1916 would not give permission for recruiting rallies to be held in the vicinity of churches in his diocese. However, a year later he personally welcomed visiting soldiers from the Canadian army.[35] Logue's position seems to have been one of compassion and concern that war was causing depravity and trauma across the countries involved, an early version (in 1916 and 1917) of the 'war as waste' criticism.[36]

At home, the economic impact of the war was decidedly unequal. The linen industry had a mixed war, although employers had anticipated profitable markets and full-time working as Austrian and German producers were cut off from the American markets. These hopes were not realized due to the fluctuating supply of flax first from Belgium and later from Russia, and also due to unsuccessful tendering for government contracts for aero linen and tents.[37] Farmers had a much better war due to the soaring prices paid for their produce. One analysis shows how prices paid for all foodstuffs in Armagh city's market between September 1914 and January 1919 more than doubled, with the sharpest rises coming in 1917.[38] Production costs rose too and, at a recruiting meeting in Poyntzpass in 1915, William Johnston argued that the 'war's costs would eat up all the profits the farming classes are now making'.[39] But Sir John Lonsdale MP did not share this view and acknowledged later that year that he did not expect many more recruits from Armagh without compulsion: 'I imagine Protestant farmers would not show much eagerness, now they are making so much money by staying at home.'[40] The high prices prompted negative reaction with even normally supportive newspapers admitting the truth of accusations of excessive agricultural profits.[41] One incident in February 1916 shone a light on reactions to war profiteering. A social evening in support of the Red Cross at Tullyallen Presbyterian church was disrupted by young men shouting and cheering during the proceedings with chants of 'what's the price of yellow meal?' directed at Portadown mill-owner M.P. Clow.[42]

Given that inflation was in double figures from the start of 1916, even those working full time had to practice 'rigid economies'.[43] As a result, there was growing pressure for wage increases, especially in the summer and autumn of 1917. Typical of those involved were road workers employed by Armagh UDC, who successfully pressed for a 1s. per week rise in August 1917.[44] However, most attention centred on the textiles industry, where the workers were organized into sectional trade unions (weavers, hemmers, veiners, tenters and so on), rather than in general unions. The tenters, who set up spinning and weaving machines, had demanded a pay rise in late 1916 and were rebuffed after a short strike.[45] This heralded an increase in industrial unrest in 1917. The tenters again struck in July 1917, demanding a significant weekly pay rise of 20s. This led to a protracted dispute that went to government arbitration which was rejected by angry employers.[46] The strikes soon spread across Portadown, Lurgan and Armagh city among women workers in the mills and textile factories, railway workers and some employed in construction. The unrest was attributed not only to union organizers coming from Belfast and a successful wave of strikes in Britain, but also to the struggle, particularly by women, 'to make both ends meet'.[47] The unrest continued into 1918 as inflation remained high, resulting in severe levels of poverty. Launching a new child welfare scheme in Portadown in April 1918, Thomas Shillington, veteran Protestant home ruler, spoke of the high mortality rate among infants and stated that assistance for new mothers was critical.[48] In his March 1918 report, CI Oulton complained that 'it is easy to start a strike now' and went on to mention four concurrent stoppages: weavers in Lurgan, hemstitchers in Portadown, cabinet-makers in Richhill, and asylum attendants in Armagh city. The strikes had begun in January in scutching mills across the south of the county for higher wages and over the use of non-union labour and then spread to various other industries, including council staff.[49] Most of the disputes were settled for higher wages, but a strike in Armagh asylum, for a change in conditions and a weekly pay rise of 10s., proved both controversial and, ultimately for the workers, unsuccessful. Newspaper coverage was scathing and largely praised the RIC and soldiers for intervening to secure patients and protect the small number of staff (4 out of 52) who continued working. The strike was broken after three weeks. Thereafter, Armagh played little part in the national strike that affected asylums in September 1918.[50]

While Oulton's reports after August 1914 repeatedly referred to the relaxation of political tensions, there were incidents that highlighted the continuing potential for conflict. In October 1914 the Armagh city branch of the National Volunteers escorted thirty of its members called up for service to the train station. The UVF was also present at the station, providing an escort for army recruits from their ranks. When both forces arrived, a group of about sixty UVF men broke away and went through the ranks of the National Volunteers, 'cursing the Pope, shouting "No Home Rule" and other insulting epithets'. According to one account, no notice was taken of the abuse which spoke 'volumes for the discipline and spirit of the Armagh City Volunteers'.[51] The destruction of a partially built AOH hall at the end of March 1916 by a large crowd, which included 200 armed UVF men, at Tartaghan or Breagh, near Portadown, also caused a stir. A fusillade of 'several hundred' shots, some of which were directed into the thatch of a nearby house, where John Donnelly, a middle-aged Catholic lived, added to the anger. Oulton maintained that local nationalists did not want the hall, which was being pushed by people from outside the area regardless of the consequences.[52] But the new MP for College Green, John D. Nugent, stated in parliament that this was the third attempt to build a hall in the locality and that the attacks were reported to have 'aroused a strong feeling in the district'.[53]

A final curious incident revealed evidence of sectarian tensions within the RIC itself. On 8 July 1915, Sergeant Denis Leonard, stationed in Keady, addressed a gathering in the Beresford Arms Hotel in Armagh city, where he allegedly stated:

> Carson is a fraud. Your Ulster Volunteers are a fraud. My father was a policeman but a good Fenian. My brother is a Fenian and I am a Fenian myself … We will have Home Rule and will never submit to you … When Home Rule comes, we will be back from the war. The Irish Brigade will be drilled and will cross the Boyne and walk on your neck.

At a disciplinary hearing, Head Constable Long of Armagh was the main prosecution witness, even though he had not seen Leonard speak (but knew his voice), and had not interviewed another RIC sergeant to confirm that Leonard was one of three RIC on duty that night, all of whom were Catholic and the subject of disciplinary proceedings. The hotel proprietor, James Best, supported Long's evidence but, it was revealed, he had been prosecuted by Leonard in Keady for a weights and measure offence.[54] Leonard protested at the obvious bias in the hearing, but refused to give evidence on his own behalf and did not deny making the comments (though he stated that in Ulster, the term 'Fenian' as used by him, meant 'Catholic' and not a rebel).[55] The RIC inquiry decided that Leonard should be dismissed but, as he had enlisted in the Irish Guards, he was instead demoted to constable.[56] After the war, Leonard transmitted plans for a raid on the RIC barracks in Cookstown, County Tyrone, where he was stationed, to IRA contacts in Armagh city and Keady. A successful attack by the IRA on the barracks took place on 16 June 1920.[57]

The split that occurred in the Irish Volunteers in 1914 has been described as a 'muted bang and a drawn-out whimper'.[58] While it appeared that the majority of those who supported Redmond would remain effective, as early as the end of 1914 the existing thirty-seven National Volunteer branches in Armagh were moribund.[59] When ordered to parade at Crossmaglen in October 1914, the Mullaghbawn members did not know which side of the Volunteer split had called them together or why. It was, in fact, a poorly attended National Volunteer event, at which loyal noises for Redmond were made, that marked the end of volunteering in that part of the county until early 1918.[60] The inactivity continued in 1915 when only 120 Armagh volunteers, including Éamon Donnelly and Frank Short, who would later join SF, attended a National Volunteer rally in the Phoenix Park, Dublin, in April.[61] To all intents and purposes, the Redmondite Volunteers as a functioning body had ceased to exist by late 1915, although occasional efforts were made to 'combat apathy', 'instil virility' and maintain some semblance of organization. They retained possession of a cache of arms and in October 1915 the Armagh city corps debated 'sending their rifles away for fear the government might seize them'.[62] This Armagh city committee was sufficiently divided politically that the members could not agree to give John Dillon a guard of honour in October 1914, and one speaker denounced him as a 'recruiting sergeant for the British army'.[63]

The radicals in the newly (re)formed Irish Volunteers were small in number, nationally perhaps 12,000, and led by two Ulstermen, Eoin MacNeill and Bulmer Hobson. Within the new leadership, a group of IRB activists, notably Tom Clarke and Seán Mac Diarmada, secretly decided as early as August 1914 to use the opportunity provided by the war to launch an armed rebellion against British rule. In Armagh, Charles McGleenan recorded that a branch of the Irish Volunteers existed in Blackwatertown in late 1914, though CI Oulton believed there was no support for the views of MacNeill and his allies in Armagh, a stance he maintained through 1915 and into 1916.[64] The efforts of Herbert Moore Pim, a colourful political figure, to address a meeting in Camlough on 20 June 1915, organized by Henry Osborne to promote the cause of the Irish Volunteers, was 'met with opposition', seemingly led by 81-year-old Canon John Quinn.[65] Oulton reported further unsuccessful attempts to establish branches of the Volunteers in Corrinshego (February 1916) and Blackwatertown (March 1916).[66] The IRB made a critical contribution towards the growth of the Irish Volunteers elsewhere, but were unable to do much in Armagh beyond expressing opposition to the war.[67] The IRB county centre, John Southwell, who was based in Newry, recalled that the county was poorly organized by 1916, outside of a few circles based in Blackwatertown and limited parts of south Armagh, notably Camlough (under Thomas Arthur Hughes).[68]

The outbreak of the rebellion on 24 April 1916, therefore, came as a surprise to the vast majority in the county, and Armagh did not feature in any significant way in the plans or the events themselves. As historian Charles Townshend has written, 'the mobilisation in Ulster was, not unexpectedly, short lived.'[69] A small group of IRB members from Blackwatertown assembled at Coalisland, County Tyrone, on Easter Sunday to meet the Belfast Volunteers only to receive instructions to 'demobilise and disperse'.[70] This group went home and gathered each night of Easter week, partially armed, to await instructions that never came. One of those who waited was Charles McGleenan. He had not gone to Coalisland and later recalled that he had not understood the importance of the events.[71] According to the original plans for the rebellion, Donal O'Hannigan, a Galwayman, was sent by Seán Mac Diarmada to Dundalk. On Easter Sunday he was to take command of all Volunteers in south Armagh, south Down, Louth and Meath. Their orders were to march from Dundalk to west Dublin, and to form part of a cordon surrounding the city. However, 'south Armagh were not expected to do anything and no allowance was made for them'.[72] Pádraig Quinn later recalled how he and his schoolfriend Frank Aiken met nightly in Newry to see what news they could gather about the Dublin events.[73]

There were a few incidental arrests in Armagh. The well-known Irish language writer and poet Pádraic Ó Conaire was travelling by train to Dundalk when he was arrested at Portadown on the grounds that it was thought he was a member of SF. He was held in Armagh gaol for three weeks before being released without charge.[74] Michael Donnelly from Silverbridge, County Armagh, was active with the Dundalk Volunteers and was part of a group who were under orders to seize National Volunteer arms held in Dundalk.[75] That operation did not come to pass. Donnelly was arrested, held in Richmond barracks, Dublin, and on 13 May deported to Wakefield prison.[76] The IRB county head for Armagh, John Southwell, was also arrested in Newry. In Blackwatertown, John Garvey, a local IRB leader, believed he too would be arrested and was shadowed at a fair in Moy. Curiously, he was then the subject of discussion between the RIC DI in Armagh city, Connery, and the local Roman Catholic administrator, Fr Ward. It was agreed that as he 'was the only man in the district under suspicion it would be better not to press an arrest'.[77]

Reaction to the rebellion was mostly hostile from both unionists and nationalists. Speaking at the opening of an exhibition in Portadown on 24 April, when news of the Rising was filtering through, Archbishop Crozier appealed to loyalists to show restraint and added:

> The eyes of England must be opened now and the ears of the deaf must be unstopped to hear what was going on and learn something of the character of the men as well as the conduct of the men to whom it was proposed to hand over the destinies of Ireland.[78]

Sir James Stronge issued a public statement that 'in a crisis like the present, it is the duty of every loyal man to be ready to place his services at the absolute disposal of the government'.[79] In response, the UVF 'offered their services' in several places and in Blackwaterstown and Newry, the National Volunteers also offered assistance to the RIC.[80] Unionist hostility in Armagh was heightened with the news that Lieutenant J. Howard Calvert, Royal Irish Rifles, son of the clerk of Lurgan Poor Law Union, James Calvert, had been killed on the afternoon of 24 April, shortly after the fighting first broke out in Dublin. Calvert, who was stationed in Portobello barracks, Rathmines, was part of a unit making its way towards Dublin Castle when it was fired on at the corner of Cuffe Street and Wexford Street by members of the nearby Jacobs' factory garrison.[81] Expressions of condolence were widespread and those from the Lurgan board of guardians also commended General Sir John Maxwell on the prompt action taken to quell the rebellion.[82] There were others with Armagh connections who were killed. Private Denis Wilson, Royal Irish Rifles, who came from Hill St, Lurgan, but lived in Glasgow with his wife and three children, was shot dead while trying to reach Dublin Castle. Wilson had enlisted in the army only a week previously.[83] A former RIC head constable and musketry instructor in Armagh, Tom Brosnan, was shot dead by a fellow soldier, having helped repel the Irish Citizen Army's attack on Dublin Castle.[84] Another man with Lurgan connections was Edward Costello who was a member of the Irish Citizen Army, fought in the GPO, and was then killed in Church Street in the retreat.[85]

The local unionist press naturally condemned the rebellion. The *Ulster Gazette* claimed that nine out of ten people would gladly pluck the events of Easter week out of the history books, 'so deep is the sense of shame and indignation with which they view the acts of a small minority of traitorous irreconcilables'.[86] Much of the blame was heaped by unionists on the incompetence of the Castle administration, Birrell, in particular, whose resignation as chief secretary was welcomed. The perhaps obligatory soft words about him from Carson in the House of Commons came in for sharp criticism from the veteran Armagh city unionist, Joshua Peel, who regarded the statement as out of touch with local sentiment.[87] The ill-feeling towards the rebels was understandable given the juxtaposition of the news from Dublin with reports of the war in Europe and the hostility intensified after the battle of the Somme in July 1916. This was summed up by the Revd R.S. Morrison of St Saviour's, Portadown:

> To talk of future compromise arrived at by the patriotic Irishmen who have fought side by side at the Somme and whose forefathers fought against each other on the banks of the Boyne was the dream of a visionary.[88]

Nationalist newspapers and local authorities in the neighbouring counties of Monaghan and Louth had also criticized both the rebels and the rebellion.[89] CI Oulton noted that in Armagh the rebellion received 'no active sympathy from the nationalists', although he believed that there would undoubtedly be some who did actually sympathize with it. John McCoy had mixed feelings, thinking the leaders were 'foolish' as they had little hope of success, but if he had been in Dublin, he would have offered his service to the rebels.[90] The *Frontier Sentinel* suggested the rebellion was an illustration of what happened when experienced leaders were replaced by men without wisdom or prudence. Yet it also called for leniency towards the rebels. While it felt inclined to apportion blame, and referred to the rebels as 'misguided dupes', it decried the calls from unionist newspapers for 'extreme punitive measures'.[91] By the time this editorial was published, eight of the rebel leaders had already been executed. A week later, the *Sentinel* called for the 'fullest possible mercy': 'it is not by a system of execution and imprisonment that normality can be restored to the country … the future will better appreciate a merciful sequel to the story of horror than a policy of drastic severity.'[92]

This editorial also reminded the *Sentinel*'s readership of the role that unionist leaders played in creating dissension, threatening civil war and 'boasting of the assistance from a powerful continental monarch to resist Home Rule'.[93] The UIL-controlled Newry No. 2 RDC passed a motion expressing their 'abhorrence of the recent deplorable occurrences in Dublin and our gratification that the rising has been so promptly quelled'.[94] By the start of June, Armagh UDC, chaired by Thomas McLaughlin, was calling for prisoners to be released, believing the arrests to be 'misguided actions, which … must alienate from the government the sympathy and support of the people of Ireland'. The UDC also demanded the immediate introduction of home rule for the whole of Ireland.[95] The CI's June report noted that there had been a shift in sympathy towards the rebels since April as 'nationalists have no doubt been upset by the executions in Dublin'.[96]

The initial reaction of the Catholic Church in Ireland was one of 'silence is the best policy'.[97] The *Belfast News-Letter* reprinted a *Daily Mail* report that the Pope was critical of the Rising and he would give instructions to all Irish Catholics, clergy and laity, to 'maintain perfect loyalty toward England'.[98] According to this report, Cardinal Logue's initial reply to the Vatican stated: 'Insurrection happily terminated. Insurgents have surrendered unconditionally. Hope peace soon re-established.'[99] In June an episcopal conference was held in Maynooth to discuss the Church's reaction to the Rising and to respond to accusations of clerical connivance with the rebels. This prompted Logue's first public response wherein he referred to the outbreak as 'foolish and absurd' and was critical of all the various Volunteer organizations. He was also critical of a 'muddled' response by the British government, especially the subsequent widespread arrest and imprisonment of suspects which he saw as an 'act of folly'. He believed the authorities should have 'let this die like a bad dream … without going to those extreme measures.'[100] In private, Logue went further and excoriated General Maxwell at a face-to-face meeting on 23 June: 'You put your foot in it' he declared and pointed out that the executions had made martyrs of the rebel leaders and gained overwhelming support for them.[101]

Northern Catholic bishops were even less impressed by the government's next moves. After the executions, Asquith gave Lloyd George the task of reaching agreement on a constitutional settlement. Lloyd George assured Redmond that the Home Rule Act of 1914 could be quickly implemented with six Ulster counties temporarily excluded, pending a final settlement at an imperial conference to be held at the end of the war. Carson, meanwhile, was assured that the six counties would be permanently excluded and was to stake his political fortunes on this promise.[102] A meeting of a committee of the UUC was held on 6 June at which Carson proposed a six-county exclusion, asserting that more was not possible and that resistance was useless.[103] The UUC members were given time to consult, which was sensible as unionists in Armagh appeared unsettled by the change in events and tactics. The first response of the *Portadown News* in June 1916 to the UUC's consideration of Lloyd George's home rule proposal was to run a story under the headline: 'Not settlement but surrender'.[104] Unionist members of Armagh County Council then proposed a resolution against (all of) Ulster's inclusion in any home rule settlement; R.J. Harden of Lurgan denounced any discussion of the issue given the recent rising.[105] However, when the UUC unanimously agreed to the proposals a week later, the Armagh unionist press accepted the turn of events, claiming it was only being done 'for the exigencies of empire', and praised the leadership of Carson and Craig and the sacrifice of delegates from Cavan, Monaghan and Donegal.[106] According to Jackson, the partition strategy that Edward Carson and James Craig had promoted since 1913 now had the mandate of the UUC.[107] Archbishop Crozier, who was more in tune with Irish as opposed to Ulster unionist views, felt the proposal was the least worst option, but still a bad one.[108] The 1916 Rising, the subsequent spread of violence across the island, and the progress of the war with its ever-growing casualty lists provided the context in which Armagh unionists grew more sympathetic to a partitionist solution.

The attitude of Armagh nationalists was even more confused. CI Oulton reported that a meeting in Armagh city on 15 June had unanimously rejected the temporary exclusion proposals, while just a week later at a convention in Belfast, a majority of the Armagh delegates voted in favour of those very proposals.[109] The Armagh city conference was described as 'fully representative of the nationalists, lay and clerical of Co. Armagh', chaired by Canon Quinn of Camlough and addressed by Dr Charles O'Neill, MP for South Armagh. It passed the customary resolution of loyalty to Redmond and the IPP, but added that 'we vehemently protest against the outrage threatened to the six Ulster counties'. Furthermore, it vowed 'never to accept a settlement by which any portion of Ulster would be excluded from the scope of the Home Rule Act'.[110] The diocesan administrator, Fr J.W. Brady, referred to the 'depth and determination' of the opposition to temporary exclusion from the 'most loyal supporters of the Irish Party in the UIL and AOH throughout county Armagh'.[111] As Eamon Phoenix has noted, 'the Armagh resolutions were the more ominous' for Redmond and Joe Devlin as they were proposed by John McGlone, UIL national director in Mid Armagh, and supported by Andrew Campbell, a prominent Hibernian solicitor in Lurgan, as well as by the veteran Protestant home ruler Thomas Shillington.[112] Their views were reportedly supported by Logue, whose hostility to the Lloyd George proposal was captured in his remark that it would be 'infinitely better to remain as we are for fifty years to come under English rule than to accept these proposals'.[113] Other northern Catholic bishops, notably Charles McHugh of Derry and Patrick McKenna of Clogher, were equally hostile to any suggestion of partition. Little wonder that John Dillon believed the northern bishops wished to defeat the settlement.[114]

At the convention held on 23 June 1916 in St Mary's Hall, Belfast, the debate exposed deep divisions among northern nationalists, including an irreversible split in the Tyrone UIL.[115] The speakers from Armagh were divided as Canon Quinn supported the motion to accept the Lloyd George proposals, while Thomas McLaughlin, chairman of the Armagh UDC, and John McGlone both spoke against. The *Irish Independent* and the *Frontier Sentinel*, both opposed to partition, carried reports of McLaughlin's comments that the proposal was 'worse than useless' and a letter from an 'Armagh nationalist' that exclusion had been denounced by Redmond in 1913 and would 'give ourselves up to a party of Orange bigots'.[116] The 113 Armagh delegates divided as follows: 62 voted for the exclusion proposal, 32 opposed it and 19 abstained (the highest number of any county).[117] Some UIL stalwarts in Armagh, including Canon Grimes of Portadown, had argued before the Belfast convention that they wanted to amend the resolution passed at the Armagh city meeting, but had been prevented from doing so and were, therefore, not bound by that meeting's decision.[118] The perception that the counties divided on an east (in favour)/west (opposed) basis placed Armagh somewhere in the middle.[119] Ultimately, the influence of Joe Devlin and the threat of resignation by Redmond were required to secure the crucial support of Ulster nationalists (475 voters to 265) for the exclusion proposal.[120]

This division and turmoil counted for nothing when Lloyd George's initiative was effectively abandoned after Lord Lansdowne declared in the House of Lords on 11 July that partition would be permanent.[121] Faced with this reality, Redmond publicly rejected the proposals on 22 July but the damage to his credibility and that of the IPP was immense. Nevertheless, the IPP brand, assisted by the strength of the AOH, continued to muster considerable support in parts of Armagh, Monaghan and Louth.[122] The dissension among Armagh nationalists was noted by CI Oulton: 'the clergy are particularly annoyed over the voting in Belfast, being entirely anti-exclusionist in the city'.[123] Éamon Donnelly (secretary) and John McGlone (executive delegate) resigned from the Mid Armagh UIL executive in September, the former indicating that 'he would be acting hypocritically if he continued in a movement controlled by leaders whose policy he no longer approved of'.[124] The same meeting heard calls for unity from the UIL organizer, James Convery, because 'a faction-riven Ireland could never accomplish anything' and from Bernard O'Neill, formerly a key IRB member in Blackwatertown.[125] Although the local UIL and AOH organizations remained largely loyal to the IPP, a series of UIL meetings had mixed results.[126] In most meetings, the speakers, including O'Neill and Richard McGhee, successfully urged loyalty to Redmond while denouncing dissidents or 'factionists'.[127] However, at Whitecross and Aghayallogue (near Meigh), both in the south of the county, meetings were abandoned or resolutions were not put before hostile crowds.[128] This attempt at a settlement also effectively marked the beginning of the end of Carson as a political force within unionism. Lonsdale became chair of the 'Ulster Party' in Westminster in December 1916 and James Craig was the effective leader of the UUC in Belfast, marking the ascendancy of those who accepted permanent partition and the abandonment of their southern brethren as the only acceptable constitutional settlement.[129]

As 1916 drew to a close, it was apparent that the UIL, in particular, was in danger of floundering; it was saved in part by the absence of a credible nationalist alternative. A new anti-partition organization, the Irish Nation League, flourished in the summer before stagnating but in its brief life it 'eased the path of many who would have found the transition from the IPP to SF as too drastic to be taken in one step'.[130] It had its greatest impact in Tyrone and Derry, where leaders of the League went on to become prominent SF politicians, but no branch seems to have been formed in Armagh.[131] The reasons for this are not clear. One of the League's promoters felt 'a very large number in Ulster were in favour of the anti-partition movement but they are afraid of the Nation League', while the lack of any senior clerical backing, unlike in the neighbouring diocese of Derry, may have been important.[132]

The views of younger Catholic clergy, read through their support for collections for dependants of those men killed, executed or imprisoned after the rebellion, may have been changing. The Irish National Aid Association and Volunteer Dependants' Fund began as two organizations, the radical Volunteer Dependants' Fund and the more moderate Irish National Aid Association, which had J.D. Nugent on its committee. They merged in early August 1916 and became a catalyst for change in nationalist opinion, offering an opportunity to create a 'vibrant local organization' in the autumn of 1916.[133] Even before the merger, the *Frontier Sentinel* called for support for Volunteer Dependants collections while the first National Aid collection occurred in Armagh city in July.[134] The collection in Armagh parish, which included the city and hinterland, was taken up in fifteen different district collections by more than forty women, several of whom (including the Hanrattys and Garveys) would later become involved in Cumann na mBan.[135] In Cullyhanna parish, the collection committee was headed by the local Catholic curate, Fr Arthur Smyth, and the national teacher, Michael Devlin, who were listed as members of SF in 1917.[136] The amounts received were never large, perhaps less than £500 from the county by the end of the year, but the collections provided an opportunity to show sympathy for the spouses and children of those killed or imprisoned. They also provided an outlet for more radical opinions.

In his review of 1916, CI Oulton suggested that the rebellion had scarcely any effect on Armagh, but then noted that among nationalists

> the old latent spirit of the rebel [emerged], and after the execution of the leaders a malignant spirit manifested itself by indifference to Allied successes, a semi-satisfaction of the first report of the Jutland naval engagement … and indifferences to supplying things for the wounded.[137]

He also pointed to an AOH county meeting on 10 December at which a 'complaint was made that owing to SF tendencies there was a falling off (of AOH membership) in South Armagh'.[138] Although recruitment levels for the army were low, the sacrifices made by loyalists fighting in the war were kept to the forefront by Archbishop Crozier and other clergymen and unionist political leaders, who were pressing for the extension of conscription to Ireland.[139] The hostility of unionist politicians towards any home rule settlement remained unflinching, and was encapsulated in an address by Sir John Lonsdale to the mid-Armagh Unionist Association in November 1916. Although Ulster unionists had accepted Lloyd George's exclusion proposals very reluctantly, in light of the broader war aims and the need to 'strengthen the empire', he did not regret that the settlement had collapsed.[140] In December, Stronge continued to criticize Lloyd George's July scheme and the (false) rumours of a fresh attempt at a settlement, before promising the Orange Order in the county that they would not again suspend the Twelfth celebrations as they had done since the outbreak of the war.[141]

5 An altering political situation?: Armagh in 1917–18

In 1917 SF became a political force to be reckoned with, winning four successive by-elections against the IPP in North Roscommon, South Longford, East Clare and Kilkenny.[1] The by-elections were important, not least as Michael Laffan has noted, because they 'facilitated the drastic change in the scale and efficiency of the SF effort ... the process snowballed and each victory facilitated the next'.[2] In its rebirth, SF emerged with new separatist principles and a new radical republican leadership made up for the most part of former internees from the 1916 Rising.[3] In May 1917 Lloyd George, now prime minister, invited delegates from all walks of life, including political parties, chairmen of county councils and representative of the Churches, to a convention to discuss how home rule could be implemented. SF declined to take part as complete independence was not on the agenda. The IPP was unable to force a settlement at the convention and was 'suffocated by its proceedings'.[4] Ulster unionists were only partially engaged, being increasingly content to concentrate on securing the exclusion of six north-eastern counties, including Armagh, from any settlement. While the nature of political discourse was changing slowly in 1917 and 1918, in Armagh the most significant episode within nationalism was the hotly disputed contest between the IPP and SF in the South Armagh by-election in February 1918. The victory of the IPP was a clear illustration of its continued dominance, at least in certain regions, for the time being.

The gradual pace of political change within nationalism in Armagh was reflected in RIC reports that recorded, month-on-month, significant growth in the numbers of SF branches and membership. In January 1917 the party had two 'moribund' branches and 32 members in the county, in Armagh city and Blackwatertown. Significant growth was recorded during the summertime and by December there were fourteen or fifteen branches with 786 members.[5] This coincided with the release of the remaining 1916 prisoners and with a revival of Irish National Aid and Volunteer Dependants' Fund collections, led by fundraising events in Armagh city and Whitecross.[6] In June, noting the revival of the Armagh city branch with a membership of 100, CI Oulton warned that 'Sinn Féinism had been spreading and is taking shape'.[7] The following month, three more branches were established; one of those was formed on 29 July after Michael Collins and J.J. Byrne had addressed meetings in Armagh and Mullinary.[8] This was one of many 'weekend jaunts' to establish SF clubs undertaken by Collins and IRB allies (including J.J. Byrne, Paul Galligan and Seán Ó Murthuile) that summer.[9] Efforts were made to revive the IRB in 1917 in Armagh as elsewhere. The return of Newry-based internees extended the reorganization into other parts of south Armagh from September.[10] The overlap of IRB circles and SF branches was clear in the early days of SF clubs in 1917 within or around Armagh city and Newry, as well as Blackwatertown and Camlough. However, as more and more SF branches were formed in late 1917 and 1918 – and with the revival of the Irish Volunteers – the influence of the IRB gradually faded. This also occurred in parts of neighbouring east Tyrone.[11]

Police reports tended to deprecate those involved in SF meetings as being of 'little importance' or 'standing'. For example, a report of a meeting held in Armagh City Hall in September 1917, addressed by Éamon de Valera, Arthur Griffith, Constance Markievicz and the new Roscommon MP, Count George Plunkett, highlighted the youth of those in attendance, de Valera's 'disloyal' language, and the belief that 'men of stake in the country still hold aloof, and are averse to revolution'.[12] The local unionist press took a similar view, emphasizing the youth of those involved in one club at Middletown or that 'no persons of importance attended' a second large SF meeting in Armagh city in November.[13] Another meeting held in Cullyhanna in December 1917 was attended by 'an ignorant lot with no leader of standing', according to the CI. However, the reality was different as a local schoolteacher, Michael Devlin, and the former UIL branch secretary, Hugh Kelly, were key figures in the club and the meeting was addressed by Éamon Donnelly, by that stage the main SF organizer in Armagh.[14]

The two largest nationalist organizations – the UIL with forty branches and 2,800 members and the AOH with forty-four divisions and a membership of 2,300 – were the main barriers to SF growth.[15] The AOH, in particular, was very capable of organizing large public events such as the traditional rally in Armagh city on 15 August 1917, when John Dillon was the key speaker. Between 5,000 and 10,000 were in attendance from all parts of the county. They heard calls for loyalty to the IPP and their critics denounced as 'cranks'.[16] Other events arranged by the AOH to mark the Manchester Martyrs commemoration held on 23 November 1917 in Keady and Derryadd, near Lurgan, were described as 'mild affairs', but attracted large crowds.[17] The UIL was weaker but Charles O'Neill held a series of meetings across south and mid-Armagh in September and October with a view to 'counteracting the spreading influence of SF' by highlighting his own experience, the role the IPP had played in land reform and the hopes for the Irish Convention. However, the CI noted that O'Neill did not appear to be 'creating enthusiasm'.[18] In north Armagh, there was more support for the UIL among nationalists around Portadown, where the dangers of 'physical force' being adopted by SF were stressed by Canon Grimes and Alex Donnelly.[19]

Charles O'Neill identified the importance of the Irish Convention in his speeches in November 1917 and expressed the hope that a home rule settlement might emerge from it. There were some Armagh connections to the convention, including three delegates from the county: Archbishop Crozier and two unionists, H.B. Armstrong, chair of Armagh County Council, and Harry

MacGeagh, long-time chair of Lurgan UDC and also a linen manufacturer in the town. Unionists were ambivalent about the Irish Convention, perhaps fearing the emergence of an agreed or near-agreed settlement to pressurize them into acceptance.[20] Lonsdale's response, as party leader, to Lloyd George's invitation to send delegates was a cautious one, indicating the necessity of approval by the UUC.[21] There were fierce discussions within the UUC with 'very many Armagh and Fermanagh stalwarts' opposed to taking part. Only Carson's persuasive powers and the promise of an advisory committee that delegates could refer to ensured participation.[22] James Stronge dismissed any fears that Lonsdale and unionists could be portrayed in England as 'a lonely group of reactionaries standing in the way of Ireland's reconcilement' if they refused to attend, and backed oversight over delegates.[23] This position was fully supported by resolutions from the Orange Order in Armagh at a meeting in June 1917.[24] In the face of unionist ambivalence, the CI reported in May 1917 that 'most people believe it will come to nothing as far as the Convention is concerned' and Lonsdale told Armstrong to 'not allow the Convention worry you much.'[25]

The experience of the three Armagh delegates reveals much about the convention. Archbishop Crozier made significant attempts to reach a compromise on home rule (including advocating provincial parliaments), but he was an isolated figure among Ulster unionists by the time the convention reported in April 1918.[26] His friend and fellow delegate, H.B. Armstrong, co-authored a memorandum detailing Crozier's errors, while Stronge told colleagues that Crozier's fears for the future of the Church of Ireland were exaggerated.[27] Harry MacGeagh sat in most sessions but only involved himself in a committee to look at urban housing.[28] Armstrong's papers reveal that he sought to establish common ground on issues such as land purchase, but also confirm his belief that no agreement would be reached on the key issue of Ireland's constitutional arrangements. He also stayed in close touch with advisory committee members.[29] In 1923, in answer to a journalist's questions about the convention, he was positive about the quality and good humour of the discussions but felt it considered something that would not satisfy those who abstained (SF) and was horrified at the reported cost of the convention which came to £12,000.[30]

As 1917 drew to a close, there was growing uncertainty about the political future in Armagh. Two experienced Unionist MPs, William Moore and John Lonsdale, resigned their seats and took up positions in the judiciary and the House of Lords respectively.[31] There would be no by-election contests. In North Armagh the local Orange leader, councillor and now war veteran W.J. Allen declared his hand even before Moore's resignation and made himself unassailable, killing any talk of a Labour candidate.[32] In Mid Armagh, the rumour that SF might stand proved unfounded and the contest became a choice between two Unionist hopefuls, Richard Best of Richhill and James Lonsdale, a brother of the resigning MP. After a meeting of the constituency organization, Best stood aside and Lonsdale, asserting his life-long association with the constituency and his priority to serve the 'interests of Ulster', was returned.[33]

Within nationalism, Cardinal Logue's pastoral letter to the Armagh diocese on 25 November 1917 caused a stir. It focused on a call by Pope Benedict XV for an end to the world war, but also called for an end to agitation in Ireland which Logue believed would result in defeat and disaster:

> And all this in pursuit of a dream that no man in his sober senses can hope to see realized: the establishment of an Irish Republic by an appeal to the potentates of Europe seated at a Peace Conference or an appeal to force by hurling an unarmed people against the might of an Empire which has five million men under arms ... The thing would be ludicrous if it were not so mischievous and fraught with such danger when cleverly used as an incentive to fire the imagination of an ardent, generous, patriotic people.[34]

The pastoral received a mixed reception within his own diocese of Armagh. The *Drogheda Independent* commented that it would be endorsed by 'every commonsense individual within the four seas of Ireland'. However, the *Frontier Sentinel* maintained

> it would be regretted by the vast bulk of the Irish race and five-sixths of the Irish Priesthood whose sympathies and activities are enlisted in the National Movement ... the Catholics of Ireland, including many distinguished ecclesiastics and at least two revered bishops, attached themselves to the Sinn Fein policy ... and they could find nothing by which the National Movement could be impeached.[35]

Logue chose to meet head-on the political challenge posed by the growing support for separatism within the Church body that had become obvious by the presence of many Catholic clergy at the funeral of Thomas Ashe in September 1917. Whether Logue's pastoral letter was intended to be a pre-emptive strike to stop Armagh priests from supporting SF in the future, or to silence those priests already advocating the separatist cause, is not clear.[36] In Camlough and Portadown senior clergy and UIL supporters (Canons Quinn and Grimes) were reported by the police as having added to the pastoral but the exact detail of what they had to say has been lost. The CI expected that the pastoral letter 'will no doubt have considerable effect against Sinn Féin in this diocese'.[37]

The test came when a by-election in South Armagh was triggered by the death of Charles O'Neill on 14 January 1918.[38] On paper the seat was in a strong IPP enclave with the AOH particularly active and there were even some initial doubts, quickly denied, that SF would even stand as its organization was quite new and weak.[39] John Dillon managed to be both optimistic and fatalistic:

> South Armagh is about the most favourable seat for us in Ireland and if the Party candidate is beaten there I really do not see any reason for believing that we could hold any seat in Ireland in a general election.[40]

The register of 6,347 voters had not been updated since 1910. It had strong nationalist majorities in the Ballybot (Newry), Forkhill and Crossmaglen polling districts, and a more evenly balanced electorate in the smaller Newtownhamilton, Clady, Milltown and Poyntzpass districts.[41] The IPP was helped by a short two-week contest which highlighted the unpreparedness of SF, whose campaign was managed from Dundalk by national organizers assisted by Louth activists.[42] Leading lights of the republican movement appeared in Armagh, including Éamon de Valera, Count Plunkett, Countess Markievicz and Laurence Ginnell. Irish Volunteers provided support, coming from Dublin under the leadership of Michael Collins and Harry Boland, and from County Clare and Cork city under their commanders, including Tomás MacCurtain.[43] For the IPP, Devlin and Dillon were the main speakers while AOH members, both local and from Belfast, Down and Tyrone, provided the organizational backbone. Both sides held dozens of meetings, and on the 'Big Sunday' (27 January 1918) over thirty meetings and large rallies were held across the constituency.[44] The SF party convention selected Dr Patrick McCartan, a Tyrone native and member of the Supreme Council of the IRB involved in planning the 1916 Rising, who had recently been arrested in Nova Scotia and deported while en route to Germany on an arms-buying mission.[45] He was nominated by two Camlough delegates: Dr James Aiken, elder brother of Frank Aiken, and Jack McElhaw, later to become an active member of the IRA in the region. The UIL convention was a show of local strength and selected Patrick Donnelly, a solicitor and native of County Derry, as the candidate. He was nominated by the veteran Canon Quinn, who highlighted Logue's recent pastoral and contrasted the 'sane' politics of the cardinal with the 'insane' politics of de Valera, which 'could only lead to bloodshed and disunity'.[46]

The campaign was predictably nasty and sometimes violent given what was at stake. On the first weekend, J.D. Nugent accused McCartan of lending his car to unionists who had run guns into Larne in 1914 (something McCartan had never denied), which would be used to shoot nationalists.[47] McCartan was referred to as 'a colleague in traitorism of the loathsome Casement', accused of running away in 1916, and of being elected as a dispensary doctor in Gortin with unionist votes.[48] The allegations against Donnelly were tamer and centred on his having supported the exclusion proposal in 1916 for the promise of future favours.[49] Speeches from both parties also played to expected class and gender prejudices.[50] These included, for instance, that SF had little support in the constituency except for servant boys, women and unionists, while Seán Milroy, for SF, condemned his hecklers in Newry as 'Belfast corner boys', who had 'always disgraced Irish politics in the past'. Countess Markievicz, canvassing for SF, was attacked on several occasions to prevent her being heard, and Donnelly's supporters were denounced as 'separation women' (who were in receipt of income as their husband or son were in the British army) and 'wee mill girls'.[51]

Violence or the threat of it was never far away. John McCoy recalled that the Hibernians adopted a 'violent attitude and made various attempts to break up our meetings', which sometimes contested for space with IPP gatherings.[52] The most infamous clash occurred at Creggan Bridge, near Crossmaglen, on Sunday, 27 January, as a SF convoy of cars approached the town for a meeting. One car, in which de Valera, Austin Stack and Seán McEntee were travelling, was forced to stop by a large crowd from a rival meeting. The car was pelted with mud and one man thrust a pike into it, wounding several passengers. In one version, SF had now met the 'sturdy voter' of Ulster, who was not afraid of 'flag waving and stampeding', while in another version it appears de Valera needed medical treatment and cars were badly damaged.[53] The mobilization of supporters by both sides led to an inevitable 'politics of disruption' and claims of voter intimidation.[54] John Grant believed 'fisticuffs were considered by some as more effective than arguments' and the Irish Volunteers were crucial to the SF campaign for canvassing, providing transport, and taking charge at the polling booths.[55] Although the *Dundalk Democrat* complained that 'from every corner of Ireland came men, some of whom could only put three words of English together', the Volunteers made an impression in their uniforms and their military bearing, armed with hurls or sticks.[56] 'Taking charge' of a booth could be intimidatory – James Short recalled how a group of unionist mill workers marching en-masse to the polling station at Cladymilton to vote for Donnelly turned away when they saw Volunteers on guard there.[57]

While nationalist in-fighting dominated the narrative, it was clear that accommodating the unionist electorate of between 1,200 and 1,500 voters was another concern. The *Armagh Guardian* initially suggested that a unionist candidate could win, given the nationalist split.[58] Unionist voters received no signal from their political leaders and there was some excitement when Thomas Wakefield Richardson, son of the founder of Bessbrook, said he had been approached by 'a number of influential Unionist electors' and would stand on a temperance platform.[59] His withdrawal two days later, after a meeting of local unionists from the Bessbrook and Poyntzpass areas, was certainly to the advantage of Donnelly.[60] The lasting belief among SF supporters was that unionists supported Donnelly. Charles McGleenan recalled that the National Volunteers removed identification flags from their cars and transported unionists voters to the polling stations.[61] According to John Cosgrove, an Armagh city Volunteer:

We then saw the unusual spectacle of Hibernians. and Orangemen travelling together in the same public conveyance with the green Hibernian flag and the Orange Union Jack flying side by side … (this was the start of an intense opposition by the Hibernians to everything republican in our area).[62]

The IPP retained the seat with Donnelly receiving 2,324 votes to MacCartan's 1,305 and Richardson's 40. There was immediate debate about which candidate unionists had favoured. One separatist newspaper claimed that over a thousand had voted for Donnelly.[63] It missed a crucial point observed by Kevin O'Sheil that SF had only added 362 votes to the votes received by opponents of the IPP in December 1910 (which had a similar turnout of 57 per cent). In effect, SF 'made no appreciable impression upon the Nationalists of the constituency, whether they voted or did not vote'.[64]

The defeat of SF, which was followed by IPP victories in Waterford and East Tyrone, threatened to halt the SF advance. The South Armagh by-election also highlighted SF's weaknesses in the northern part of the country and de Valera's comment that their defeat was due to 'over-confidence' and neglect of Ulster was prescient.[65] SF had exploited the recruiting and conscription issues and the IPP's vulnerability on partition. But SF had little to say about partition beyond arguing that it would be a creation of the British government rather than of unionists. This sat oddly with de Valera's phrase, used in Bessbrook and replayed for years afterwards, that unionists were a 'rock in the road', which might have to be removed by blasting powder.[66]

The by-election revealed a small shift in the political leanings of some Catholic clergy and added strength to the separatist cause, not least in the formation of Volunteer companies, Cumann na mBan branches and SF clubs. Senior clergy, including Canon Quinn, Canon Corr and Fr Patrick Vallely, publicly continued to support the IPP and, on balance, Cardinal Logue's influence meant that Armagh clergy were not supporting SF in the same numbers as clergy in other dioceses.[67] However, there were exceptions such as Fr Smith, a curate in Newtown, who took down posters for an IPP meeting at one of his chapels and then supported McCartan's nomination.[68] De Valera regularly claimed that he had been pledged the support of younger clergy and this provoked some IPP speakers to denounce priests for becoming too involved in politics in a throw-back to the Parnell split.[69]

Putting best face on the loss, Countess Markievicz announced that 'the result was only a battle lost, not a defeat', which chimed well with supporters of SF and the Volunteers.[70] Not entirely disagreeing, but in an interesting commentary on the bitterness that the election generated, John McCoy maintained that 'we were not expecting to win the election but made a marvellous showing'. However, it created a lasting hostility between SF and Hibernians, who even refused to play Gaelic football together.[71] The activity of the Irish Volunteers in the South Armagh by-election provided the impetus for expansion of the organization. Companies and drilling may have begun in 1917 in Armagh city, Blackwatertown and Camlough, but the evidence is clearer that the Volunteers emerged strongly in February and March 1918.[72] During the by-election campaign, James McGuill (Dundalk), Michael Brennan (Clare) and George Plunkett (Dublin), brother of Joseph Mary Plunkett executed in 1916, helped to organize companies in places such as Crossmaglen, Dorsey, Mullaghbawn, Dromintee, Killeavy and Camlough (where Frank Aiken was appointed company commander).[73] McCoy recalled that the Mullaghbawn company was instructed 'not to recognise the authority of the Royal Irish Constabulary and, when necessary, to deal with them as our officers directed'.[74]

Drilling began soon after in a sign of growing defiance.[75] In March 1918, CI Oulton recorded that 'a man named Francis Aiken has been arrested for drilling at Camlough and remanded till 3rd inst. when he will be brought up at Newry petty sessions'.[76] At the hearing, the courthouse was rushed by SF supporters and, after Aiken was sentenced by the resident magistrate Woulfe Flanagan to a month's imprisonment, it was reported that 'wild scenes ensued, there was booing and cheering and shouts of "Up the Rebels" and the "Soldiers Song" was given'.[77] Soon afterwards, Jack McElhaw was also arrested for the same offence and, in response, there was an attack on Camlough RIC barracks by a crowd throwing stones.[78] When brought before the court, McElhaw was served tea in a cell by members of Newry Cumann na mBan, while a large crowd gathered outside and inside Newry courthouse. Woulfe Flanagan imposed a sentence of two months with hard labour, warning that McElhaw could have been sentenced to twelve months' imprisonment and that prison terms would continue to increase 'until they inflicted really heavy sentences'.[79] Large numbers of supporters and police confronted each other in Newry town as McElhaw was taken away and, in a further act of defiance, Irish Volunteers from Camlough marched back in formation through Newry to their home village.

In the face of these developments, Oulton finally acknowledged the existence of the Irish Volunteers in Armagh in April 1918, but merely mentioned that one branch had been established near Middletown with a membership of seventy. In addition, he reported that SF now had nineteen clubs with 1,309 members.[80] Companies of Volunteers formed in the Mullaghbawn, Dromintee, Crossmaglen and Cullyhanna areas, which directly bordered Louth, initially came under the command of the Dundalk Battalion, while other companies were linked to the Newry Battalion. By the end of 1918, all of the south Armagh companies were organized around the Camlough Battalion under the command of Frank Aiken. Shortly afterwards, this battalion in turn became part of the newly formed Newry Brigade under the command of Paddy Rankin, who had fought in Dublin during the Rising, with Aiken as his deputy.[81]

In late March 1918 the conscription crisis erupted. Conscription had been introduced in Britain in early 1916, but had not been extended to Ireland, much to the annoyance of some Armagh unionists.[82] The question was reopened when a massive German offensive on the Western Front, beginning on 21 March 1918, threatened to turn into a rout of the allied armies. There were 1.5 million trained men available in Britain for immediate service to combat the German onslaught, but Lloyd George refused to release them, and instead extended the terms of conscription in Britain which would be offset politically with the implementation of conscription in Ireland and in turn would be linked to the introduction of home rule. Given that any new recruits would need a minimum of six months training to bring them up to an acceptable level of proficiency, this was a proposal of bewildering political and military logic, especially as the final report of the Irish Convention, which advocated a home rule settlement, was also under consideration by the British cabinet.[83] The Dublin Castle administration had hoped the recent by-election defeats in South Armagh, East Tyrone and Waterford signalled that the popularity of SF had peaked and strongly advised against the proposal. Nevertheless, the conscription bill was introduced on 9 April 1918 and immediately sparked a political storm, which saw the IPP withdraw from parliament and make common cause with SF in opposition to the proposals. On the same day, the Catholic bishops issued a statement warning that conscription 'would be a fatal mistake, surpassing the worst blunders of the past four years' and advised the government 'against entering upon a policy so disastrous to the public interest, and to all order, public and private'.[84]

In Armagh the public response to conscription came quickly from the diocesan administrator, Fr J.W. Brady, who organized an anti-conscription covenant, modelled on the Ulster Covenant of 1912, for signing after Sunday Masses in the diocese on 14 April. He advertised his intentions in a letter to the *Irish Independent* on 13 April, advocating passive resistance and the need to avoid illegal drilling.[85] On Sunday 14th, a series of meetings were held in Armagh city, Keady, Ballymacnab, Portadown, Silverwood (near Lurgan), and in Drogheda and Dundalk. The meetings were mainly chaired by local Catholic clergy with speakers drawn from the UIL, AOH and SF, after which anti-conscription 'covenants' were signed. In Armagh city, the football field at St Patrick's College was the venue for Brady and T.J. McLaughlin of the UDC to lead a meeting, followed by various speakers, including Éamon Donnelly of SF, who declared his support for the meeting 'in so far as it served its purpose'.[86] After meetings during the following week in Dublin and Maynooth between the Catholic bishops and the leaders of the IPP and SF, the local anti-conscription campaign became a national one.[87] On Sunday 21 April anti-conscription pledges were signed across Ireland, often after Mass. CI Oulton noted that at 'every chapel in the county the pledge has been taken to offer resistance to the measure' and that some clergy 'have given utterance to most disloyal sentiments regarding the Government and the army'.[88]

Cardinal Logue has been cast as a reluctant figurehead of the anti-conscription movement, outmanoeuvred by the more radical Archbishop William Walsh of Dublin, and his secretary, Fr Michael Curran.[89] Logue's biographer, however, points out that the Church's position had 'something for everybody' by condemning conscription as 'oppressive and inhuman', which could be resisted 'by all means consistent with the laws of God'. The anti-conscription pledge that bound people to resist 'by the most effective means at our disposal', left the door open for SF to advocate military resistance if necessary. Dislike of government policy and a desire to avoid fresh rebellion overcame distrust of SF motives to the extent that rarely were the 'Church's manifestation so overt or controversial'.[90] At numerous meetings across the county in April and early May, the anti-conscription forces presented a united front.[91] This did not last, with some distrust arising over the 'national' or anti-conscription fund and where this might finally find a home.[92] The sums were large, with suggestions of perhaps up to £1,000 being raised in Armagh parish alone. By mid-June, almost £3,000 had been raised from 15 parishes across the county.[93] The IPP/AOH remained a formidable political force to be reckoned with in Armagh, but it is hard to escape the conclusion that the conscription crisis offered SF more benefit by expanding its membership and organization. In addition, campaigning alongside Church and IPP/AOH figures offered SF a respectability and 'appeal beyond the militant and the young'.[94]

By linking conscription to home rule to offset nationalist opposition, the British government also managed to alienate unionists. Carson stated in the Commons that while he supported the bill, he regretted that 'the Government should have mixed it up with the question of Home Rule'.[95] James Stronge, at a county Orange meeting in Portadown, argued that to consider home rule and conscription together was an impediment and contrary to the wishes of all parties.[96] The Armagh Black Chapter later unanimously passed a motion condemning the fresh attempt to introduce home rule and called on the government to 'enforce' conscription immediately in all parts of Ireland. The meeting also reaffirmed their trust in Carson's leadership and criticized the Catholic Church for involving itself in these affairs.[97] CI Oulton discerned that unionists in Armagh were 'not particularly keen for conscription, the slackers generally now remaining in the country. It is believed that Home Rule and conscription will collapse together.'[98] He was prescient. The conscription proposals collapsed as suddenly as they had been introduced.

Just as the crisis ended, the government announced, without evidence, that certain persons had entered into a treasonable communication with the German enemy. As a result of the so-called German Plot, the arrest and imprisonment without trial of more than 100 republicans further enhanced the relative advantage gained by SF during the conscription crisis and perhaps further radicalized the organization as more moderate leaders were arrested.[99] While there were no arrests in Armagh, this latest crisis provided a fillip to SF, which called a fresh round of protest meetings.[100] It also re-invigorated the contest within nationalism. In the aftermath of Arthur Griffith's by-election victory in East Cavan in June 1918, there were clashes in Newtownhamilton and Crossmaglen between AOH and SF supporters, and conflict over band instruments and bonfire materials in Mullaghbawn. In August, there were further clashes in Middletown as Hibernians returning from Monaghan began to pull down tricolours.[101] The AOH could still gather a large crowd. Its county demonstration at Crossmaglen on 15 August drew 2,000 people but 'came off quietly and there was no interference on the part of Sinn Féiners'.[102]

As a face-saving device for dropping conscription, a fresh recruiting drive was initiated. A statement from the lord lieutenant announced measures to encourage voluntary enlistment 'in the hope that without resort to compulsion the contribution of Ireland … may be brought to its proper strength and made to correspond to the contributions of other parts of the Empire'.[103] A target of 2,000 new recruits by 15 October was set for Armagh but CI Oulton believed there would be few new recruits as 'all those who desired to join have done so and unionists will not join till they see the nationalists coming forward'.[104] The Twelfth celebrations in Milford, outside Armagh city, heard both James Lonsdale and James Stronge urge those present and able to enlist to do so.[105] By September, Lurgan was the only place 'where the men have come forward in any respectable number' and by November a mere 380 new recruits were enlisted in Armagh (out of a total of nearly 10,000 newly recruited in Ireland as a whole).[106] There was also opposition to the recruitment campaign. Irish Volunteers from Camlough and Whitecross took part in breaking up a meeting in Newry in August, after which seven men were jailed for unlawful assembly.[107]

With the Armistice of 11 November 1918, a general election was called for 14 December 1918, the first in eight years. Initially, there was discussion that SF would oppose Unionist candidates in every constituency in Ulster, perhaps backed by elements of the labour movement, but the Catholic hierarchy feared that three-cornered contests would hand seats to unionism.[108] The northern Catholic bishops called on SF and the IPP on 26 November to convene a conference to agree a pact on eight marginal nationalist seats in Ulster, one of which was identified as South Armagh. Both sides had their reasons not to agree to the proposal, which infuriated Logue. John Dillon's public foot-dragging provoked the cardinal to inform a correspondent from the *Freeman's Journal* that he would 'advise the people to go straight to work and vote for Sinn Féin candidates', if Dillon did not agree to an electoral pact in Ulster.[109] Meanwhile, the SF standing committee initially made demands about local plebiscites to select candidates and abstention pledges, and only agreed to Logue's proposal after a final meeting at which Michael Collins dominated the discussion.[110] By this point, Logue was fed up with the whole 'ugly pie'.[111] South Armagh was given to the IPP candidate and incumbent, Patrick Donnelly. Although a SF candidate – Dr James McKee – appeared on the ballot paper, he only received 79 votes to 4,345 for Donnelly.[112] The numbers tell us nothing about vote shares and the pact certainly did not please everyone. John McCoy later made the point that it was a 'bad policy as it gave the Parliamentarians a representation which they could not otherwise obtain' and, he believed, alienated 'those former Unionists with Republican inclinations'.[113] Joe Devlin and Donnelly himself had not been confident that they would win a contest with SF, the former pinning his hopes on an election pact and the latter refusing to concede defeat:

> Whatever the result it is clear that the Nationalists of South Armagh will never consent to a Sinn Féin representative until they are beaten at the polls and not even then.[114]

The *Frontier Sentinel* recorded the disappointment of those who had been confident of a SF victory in South Armagh and stated that further explanations would follow as to why Donnelly should be supported – these never came.[115] Donnelly's election campaign saw clashes between his supporters and SF activists at meetings in Jonesboro and Dromintee.[116] When it was rumoured in early 1919 that Donnelly would resign the seat in favour of John Dillon or J.D. Nugent, he claimed his local supporters would not tolerate any change of representative. That said, he did not attend the Commons regularly up to 1922, much to the frustration of Joe Devlin.[117]

SF also contested the more challenging constituencies of North and Mid Armagh, through Ernest Blythe and Liam Ó Briain respectively. In November 1918 the CI reported little interest in the election and, in the event, the sitting Unionist MPs, W.J. Allen and James Lonsdale, were returned comfortably.[118] In North Armagh, Allen won over 80 per cent of the 13,099 votes cast. A SF appeal to voters in Lurgan to cast their votes 'against Carsonism, Unionism and Partition' proved of limited appeal.[119] In Mid Armagh, Lonsdale took 60 per cent of the 14,300 votes, Ó Briain showing a respectable return for a non-unionist candidate.[120] Ó Briain's rhetoric in a speech to supporters in Armagh City Hall – where he argued that 'the land of Ulster was Irish' and that the 'people who opposed Ireland's demand for independence were planters' – was not, however, designed to appeal beyond a core nationalist constituency.[121] The IPP/SF antipathy was highlighted when Ó Briain was heckled at Blackwatertown by James Donnelly, the constituency UIL director, about 'the absurdity of the Republican idea', casting back to Logue's pastoral of the previous year.[122] In his review of the elections, CI Oulton remarked that SF had been active in the county but not with the same 'enthusiastic conduct as witnessed at other elections'. He believed that 'the AOH is sided with Sinn Féin' in North and Mid Armagh, but, contradicting himself, argued that nationalists had not polled strongly for the SF candidates and that a small number had voted for a unionist candidate instead.[123]

The elections at the beginning and the end of 1918 showed the strong antipathy or suspicion with which a substantial part of the nationalist population in the region continued to regard SF. In the general election in Louth, the SF candidate won a narrow victory over the IPP candidate by a margin of only 255 votes out of more than 23,000 cast. The election results in Armagh, Down and Antrim, where SF failed to take any seats, highlighted the potential for exaggeration of the level of any swing in support from the IPP towards SF in those constituencies. Tom Garvin's analysis of the SF vote in the 1918 general election, which suggests that it was based 'in communities rather than on generations or any distinction between old and new voters', has been upheld by recent research.[124] While the results in east Ulster and Louth emphasize the continuation of nationalist factionalism, David Fitzpatrick was probably correct in concluding that Cardinal Logue's pact may indeed have favoured SF which won ten seats to five for the IPP across Ulster.[125] Unionists returned twenty MPs and three Labour Unionists were also elected in Ulster, all in the six north-eastern counties. After the votes had been counted, Sir James Stronge wrote to the *Church of Ireland Gazette* to give his verdict that the election results had strengthened the case for the exclusion of six counties in order to have a majority of Church of Ireland members outside home rule and to protect the Church and support southern brethren.[126]

The two years of 1917 and 1918 were pivotal to Armagh in relation to the Irish Revolution. The defeat of SF in the January by-election and its squeezing out at the December 1918 general election by the Catholic Church were political setbacks and a reminder of the continued strength of Redmondism that existed, not only in Armagh but also in the surrounding counties of Monaghan, Louth and Down. The election campaigns had, however, served to radicalize many nationalists who went on to invigorate SF and to establish the Irish Volunteers/IRA as a force in the county, the results of which would be seen between 1919 and 1923.

6 Armagh and the War of Independence, 1919–21

In the generally accepted timeline, the War of Independence began on 21 January 1919, with the shooting dead of two RIC constables in Soloheadbeg, County Tipperary, and ended with the truce two-and-a-half years later on 11 July 1921. The war was experienced with varying degrees of intensity from county to county, depending on the effectiveness of local IRA leaders and the consequent military and civil responses.[1] The conflict also spread slowly because the IRA in most places was unprepared in 1919 and it did not have the capacity to engage in serious offensive activity until late 1920.[2] To assess the IRA campaign in Armagh, it is useful to use the three phases of the conflict identified by historian Charles Townshend. The first phase from 1918 to the winter of 1919–20 consisted of open drilling, low intensity operations, arms raids and attacks on individual policemen. In the second phase from January until the autumn of 1920, organized attacks and killings increased, police barracks in outlying rural areas were abandoned by the RIC and then destroyed by the IRA, allowing space for the extension of SF law through the operation of Dáil courts. In the last phase from the winter of 1920 to the truce in July 1921, the IRA, reorganized into regionally based divisions, was increasingly willing and able to undertake larger-scale offensive operations and, in response, Crown forces intensified counter-insurgency operations.[3] This chapter will examine how closely the war in Armagh followed this pattern.

If the level of violence as indicated by the number of fatalities was the yardstick to measure involvement in the revolution, then the bulk of the burden was borne by about half a dozen counties. More than half of the estimated 2,300 fatalities during the period 1917–21 occurred in only six counties: Cork, Dublin, Antrim, Tipperary, Kerry and Limerick. Armagh, with thirty-three killed,[4] was in the middle ranks of the other counties, but was comparable to the neighbouring counties of Down (twenty-eight), Louth (twenty-seven) and Monaghan (twenty-five). The victims in Armagh were a mix of combatants and civilians, similar in profile to other parts of Ulster (excluding Belfast where non-combatants were most prevalent) and the parity of terror revealed the effectiveness of the comparatively late intensification of the state's response. In the year to July 1921, the IRA was responsible for the killing of twelve people, six civilians and six members of the Crown forces. In the same period, Crown forces killed thirteen people, ten IRA volunteers and three civilians, almost all of these in June 1921, the last month of the conflict before the truce. The ferocity of the response by the newly established government of Northern Ireland in 1921–2 was such that the IRA increasingly struggled to pose a sustained threat from within Armagh.

A crude headcount of fatalities by county can offer a false picture of the geographical patterns of violence in Armagh. Over the period of the War of Independence, the organizational profile of the IRA in Armagh evolved and for practical operational reasons was never defined or constrained by county boundaries. Newry and south Armagh became effectively a single operational region and the casualties in that area account for two-thirds of the total for Armagh and Down combined. In 1918 the Volunteer companies in Camlough, Bessbrook, Corrinshego, Killeen and Meigh, all in Armagh, were part of the Newry Battalion. Companies further south in Mullaghbawn, Dromintee, Crossmaglen and Cullyhanna were originally in the bailiwick of the Dundalk Battalion. Later in 1918 a battalion was formed within the newly-formed Newry Brigade, centred on the Camlough company (under the command of Frank Aiken) and around which most south Armagh companies coalesced. The exceptions were Dromintee and Crossmaglen companies, which remained with the Dundalk Battalion. Aiken took over as Newry Brigade O/C in October 1920, when Patrick Rankin was arrested. He retained this position until January 1921 when he was appointed inspection officer.[5] In March 1921 the 4th Northern Division (4th ND) was established with Aiken as O/C, comprising three brigades with ten battalions in total. No. 1 North Louth Brigade had four battalions, two in Louth and two in south Armagh, one of which was in a district south of a line drawn from Crossmaglen to Poyntzpass and the other in the Newtown/Whitecross area. No. 2 Newry Brigade had three battalions taking in south and west Down, and No. 3 Armagh Brigade had three battalions covering north and mid-Armagh (Armagh city and hinterland, the north-west centred on Blackwatertown, and the north-east taking in Lurgan and Portadown).[6]

Estimates of IRA and Cumann na mBan membership in Armagh during the War of Independence vary wildly. According to the CI, in July 1921 there were three 'branches' of the Irish Volunteers in Armagh with a total membership of 155, two branches of Cumann na mBan with 190 members, and one branch of Na Fianna with sixty members.[7] Aiken stated that total membership of the 4th ND at the truce, embracing all of Armagh and parts of Louth and Down, was 1,200.[8] According to figures supplied by veterans in detailed nominal and organizational rolls provided to the Military Service Pensions Board in the 1930s, total IRA membership in Armagh alone in July 1921 was 1,136. On Aiken's own evidence, this seems an overestimation.[9] The organizational rolls provided to the pensions board provide a picture of the five battalions within Armagh in July 1921 and show that half of the IRA strength belonged to companies located south of Newtownhamilton.

Cumann na mBan membership rolls point to the political and military activity of some women during the period.[10] According to figures compiled by the pensions board, there were thirteen branches of the women's organization in two 'councils' in mid and south Armagh with 256 members in July 1921, rising to 273 by 1 July 1922. There were also Cumann na mBan branches in north Armagh, including Lurgan, but there is little further detail as to either numbers or officers beyond a suggestion that activity began in 1918 and had ceased by 1922.[11] The organization appeared at the time of the South Armagh by-election in January 1918 with the central Cumann na mBan organizer, Alice Cashel, playing a key role. The emergence of Cumann na mBan in Armagh occured later than in Monaghan (1917) and Louth (1915 in Dundalk), and was in line with neighbouring Tyrone (March 1918).[12] The South Armagh Council, of which Mrs Hugh Cooney of Whitecross was president and Róisín Ní Bheirne of Camlough was vice-president, had seven branches with 145 (and later 162) members, the largest in Camlough, Whitecross and Mullaghbawn, with smaller ones in Newtownhamilton, Jonesboro, Clady and Corrinshego. The mid-Armagh council had Mary McGleenan of Loughgall as president and Róisín O'Reilly of Armagh city as vice-president. There were six branches – in Armagh city, Keady, Middletown, Blackwatertown, Lislea and Ballymacnab – with 111 members between them.[13]

Cumann na mBan in Armagh played similar roles in the War of Independence as elsewhere.[14] They carried despatches, conducted scouting operations, gathered intelligence, transported arms and guarded arms dumps; they also manufactured first-aid kits and trained in first-aid skills that were utilized in larger operations.[15] As IRA volunteers were increasingly on the run, Cumann na mBan maintained safe houses, offering food and accommodation to known and unknown men who would stay for a few days and then move on.[16] Women were also engaged in political and propaganda work, fundraising, helping at concerts and aeríochta (outdoor gatherings). According to John Grant, 'their usefulness was so great in the military sphere that it would be impossible to give even a small idea of the various ways the Cumann na mBan helped'.[17] He repeated these views about their importance in the military arena in a letter supporting the pension applications of Mary-Ann McCreesh (née Muckian) and Brigid McDermott (née McCoy), whose family homes in Mullaghbawn were used as a brigade and then divisional headquarters after December 1920. The provision of safe houses was highlighted both due to the physical risks involved and because the provision of shelter and meals had an economic cost, 'so much so that [McCreesh's] home was reduced from being in a comfortable position to a position bordering bankruptcy'.[18]

Of the 62 Cumann na mBan pension applications from Armagh, all now released online by the Military Service Pensions Collection (MSPC), fourteen secured full pensions, twelve of these at the lowest 'E' grade (including two that were appealed) and only two at the higher 'D' grade.[19] One of the latter was awarded to Róisín Ní Bheirne, who had served on the Cumann na mBan national executive from October 1918 until early 1923. After an ambush on an RIC patrol near Camlough barracks in January 1921, her house in Camlough was burned.

She later lost her job and moved to Louth.[20] By then she was targeted for internment in Northern Ireland, having been earlier warned by Frank Aiken not to get involved in any military duties because of her public profile.[21] The second to receive a 'D' grade pension was Nano Aiken, sister of Frank, who was first president and then treasurer of the Camlough branch of Cumann na mBan. From December 1920, after the burning of their family home in reprisal for the attack on Camlough RIC barracks, she went on the run with a group of IRA officers and carried out full-time courier work, maintaining contact between the officers of the brigade and the local companies, until her internment in Armagh gaol for fifteen months from February 1923.[22] Many of the Armagh applicants found it impossible to prove service before 1920, while Róisín Ní Bheirne's political work after the truce was also judged as 'nil service'. This caused her to complain that public work with Cumann na mBan was deemed less important.[23]

The CI reported in 1919 and in the first half of 1920 that the county was generally peaceful. It was not until June 1920 that south Armagh was described as 'disturbed'.[24] Volunteer drilling continued into 1919, and there were clashes with the police in the Bessbrook district in late 1919.[25] The general peace in Armagh was reflected in the local press until April 1920, after which reports of republican violence – including attacks on RIC men and abandoned barracks – increased.[26] This relative peace after Soloheadbeg was not unique to Armagh as the IRA was generally unable or unwilling to take the initiative due to a combination of a shortage of arms, uncertain leadership and lack of public support.[27] To build credibility, the IRA adopted tactics that made the greatest public impact while posing the lowest risk to themselves. For instance, the IRA enforced an effective boycott of the RIC by mid-1920 in Monaghan, using threats and intimidation, reducing the police to commandeering food and generally living in wretched conditions.[28]

A key factor remained a lack of arms. John McCoy of Mullaghbawn recalled that in 1919 in the south Armagh and south Down area, the IRA had just six rifles capable of firing modern .303 calibre ammunition, in addition to which they had a motley collection of small bore and obsolete handguns.[29] Arms could be, and were, obtained from GHQ, but had to be paid for and areas that were showing the greatest initiative got priority.[30] They could also be obtained through traditional IRB channels but these delivered little, except to some companies in north Armagh who sourced arms through Belfast connections.[31] The alternative was raiding for arms from houses, halls or individuals, especially those believed to have stores of weapons belonging to paramilitary organizations, particularly the UVF, which was reported to have 4,189 rifles in Armagh in 1917.[32] The first arms raid was on an Orange hall in Adavoyle in January 1919, which yielded nothing; the next in May on a house owned by Robert Turner, also of Adavoyle and a prominent member of the Orange Order, was scarcely better and yielded only a single-barrel shotgun.[33] Other raids took place around Whitecross, including one on Glenanne Orange hall that was said to have netted fourteen revolvers.[34] A larger raid took place on Ravensdale House, County Louth, on 1 February, which had an interesting aftermath. The few arms that were seized, antique sporting pieces, swords and spears, were stored in a dump in nearby Jonesboro, where they were quickly recovered by a RIC patrol, along with some more modern arms. It was not long before Michael Collins and the O/C north Louth IRA, James McGuill of Dundalk, were speculating on the identity of the informer who had offered up the dump. By means of assisting McGuill in his investigations, Collins supplied him with an internal confidential report from the RIC in Bessbrook, Armagh, giving details of the recovery operation, a clear illustration of the thorough nature of Collins's intelligence machine even at that early stage of the conflict. Ominously, Collins noted that the constable who received the information, Michael McKeefry, had received a reward of £2 and McGuill was told 'do not forget it for him'.[35]

A second large operation took place on 11 May 1919 at Ballyedmond Castle, County Down, which was thought to hold an arsenal of UVF rifles. The raiding party, led by Frank Aiken, included men from Armagh, Down and Louth.[36] However, the intelligence was old, the IRA's intentions in relation to the arsenal well known to the authorities and, consequently, whatever arms were in Ballyedmond had long been removed.[37] Another unsuccessful large-scale raid for UVF arms was led by Aiken in August 1919 on the house of J.G. Cope in Loughgall. Edith Cope, the well-known suffragette, reportedly shot and wounded one of the raiders, though a less dramatic version of the story was that she had fired into the ceiling with a shotgun, which a raider then took from her. According to local lore, the UVF arms had already been removed beforehand and the shotgun was later returned as it was useful only for shooting vermin.[38] Arms raids could go wrong and one strange episode in November 1919 seemed to point to this when the Revd Edward Foy of Lisnadill was injured. However, the local IRA company denied involvement and the RIC were unsure whether this had been a domestic matter.[39]

Seizing arms from policemen was another tactic, though one which was dangerous for all concerned and led to the first fatality of the War of Independence in Armagh on 6 June 1920 in Cullyhanna. During a sports day, an attempt to disarm three RIC men resulted in the deaths of Sergeant Timothy Holland and IRA Volunteer Peter McCreesh, and the wounding of Constable Rossdale and IRA Volunteer Michael Donnelly.[40] The RIC constables were carrying their service revolvers, while the IRA volunteers had a small automatic revolver and two small revolvers of 'antique pattern'.[41] Sergeant Holland had apparently refused to surrender his weapon and there was an exchange of gunfire.[42] The local Catholic curate, Fr Gogarty, condemned the fact that the attack had taken place in the presence of so many civilians and pointed out that 'everybody knows perfectly well no policeman would suffer his revolver to be taken from him without a fight'.[43]

Despite the many raids in Armagh, there was no substantial or significant seizure of arms. Indeed, the capture by the north Louth IRA of twenty modern rifles at Greenore in 1919 was the largest in the region during the conflict. So precarious was the arms situation that the addition of these rifles and the other arms held by the Louth IRA was regarded as a 'godsend' for the 4th ND arsenal when divisionalization occurred in March 1921.[44] As was the case elsewhere, for instance in nearby Louth, the IRA did not consider targeting the substantial arsenal of 276 rifles held by the Armagh National Volunteers. On the face of it, they would have made a less dangerous target than the UVF or RIC. It was curious that the National Volunteers in Armagh city held their rifles in storage in the Hibernian hall until January 1921 when a raid by the RIF finally removed them from the reckoning.[45] Arms, or the lack of them, remained a continuous problem for the Armagh IRA. By the time of the truce, the 4th ND only had thirty-three rifles for 1,200 men.[46]

The abandonment of three RIC barracks at Whitecross, Derryadd and Edenderry, which were 'closed temporarily in order to strengthen other stations', marked the start of the second phase of the War of Independence in Armagh in November 1919.[47] In early 1920 the barracks at Milford, Clonmakate, Cullyhanna, Blackwatertown, Queen Street (Lurgan), Birches (Portadown), Forkhill and Middletown were all closed. GHQ ordered a countrywide conflagration of abandoned barracks and tax offices to mark Easter 1920. As a result, 103 vacated barracks were burned over the first weekend of April 1920, including those at Cullyhanna, Whitecross and Blackwatertown.[48] On 1 July Forkhill was burned, followed by Moy on 15 July and by Birches on 8 December. These setbacks for the Crown forces proved temporary because rebuilding of abandoned and burned barracks took place from late 1920. By the time of the truce, Queen Street (Lurgan), Birches, Forkhill, Cullyhanna and Middletown were re-opened and a new barracks was built at Tynan, all for members of the new Ulster Special Constabulary (USC).[49] These were augmented by a number of army outposts established in mid and south Armagh at Markethill, Belleeks, Urcher, Heathhall and Forkhill.[50] The burning of barracks did not, therefore, have the same impact in Armagh as it did in other places, where the destruction of government buildings signified the abandonment of large swathes of rural Ireland by the authorities, a void that SF and the IRA tried to fill with varying degrees of success. In Armagh, because of overwhelming opposition from unionists and some nationalists, the alternative republican administration never took hold to the same extent.

Unionist opposition was bolstered by the Government of Ireland bill, which was making its way through the House of Commons in Westminster in 1920. The British government actually discussed whether the bill was a 'dead letter' during the summer of 1920, given the levels of violence across the country. Sir James Stronge, county grand master of the Orange Order, was one of several unionists who were sceptical about the bill. He had much less of the 'Ulsterman' about him than Armagh's Unionist MPs and was critical of those 'Belfast men', like Dawson Bates, who disliked the Irish Unionist Association. However, Stronge's views slowly changed and by the end of the Irish Convention in 1918 he conceded that the behaviour of some of the IUA 'had reconciled us to partition':

> One felt that if we have no friends south of the Newry Mountains, it might be better to draw the boundary line there and be frankly "West Britons" and not Irishmen. It may come to that. But we ought to do our best to keep Ireland as a whole under British influence.[51]

Stronge's comment in March 1920 that unionists in the three counties of Cavan, Donegal and Monaghan 'have been thrown to the wolves without compunction' by the UUC has often been quoted.[52] However, while he voted for the resolution supporting a nine-county partition rather than a six-county version, Stronge's hope was that delegates from the three excluded Ulster counties would regard the 1912 Covenant as now irrelevant and stand aside, rather than splitting the UUC. He was content that Lord Farnham's resolution to make Northern Ireland the nine-county province of Ulster had been defeated, 'because to carry it would possibly have killed the last chance of unionism in Ireland'.[53] When a further meeting was called in May to revisit the vote, Stronge opposed it as a divisive measure and was pleased at the size of the majority (301 votes to 80) in support of the six-county option as this minimized potential division.[54]

Stronge's agonizing, which probably reflected a lifetime of unionist and Orange Order friendships and alliances across Ulster and Ireland, was something of an exception among his Ulster and Armagh unionist colleagues. By 1920, most had fully endorsed the idea of partition as correspondence with the UUC secretary, Dawson Bates, before the May 1920 meeting shows. In one letter to J. Patterson Best, an Armagh city solicitor, Bates denounced those who had forced a recall meeting and hoped Best would be in attendance to defeat the 'nine county' people. Another letter deplored the same group as 'having no regard to the interests of our old cause'.[55] The *Armagh Guardian* approvingly quoted a London correspondent as saying that 'the choice was between a large Ulster and a solid Ulster', a position echoed by Sir John Lonsdale.[56] William Moore expressed 'satisfaction at being cut off from southern Protestants, whom he denounced vehemently as cowards'.[57] Stronge was less dismissive of the abandoned unionists, and remained hopeful that the Government of Ireland bill would never be implemented, as he opposed home rule for any part of Ireland. His overarching fear was that a Belfast parliament would have jurisdiction over disloyal regions, including south Armagh, 'with sedition organized over the border and little or no support from England'.[58]

Any idea that the separation of Ulster would isolate it from the rest of the island received a brutal rejoinder in the response to the murder in Cork on 17 July 1920 of RIC Divisional Commissioner Colonel Gerard Smyth, a Protestant from Banbridge, County Down. This provoked an outbreak of violence in Ulster at a time of year when, even in comparatively peaceful times, sectarian tensions were at their highest.[59] His funeral was held in Banbridge on 21 July 1920, after which Catholics and Catholic-owned property in Banbridge and nearby Dromore were attacked.[60] Catholic workmen were expelled from Belfast shipyards and nationalist enclaves were also attacked. After five days, eleven Catholics and eight Protestants had been killed, while large numbers on both sides of the sectarian divide were injured or made homeless.[61] A few weeks later, on 22 August, DI Oswald Swanzy, who was believed to have killed Tomás MacCurtain, the lord mayor of Cork, on 20 March 1921, was shot and killed by the IRA in Lisburn.[62] In the ensuing violence, almost the entire nationalist population of Lisburn was expelled (before gradually returning) and 300 houses were destroyed. The rioting spread to Belfast where seventeen people were killed over the following ten days.[63]

These levels of sectarian violence did not reach Armagh. The shooting at a group of SF supporters at Bannfoot on 15 August, when Francie McNeice was killed and another person wounded, was unusual for the county in 1920. Some unionist newspapers placed the blame on the victims who chose to travel through an area known to be antagonistic towards nationalists.[64] The danger of clashes escalated over the summer. In June the Ulster Unionist Labour Association in Portadown advised its members to 'be prepared to take a stand against the forces of disorder'. This was followed by a report that unionists were 'organising for their own protection to resist SF activities'. This was a euphemism for the reorganization and mobilization of the UVF, which was progressing in August when persons of means were 'forming committees in the towns for the protection of property in the case of an outbreak'.[65] These efforts had actually begun earlier and were known to the local police. In Armagh city, in the spring of 1920, former UVF members, led by John Webster, secured arms from Belfast for the use of so-called 'Protective Patrols'. Openly patrolling in and around the city by the summer of 1920 under the nose of the RIC, they served to revive the UVF across south Armagh, and later became members of the USC.[66] By the autumn of 1920 a number of Ulster Protestant 'vigilance patrols' were also in operation across Ulster.[67] In Lurgan, 330 men were sworn in as special constables (not as members of the USC) in October 1920 to keep the peace in the town in what appears to have been a cross-community effort.[68]

When the plans of the UUC to revive the UVF as a 'special force' to supplement the distrusted RIC and the army began to falter, Craig demanded that the British government establish and pay for a special constabulary for the six excluded counties.[69] The initial plan for the USC was for three classes of constables: 2,000 full-time A Specials, organized in mobile platoons, who were expected to serve for at least six months after training; 18,500 B Specials who were paid an allowance to serve in local patrols at least one night a week; and an unlimited number of unpaid C Specials who could be called up in an emergency.[70] Recruitment to the USC in Armagh began on 15 November 1920 when Lonsdale, now Lord Armaghdale, announced the county's scheme.[71] By the end of March 1921, the official returns identified approximately 290 A Specials and 2,300 B Specials enrolled in Armagh (more than half of these joined in November 1920 alone).[72] At the time of the truce in July 1921, the number of B Specials in Armagh had swelled to more than 2,500. This dwarfed the combined strength of the RIC and military of about 400 men and represented a dramatic militarization of the county. While they were 'waiting for the Specials', Armagh County Council decided at its December 1920 meeting to continue with the armed guard that had been placed on its buildings in the city since the previous summer.[73] This guard was presumably made up of Webster's 'Peace Patrols', which may also have been involved in an incident when a military lorry was stopped by three armed men outside Killylea. The three were arrested and taken to the police barracks in Armagh city.[74]

Few Roman Catholics enrolled in the USC, sparking a debate as to whether they were wanted or not, or were intimidated out of doing so.[75] When Joe Devlin asked how many Catholics had joined the USC by November 1920, W.J. Allen claimed that Catholics had already enrolled in Armagh (although the scheme had not been launched).[76] Allen may have based his claim on the experience in Lurgan, which was a telling case where three local Catholic magistrates, including the local GP and independent county councillor, Dr Michael Deeny, had supported the swearing-in of special constables in October 1920.[77] The three men then wrote to the senior civil servant in Belfast, Sir Ernest Clark, requesting that potential Catholic recruits to the new USC have their own selection committees and be able to patrol in their own areas. Clark wrote to Lord Armaghdale wondering whether this segregation might persuade Catholics to join the USC.[78] The proposal was never adopted (though it did appear in the second Collins/Craig pact in 1922), and the discussion closed without encouragement of the Lurgan correspondents.[79] Christopher Magill's work on a sample of B Special recruits in County Down shows that less than 2 per cent were Catholic in the earliest years. In the absence of USC recruitment data for Armagh and allowing for the fact that the ratio of Catholics to Protestants was higher in County Armagh than in Down, one could estimate that Catholics would have amounted to less than 50 in number out of 2,500 B Specials in the county in July 1921.[80] The evidence from newspaper reports is that the leadership of the Armagh B Specials, who were under the command of Captain

C.H. Ensor, was exclusively Protestant. The leaders were drawn from younger men aged under 35, single, recruited locally with few having military service. In Armagh city, the local district B Special commanders were hardware merchants, commercial painters (Webster) and a commercial clerk. All, notably, were involved in the Orange Order.

The reaction to this was unsurprising. Nationalist concerns about the USC were clear from the first mention of the force in September. The *Frontier Sentinel* referred to 'pour-parlers [sic] between Orangemen and the Government with a view to the enrolment of Ulster Volunteers as a police force'.[81] In November 1920 the CI reported that while the formation of the USC had created 'a feeling of security among the law-abiding inhabitants, resentment is manifesting itself in the depleted ranks of the AOH who are discouraging Catholics from joining.'[82] In December 1920 the entire AOH leadership in the county, supported by John D. Nugent, publicly protested against the plans to have the USC out on patrol and warned the CI that 'if this course is persisted in serious trouble will ensue'.[83] Officials noted the protest, but decided that it was not to be acted on or further investigated.[84] The publicity given to Cardinal Logue being stopped 'by a group of armed men' on his way to Armagh after Christmas services added to these concerns and provoked angry denunciations to the British government.[85] These protests intensified as the USC quickly became involved in violence against IRA suspects and civilians. In late December 1920 they were accused of shooting dead Michael Smith and wounding Peter Mackin, two IRA volunteers, at Belleeks, while allegedly trying to escape.[86] By the time of the truce in July 1921, the USC in Armagh were believed to have killed as many as ten men.[87]

With the creation of the USC and the realization that the local IRA lacked the numbers and material to respond, other strategies were adopted to relieve the pressure on northern nationalists. Seán MacEntee, the son of a Belfast city councillor, proposed in the Dáil that an embargo should be placed on all trade and commerce by the 'citizens of the Irish republic' on the manufacturers of Belfast who were believed to condone attacks on nationalists in the city.[88] The proposal was carried but drew criticism from Ernest Blythe, a fellow Ulsterman, who presciently claimed that the boycott would destroy forever the possibility of any union as 'Belfast could not be brought down through the banks'.[89] Rather than demonstrating the economic cost of partition, the boycott provoked the withdrawal by Belfast-headquartered companies from the south and created closer economic and trade links with Britain.[90] In Armagh, from a practical point of view, the boycott was scarcely noticed by either the CI or the local newspapers, despite some claims as to the effectiveness of the campaign.[91] It did, as elsewhere, provide the basis for a ready supply of targets, which could be attacked with minimum risk to the IRA. On 19 August a breadman's cart was burned outside Middletown and the driver warned against selling Belfast bread in the district again.[92] The next report of an attack on a bread-server was on 5 February 1921 outside Armagh city.[93] One breadman refused to be intimidated; pointing out a new cart that replaced one that was burnt out, he reportedly said to an IRA volunteer: 'This is another cart you can burn tomorrow', while another breadman armed himself with a revolver to ward off attacks.[94] In Monaghan the boycott was enforced mostly by traders seeking local economic advantage. It 'was seen by many Nationalists as another effective instrument to weaken the economic position of their Unionist rivals', and led to a significant rise in the cost of living.[95] The boycott also provoked a counter-response in Armagh. It was alleged that a Catholic horse-dealer who sold a horse at a fair in Armagh city to a Protestant was forced to refund the money and his customer compelled to return the horse in retaliation for Protestant dealers not being allowed to trade elsewhere in the south in the country.[96] The Belfast boycott marked the beginning of a period when the Dublin-based leadership of the IRA took an increased interest in Ulster matters. This had a greater significance for Armagh with the divisionalization of the IRA in 1921 when attacks on trains, lorries, boats and shops selling goods made in Belfast, already common in Louth, became more widespread.

The Belfast boycott came at a time when republicans were already enforcing a ban on the movement of 'munitions of war' by rail. This followed a national strike, called by the ITGWU in support of hunger strikers in Mountjoy prison, on 13 April 1920 which was widely observed in Louth, fitfully in the Newry area, and made no impact in Armagh.[97] In May, Dublin dockers refused to unload munitions ships and when the military transferred the material to trains, railway workers refused to work. The subsequent country-wide railway strike, which involved a ban on driving or facilitating munitions trains, or trains carrying troops or armed RIC men, received the backing of the National Union of Railwaymen and lasted from July until December 1920.[98] Those who did not honour the strike received some brutal attention. Two engine drivers were tarred and feathered in Dundalk and Newry in July and August. This was followed on 15 September by the tarring of William Tutt, an engine driver, in Armagh city.[99] Others who offended the republican cause were also harshly treated, including Thomas Maguire, a carpenter from Middletown, who was tarred for 'working with Protestants' in the county council.[100] Women, too, came in for harsh treatment. In January 1921 Letitia Forsythe, about 18 years old and a member of the Church of Ireland, was delivering a telegram from the post office at Newtownhamilton when she was stopped by armed men near Camly. She had her hair roughly cropped and was told to 'join the special police like her two brothers'. It was reported that a number of houses closed their doors to her when she sought help, before a local farmer took her in.[101] The following month 56-year-old Mrs Martha Cooke of Armaghbrague was tarred and had her hair cropped, the reported reason given was that her son was in the USC.[102] In March

1921, Louisa Hyde, also of the Church of Ireland, had her hair cropped by persons unknown, for reasons unknown, as she cycled alone near Newtownhamilton.[103] This type of punishment was usually inflicted by the IRA as a warning to the nationalist community to highlight the consequences of fraternizing with the enemy.[104] However, the three recorded female victims of these attacks in Armagh were from the Protestant community and it would hardly have been unusual or unexpected that they would have had relatives in the USC. Why these women were selected above others for this brutal punishment remains unresolved.

Opposition to the IRA campaign also came from within the nationalist community. John McCoy noted the presence of a 'big percentage of Hibernians who did not subscribe to the republican doctrine and were not enthusiastic about republican activities'.[105] John Cosgrove, speaking about the mid–Armagh area, recalled that in 1918 and 1919 the IRA 'got more annoyance and opposition from Hibernians than from the unionists' and that 'this intense hatred by the Hibernians to everything republican did a lot of harm from 1918 up to the truce'.[106] Major confrontations between republicans and nationalists were frequent during the election campaigns of 1918; thereafter the two sides seemed to give each other wide berth. However, offending the IRA was not to be excused and on the night of 8 June 1921, two farmers from the Camlough area, Hugh O'Hanlon and James Smith, both members of the AOH, were shot as spies. O'Hanlon had been warned by the IRA that he had been convicted and would be visited: 'the arm of the IRA is long and spies, informers and traitors must suffer the consequence'.[107] Both were alleged to have been involved in the killing of one SF member and the wounding and arrest of John McCoy in April 1921.[108] These were the only recorded killings in Armagh of alleged 'spies' during the War of Independence – though other expulsions and warnings were noted in recollections and there was debate about one killing soon after (whether it was a reprisal or part of the same campaign).[109] They mirror similar campaigns in the region, particularly in Monaghan, often against civilians who held differing nationalist opinions and against whom allegations of treachery were made.[110] The killings in Armagh in 1921 reflected the countrywide IRA response to the success of the Crown forces' military and intelligence-gathering campaign, and highlighted that warnings and intimidation were no longer always effective.[111]

In Armagh the second phase of the War of Independence did not see the IRA achieve a lasting military success, owing to the imbalance in manpower, materials and experience, and the level of popular support for their enemies. Nor did their operations provoke reprisals on the scale witnessed elsewhere from the summer of 1920.[112] A number of attacks on occupied RIC barracks marked the key operations during the second phase. One example was a determined attack on the night of 9 May 1920 on Newtownhamilton barracks, which lasted for four hours.[113] The IRA attack was resisted by a garrison of one sergeant and five men (the sergeant's wife and two children were also present). When the main barracks was on fire, the garrison continued to fight from outhouses at the back of the premises before the IRA withdrew as dawn broke. The incident highlights a number of interesting aspects of both the local IRA tactics and the loyalist response. IRA companies from across much of Armagh (including Camlough, Ballymoyer, Mullaghbawn, Armagh city and Cullyhanna) were mobilized together for the first time in one operation. Newtownhamilton was deliberately chosen as a target primarily because an attack in such a strongly unionist district would not have been expected by the RIC or the minority nationalist population, a significant proportion of whom were strongly opposed to SF. This logic was undermined by the fact that the barracks had been targeted a few months earlier and might, therefore, be on heightened alert.[114] Local unionists had also shown themselves to be strongly anti-SF in the recent south Armagh by-election, and the IRA rationalized that it was time for them to show 'their mettle when up against a serious local attack on what they had sworn to defend'.[115] The RIC garrison fought with a bravery acknowledged by John McCoy. No armed loyalists in the area came out to support them, nor it seems did anyone in the locality alert the RIC elsewhere of the attack. There were three major reasons why the IRA operation failed: insufficient explosives were used; the IRA failed to anticipate the defensive tactics that could be deployed; and they were unprepared for the challenge of maintaining efficient communications between the attacking groups. Furthermore, the attack virtually used up the IRA's reserves of modern ammunition and grenades, limiting their future operational potential. In addition, McCoy was puzzled that the Newtownhamilton attack was not taken more seriously by the authorities, who apparently were content to place responsibility on outsiders. McCoy's local RIC sergeant in Mullaghbawn approached him after Mass the morning following the attack and virtually offered to support his alibi if he was questioned about his activities the night before. Later that day at a GAA match, where a good number of the players had been at Newtownhamilton, a company of British soldiers in full battle gear cheered 'up Newtownhamilton' from the sideline 'until the repetition became monotonous'.[116]

Attitudes changed after the killing of Sergeant Holland in Cullyhanna the following month and there was a different response to another attempt on an RIC barracks in December 1920. An elaborate plan was devised in conjunction with IRA GHQ to lure Crown forces into an ambush at the Egyptian Arch railway bridge near Newry, timed to coincide with an attack on nearby Camlough RIC barracks. The operation failed primarily because not enough arms were moved from one side of Newry to the other for the use of the IRA at the ambush. The ambush was then given away when one volunteer prematurely dropped a primed grenade, killing himself and fatally wounding two others and forcing the IRA to withdraw under fire. The result was a disaster for the IRA with one volunteer killed at the Egyptian Arch, and five others wounded, two fatally. Meanwhile at Camlough, a homemade flame-thrower designed to ignite the reinforced barracks was damaged by the IRA's own grenades and failed in its intended purpose. With little hope of taking the barracks by storm, the attack at Camlough was called off after a short firefight. Unlike the Newtownhamilton attack, there were immediate reprisals. Three houses opposite Camlough barracks, which were used by the IRA during the attack, and another house at the end of the village, were burned by Crown forces. The family homes of Frank Aiken and Jack McElhaw were also burned down and property in Newry was damaged.[117] Senior IRA officers, including Aiken, McCoy and McElhaw, went on the run until the truce. They established their brigade headquarters in Mullaghbawn.[118]

Political battles continued alongside growing violence in the county. The local government elections in January and June 1920, which used proportional representation, had left unionist politicians unhappy at the results. They maintained firm control of Armagh County Council, two UDCs (Portadown and Tandragee) and four RDCs (Armagh, Lurgan, Portadown and Tandragee), but Labour won a majority in Lurgan and seats, to a lesser extent, in Portadown.[119] In December 1920, Sir Wilfred Spender outlined the Unionist strategy for the expected Northern Ireland parliamentary election to a large Women's Unionist Association meeting in Portadown. He expressed his dislike of proportional representation, the need for Labour to be forced to stand aside and stressed the necessity of strong unionist organization to win a predicted 32 out of the 52 seats.[120] The non-unionist bloc was more divided, with SF controlling Newry No. 2 RDC and Nationalists controlling Keady UDC; SF and Nationalists had a slim joint majority on Armagh UDC and had joint control of Crossmaglen RDC. Across all three local government elections, two-thirds of SF's 19 seats were won in south Armagh councils while their nationalist rivals won 24 seats in the other constituencies.[121] Nationalist party and AOH political strength remained centred in Lurgan, around Armagh city, Keady, and parts of south Armagh close to Crossmaglen. Another indicator of this pattern were the returns for the Dáil Éireann Loan of 1919–20 with £1,665 collected in South Armagh (or £0.07 per head of nationalist population), £527 in Mid (£0.03 per head) and £322 in North (£0.02 per head).[122]

The attack on Camlough barracks and the Egyptian Arch ambush signalled the beginning of the third phase of the War of Independence as identified by Townshend. Offensive action by the IRA was met with reprisal and counter-insurgency operations by Crown forces. According to John McCoy, this was designed to subdue the IRA in the months before the establishment of Northern Ireland and to validate unionist claims that the six counties were predominantly loyal and defensible.[123] The now inevitable partition provided the impetus behind the increase in IRA violence. For IRA GHQ, Ulster presented 'special

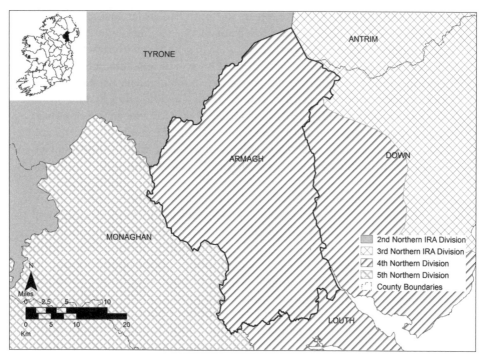

3 IRA divisions in July 1921

problems' in that the IRA there, unlike the rest of the country, operated in a theatre where the majority of the population was hostile to its aims and operations, making it difficult to organize, supply and motivate. The difficulties intensified as partition and the establishment of a hostile unionist-led government loomed. These factors prompted the country-wide reorganization in March/April 1921 of the IRA that saw Ulster divided into five divisional areas. Divisionalization offered a clearer command structure and enabled the IRA locally to deal with their particular issues 'in a more comprehensive way'.[124] Of the five Ulster divisions, only the 2nd (Derry/Tyrone) and 3rd (Antrim/ north Down) Northern Divisions had their areas entirely within the boundaries of Northern Ireland, with the 4th ND covering south and west Down, Armagh and north Louth (see map 3). It is unclear what factors, military or political, fed into the decision that three of the five Ulster divisions would be 'cross-border' in organization. Frank Aiken, as O/C 4th ND, now had control of the north Louth area, which was effectively part of the natural geographic, economic and cultural hinterland of Armagh.

SF was well-organized there but faced similar problems to Armagh and south Down where the AOH retained significant support among nationalists.

Furthermore, while the Irish Volunteers in Louth had, as far back as 1914 and the IRA from 1918, been to the forefront of the national organization, its leadership and efficiency had slipped. By 1920 they had been overtaken in terms of aggression by IRA units in Armagh and Down. The appointment of Patrick McKenna from Monaghan as GHQ organizer to the Dundalk Battalion in late 1920 was intended to address this. One of the first actions taken by him was to lead an ambush party in Dundalk, which killed Henry Murray, an ex-serviceman from Carrickmacross who was accused of being a spy.[125]

There is evidence of tensions existing within the division from the outset. Patrick Casey, an officer in the Newry Brigade, was withering in his criticism:

> the men of north Louth took little if any part in the fight for Independence. It was necessary to take men from all parts of Armagh and Down to do the work that should have been done by the Dundalk men.[126]

Other witnesses disagree with Casey: a number of the Dundalk IRA were in the ambush party at Creggan on 10 April 1921, when one constable was killed and three others injured.[127] Contrary to Casey's specific recollection, others were present at an ambush on 18 April at Plaster, County Louth, which failed due to premature firing by a contingent of Armagh or Down IRA men.[128] According to John McCoy, the Plaster ambush was set up to give the Louth IRA experience and they were strongly represented at the ambush site.[129] Nevertheless, Casey's comments revealed the underlying tensions prevalent within the 4th ND. On its establishment no one from Louth was appointed to a divisional command position. Even when Aiken moved his headquarters to Dundalk, his divisional staff was made up of men from Down and Armagh. In March 1922, the north Louth IRA openly opposed the Treaty settlement and repudiated Aiken's leadership. Their increasingly aggressive actions did much to undermine Aiken's attempts to remain neutral when the Civil War erupted.

The death of Constable John Fluke at the Creggan ambush marked the targeting of the USC in Armagh. It sparked reprisal burning of houses in Killylea, his home place, which in turn prompted further attacks on loyalist property.[130] However, the level of targeting was variable. Frank Donnelly, a battalion O/C, recalled that most of the young men from a predominantly unionist area of Todd's Corner, near Armagh city, joined the USC after its formation. His memoir states that there was no initial friction with their nationalist neighbours and, as late as June 1921, six months after their first deployment, the IRA saw 'nothing officious or aggressive in the manner they carried out their patrol duty'.[131] However, a raid for USC arms on the Georges' house in Todd's Corner on the night of 19 June 1921 changed this. The IRA were surprised to encounter a vigorous armed defence by Robert and Douglas George, both teenaged members of the USC, assisted by their even younger brothers. After one of the raiders was seriously wounded and the arrival of USC reinforcements, the IRA broke off the attack and the George brothers escaped from their burning home.[132] This was followed a week later by the attempted murder of one of the brothers, Robert, as he left a relative's house to go on a USC patrol.[133]

The killing at Creggan and the attack on the George homestead highlight the changing pattern of violence during the third phase of the War of Independence in Armagh. After December 1920, IRA attacks prompted official and unofficial reprisals that had spread to most areas by mid-1921.[134] The months from December 1920 to July 1921 witnessed two-thirds of the thirty-three killings that occurred in Armagh during the War of Independence, the vast majority in the last six weeks of the conflict. The IRA was responsible for eleven of the deaths, including the killings of Hugh O'Hanlon and James Smith of Camlough mentioned above. The other killings took place in a series of ambushes of USC and RIC patrols, and an attempt to kill Great Northern Railway staff believed to be B Specials. There was also an exception to this type of operation, the spectacular derailing of a troop train at Adavoyle. The Crown forces killed nine people in the same period, almost all in June and July 1921, each one targeted as being an IRA volunteer, associated with SF or having a family link to them.[135] These extra-judicial shootings of republicans by Crown forces began with Michael Smith in December 1920, followed in January 1921 when John Doran, a 'prominent Sinn Féiner', was taken from his home near Camlough and shot dead.[136] This pattern continued until the truce. A similar picture can be seen in Louth, where seven unarmed IRA volunteers were killed by Crown forces in extra-judicial operations between November 1920 and June 1921.

The violence in the 4th ND's area was particularly intense during the six-week period before the truce, with twenty-four deaths. Hence McCoy's downbeat recollection of a time which was 'frequently punctuated with happenings that could profitably be forgotten'.[137] The deaths were marked by close proximity in time and geography, making their delineation by county boundary meaningless and suggesting how, across the region, one killing fed off another. The Adavoyle ambush in south Armagh, close to the Louth border, took place on 24 June 1921. It was the most deadly Armagh IRA operation of the 1919–21 period, and one that Aiken personally directed and actively led. The target was a train carrying horses and more than 100 soldiers returning from the official opening of the new Northern Ireland parliament. Three soldiers in the 10th Hussars – Sergeant Charles Dowson, Privates C.H. Harper and William Telford – and Francis Gallagher, a railway guard, died in the derailment and up to eighty horses were killed.[138] Dozens more animals were injured, some seriously: the *Newry Reporter* recounted that 'the scene resembled a battle-field' and photographs of the scene captured the carnage of dead and dying horses and soldiers searching through the wreckage (see plates 10 & 11).[139] Either in confusion or due to indiscipline, troops on the train opened fire on civilians who were working in nearby fields. Three men were severely injured, Patrick McAteer subsequently died in hospital in Dundalk.[140] This highly complex operation was devised in GHQ. As originally envisaged, two other troop trains that preceded the one attacked by Aiken were to have been derailed further down the line, but the local IRA units failed to carry out their missions.[141] Aiken's tactics on the day demonstrated an intelligent use of men and material. Rather than depend on force to stop the train, Aiken reasoned that the weight and speed of the train could be the key factor in its destruction. No explosives were used in the derailment (though some reports referred to a mine exploding under the guard van). Aiken had filed spikes holding the rails so that they could be quickly and easily removed. Once the first two troop trains and a civilian train had passed the ambush site, the spikes were lifted, the rails removed and the small group of IRA involved departed the scene. The engine, tender and first carriage crossed the gap safely but the third carriage and those following fell down an embankment.[142] Aiken's tactics were to maximize the damage to the target with the minimum danger to his forces. By way of comparison, an ambush at Hazelhatch, County Kildare, planned by Seán Boylan, O/C Meath Brigade, was called off after being discovered. Had it been followed through, it may have posed as much risk to the attackers as the troops given the plan to use explosives to derail the train and then to open fire at close quarters on the surviving troops.[143] The timing of these ambushes was significant in light of the advanced nature of secret negotiations that would lead to a truce. IRA successes in the field would mean negotiating from a position of strength, while the propaganda effect of an attack on soldiers returning from an event featuring the British monarch, as the reportage on the Adavoyle attack showed, was immense.[144] However, had all of the ambushes achieved their objectives, and four troop trains been destroyed within a week, the death toll might have been so great as to derail the burgeoning peace moves.

The killings of four men on 6 July 1921 was probably in reprisal for either the Adavoyle ambush or the killing of Special Constable Hugh Gabbie in Newry market.[145] Three of the four (Peter McGennity, and brothers John and Thomas O'Reilly) were taken from their homes by men in uniform to nearby Altnaveigh and shot at the side of the road, close enough for the report of the shots to be heard by McGennity's sister who rushed out to discover the three bodies.[146] Patrick Quinn was shot in a house belonging to a former RIC head constable, about a mile distant at Carnagat, where he was staying for the night. All four victims were active IRA volunteers and the killings in Altnaveigh were, according to John Grant, perpetrated by people who were 'all most antagonistic to everything national and republican'.[147] There were immediate and longer-term repercussions to these reprisals. Three days later, an IRA ambush was put in place; its objective was to kill a number of B Specials who were employed as linesmen on the Great Northern Railway near Newry. The ambush was

1 Anti-home rule meeting in Armagh City Hall, October 1913.

2 Cardinal Michael Logue, Roman Catholic archbishop of Armagh, 1887–1924, and primate of All Ireland, speaking at Station Island, Lough Derg, on 30 June 1913. Logue was a reluctant supporter of the third home rule bill due to concerns about the threat of partition. In a speech in Fermanagh in 1913, he played down any serious threat of Ulster unionist rebellion.

3 John Crozier, Church of Ireland archbishop of Armagh and primate (1911–20), opposed both home rule and partition due to fears of their impact on the Church of Ireland. He was a strong supporter of the British war effort.

4 Sir James Stronge, of Tynan Abbey, county grand master of the Orange Order in Armagh, and grand master of the Orange Order in Ireland. Determined to oppose home rule, he promoted the expansion of the Ulster Volunteer Force. Stronge eventually agreed to partition but noted: 'One felt that if we have no friends south of the Newry Mountains, it might be better to draw the boundary line there … But we ought to do our best to keep Ireland as a whole under British influence.'

5 Henry B. Armstrong, unionist chairman of Armagh County Council, MP for Armagh, and later senator in the Northern Ireland parliament. He was one of the Armagh delegates to the Irish Convention in 1917, along with Archbishop Crozier and Harry McGeagh. He later recalled the quality and good humour of the discussions but that they would not satisfy Sinn Féin, which had abstained from participation.

6 Reverend Edward Foy of Lisnadill, local commander of the UVF in 1913. When his house was raided for arms, the IRA was blamed but the RIC pointed towards a domestic disagreement being the likely cause.

7 Éamon Donnelly with his daughter Nellie Donnelly-Wood. Donnelly was a key organizer of the Irish Vounteers in Armagh city in 1913–14 and from 1917 an organizer and director of elections for Sinn Féin at county level in Armagh and at provincial level in Ulster. He was elected Sinn Féin MP for Armagh (1925–9) but did not take his seat.

8 Camlough barracks, May 1921, attacked 12–13 December 1920 as part of the Egyptian Arch operation.

9 Following the Camlough/Egyptian Arch operation, Frank Aiken's home in Camlough was destroyed by Crown forces in December 1920.

10 & 11 Photographic and newsreel images of the carnage of the Adavoyle ambush on 24 June 1921 were widely circulated. Had the operation proceeded as originally planned, two troop trains, which preceded this one, would have been attacked north of Dublin.

12 Armagh meeting, 4 September 1921.

Front row l–r: Michael Garvey, Armagh; Seán Ua Muirthile, Cork (GHQ and IRB); Éamon Donnelly, Armagh; Michael Collins; Harry Boland; Tom Collins, bodyguard; Joseph Dolan. *Second row l–r*: George Murnaghan, Omagh; Michael Short, Armagh; Cornelius MacElroy, Armagh; Patrick Beagan, Armagh; Eoin O'Duffy, Monaghan and GHQ; Seamus Reilly, Armagh; Thomas Duggan, Armagh; Samuel Johnston; Malachy Kearney; Dr Walter MacKee; Mrs Unah McGuill, Dromintee. *Third Row L to R*: Charles Rooney, Peter Hughes; Peter Teigue, Dundalk; Seamus McGuill, Dromintee; John Garvey, Armagh. *Fourth row l–r*: James Mullen, Armagh; Frank McKee; Edward Fitzpatrick; Charles Garland; —— McStravick; Liam Healy; Not known; James Trodden, Armagh; Joseph McKelvey, Belfast IRA; John Henry Collins, Newry. Mrs Unah McGuill (second row, first from right) and other women were attacked by a USC patrol in her home in Dromintee on the night of 13 June 1922, which prompted a retaliatory ambush led by Frank Aiken (see page 105). Michael Collins and Harry Boland took opposite sides in the Civil War and were killed during the opening weeks. Joseph McKelvey opposed the Treaty and was captured in July 1922 at the Four Courts. He was executed on 8 December 1922 along with Rory O'Connor, Richard Barrett and Liam Mellows on the orders of the Irish government in retaliation for the killing of Seán Hales TD.

13 Michael Collins at Armagh, September 1921. The moustachioed figure on the bottom right of the picture is Peter Hughes, TD for County Louth.

14 Camlough, County Armagh, power base of the 4th Northern Division.

15 Members of the 4th Northern Division imprisoned in Dundalk gaol during the Civil War. (*Back l–r*) Peter Boyle, Frank Monaghan, Peter Murney, Martin O'Donnell. (*Front l–r*) Eiver Monaghan, Willie Lawless, Jimmy Goodfellow.

16 John Quinn, O/C 4th Northern Division, January–May 1923. Severely wounded at Tallanstown, County Louth, he died on 22 May 1923, two days before the 'dump arms' order.

17 Boundary Commission in Armagh on 9 December 1924. Dr Eoin MacNeill (Irish Free State representative); Mr Joseph R. Fisher, BL (Northern Ireland representative); Mr T.E. Reid, OBE, JP, secretary of Armagh County Council; Thomas Montgomery, chairman of Armagh County Council; and Mr Justice Feetham, chairman of the Boundary Commission.

18 Funeral of Cardinal Logue on 25 November 1924. The coffin was blessed by his successor, Patrick O'Donnell, coadjutor archbishop of Armagh.

19 Frank Aiken in 1925. By this time, he was inclined towards politics despite strong opposition from within the IRA. Ousted as IRA chief of staff in December 1925, Aiken joined Fianna Fáil when it was launched in 1926. He was appointed minister for defence in the first Fianna Fáil administration in 1932. Drawing is probably by Estella Solomons.

20 Nano Aiken was interned by the Northern Ireland government in February 1923. Her continued detention long after the threat from the IRA had subsided became a source of political embarrassment, and she was eventually released 'on health grounds' in May 1924. This group photograph from 1926 shows from the left: Nano Aiken, Sarah Ann 'Nannie' Magennis, Evy Magennis, Aileen Grogan, Marcie Quinn and Theresa Magennis.

abandoned when another linesman, Draper Holmes, made enough noise to warn off others coming behind and, as a consequence, he was shot dead.[148] This operation took place on 9 July, a day after the announcement that a truce would come into force on Monday 11 July. The intention of the ambush was clearly one of reprisal. In this deadly arithmetic, John Grant noted that 'our score was on the losing side'.[149] Twelve months later the IRA returned to Altnaveigh with lethal effect.

In the peace talks that were shortly to follow, SF was in the driving seat to the exclusion of other nationalist, labour or interest groups. In Ulster, however, SF and the supporters of Joe Devlin battled to remain the dominant voice of nationalism. In April 1921 de Valera and Devlin agreed a pact on the basis of abstention from the new Northern Ireland parliament, the elections for which were due the following month. De Valera had questioned whether or not to put up candidates – identifying 'the real question is whether or not we can get the people in the North to favour abstention at all' – but then decided on nominating twenty SF candidates, including two for Armagh.[150] The pact's recommendation on the transfers of second preferences between the two blocs displeased some, the *Frontier Sentinel*'s initial favour turning into a belief that the Devlinite tail was wagging the SF dog.[151] SF and the Nationalists were reluctant to put their usual hostility on hold and abide by the pact.[152] Behind the scenes there were also problems with candidates. Patrick Donnelly, the sitting MP for Westminster, wanted to stand and was only prevented by the convention that chose Devlin or Nugent as a compromise.[153] For SF, Collins was certainly not the choice of the clerical delegates (who wanted de Valera), and there was talk that Cardinal Logue might publicly oppose his candidacy. Meanwhile, Aiken did not want to stand and was reportedly going to ask the SF standing committee in Dublin to withdraw his name. Some delegates at the convention 'believe he might be the first candidate returned and even best C[ollins]'.[154] During the campaign neither Collins or Aiken canvassed. Nugent was particularly active and this, as well as his known reluctance to take part, might explain why Aiken got fewer votes than he had in the Forkhill district alone in the 1920 county council elections (1,427).[155] Expectations of up to twenty combined seats between SF and Nationalists were shattered when the results showed that only six SF and six Nationalist would oppose forty Unionist MPs.[156] In Armagh Michael Collins famously won one of the four Armagh constituency seats for SF with the final seat taken comfortably by John D. Nugent ahead of Frank Aiken, who lost his deposit, winning only 1,301 first preference votes. The bigger winners were Richard Best and D.G. Shillington, who won two seats for the Unionists, taking 55 per cent of the first preference votes and dominating in the electoral districts around Portadown and Lurgan.[157]

The pattern of violence during the War of Independence in Armagh broadly followed that which occurred elsewhere. Slow beginnings in 1919 and in the first half of 1920 were followed by intensified violence as IRA columns emerged in December 1920 and the 4th ND was created in March 1921. This chronology was also evident in other counties in Ulster but the third phase of the war in Armagh was markedly more violent than elsewhere in the north-east with the exception of Belfast. However, the War of Independence in Armagh had other aspects that were distinctive, not least the response of the unionist population, which politically and militarily (mobilizing the UVF and then joining the USC in significant numbers) provided protection to the unionist population ahead of the formal establishment of Northern Ireland. The growing threat posed by the IRA offensive from December 1920 was countered by a policy of reprisals that were particularly ferocious in the first seven months of 1921. Despite well-publicized attacks on RIC barracks, by the truce of July 1921 none had been taken by force. Some abandoned stations were recommissioned, some new barracks had been built and a line of army outposts had been established in the south of the county. With the addition of the local USC from late 1920, the IRA in Armagh faced Crown forces that had the ability to absorb and rebound from attacks. By July 1921 the republican movement in Armagh not only faced resilient nationalist political opponents but a new hostile administration in Belfast that would adopt ruthless security policies with strong military support from Britain.

7 'A dirty type of peace': truce and Treaty, 1921–2

The months after the truce of July 1921 was a period of comparative peace in Armagh, though this had effectively ended by the first quarter of 1922 as the threat of a serious outbreak of violence loomed over the county. Republicans, at the time and afterwards, questioned whether a truce had ever existed or if it was merely an interlude in which armed groups prepared for a resumption of war. For the population more generally, there was a sense of peace being restored and a space for an Anglo-Irish Treaty to be negotiated, debated and voted on. Uncertainty remained about whether Armagh would stay under the jurisdiction of the Belfast government, or be absorbed, in whole or in part, into the Irish Free State (IFS).[1] In this light, a public meeting held in September 1921 in Armagh city, addressed by Michael Collins, took on special significance.

The truce came into effect at noon on Monday 11 July 1921 as members and supporters of the Orange Order prepared to commemorate the Battle of the Boyne. Just after midnight on that day, an attempt was made to burn the coastguard station at Greencastle, County Down, and at 8 a.m. military correspondence was carried away when the post office in Armagh city was raided.[2] In Lurgan there were some nationalist celebrations of the truce that coincided with an Eleventh Night riot during which the convent in the town was fired on.[3] At a subsequent protest meeting, ex-British soldiers demanded to be supplied with arms to protect the nationalist population and the convent. To bolster their credibility, the IRA established a permanent guard on the convent and on outlying nationalist areas for several months. Despite being curtailed by a lack of numbers, the local IRA leadership preferred to draw on units from outside the immediate area to complete the task rather than utilize the cohort of trained ex-soldiers available in the town.[4]

Unionist responses to the truce ranged from caution to outright hostility. Speaking at the county's Twelfth celebrations at Tynan, James Stronge noted that while the king had called on people to forgive and forget, 'if their enemies would cease committing murder, they … were ready to forgive … and the time might come when these things … would be forgiven … but the prospects at the present moment were hardly as good as they could wish'.[5] Speaking at the same event, Revd Henry De L'Harpur 'hoped and prayed that they might have peace, but it was a dirty type of peace which was to be got by shaking hands with murderers and assassins', while William Marshall JP emphasized that he had no faith in the 'armistice' and that the government should have said that the laws were for obeying instead of 'truckling to murderers and assassins'.[6] At another Twelfth gathering in Armagh city, the chairman William Pinkerton asserted that the happenings of the past few days should awaken in them a new spirit of loyalty. They all saw that the British Government had humiliated itself by arranging a truce with the rebel leaders. They were aware how that truce had been kept. It had been dripped in blood.[7]

Elsewhere in the county, the general call was for unionists to stand behind their leaders and protect the fledgling Northern Ireland institutions.[8] Speakers stressed that the truce must be tested and not relied on, while others, conscious of looming negotiations between SF and the British government, put down a marker that the continuation of the new northern parliament was the limit of unionist concessions.[9] Unionist hostility in Armagh and other parts of Northern Ireland was compounded by the fact that, under the terms of the truce, the USC was to be immediately demobilized. This, in fact, never occurred. In the words of the *Impartial Reporter*, '[the USC] will be kept going as a Volunteer force for the preservation of order as it did in some districts before it was recognised officially'. Inevitably, it was reported that Cardinal Logue's car had once more been stopped and searched on 13 July.[10] By November, when violence engulfed Belfast, as an emollient for unionist fears about the ongoing Treaty negotiations, the official suspension of the USC was lifted. The Northern Ireland government also assumed responsibility for internal security and, with that, control of the USC and any RIC members who were operating within its jurisdiction. Recruitment of almost 6,000 additional special constables was agreed at a Northern Ireland cabinet meeting in early December.[11]

Republicans in Armagh also tested the truce in the second half of 1921. Oliver Knipe, an off-duty USC constable, was shot and wounded on 3 August on the Armagh/Tyrone border, and in September it was reported that four men known to be SF supporters were 'kidnapped' in Jonesboro, a term used by officialdom to denote an arrest by the Irish Republican Police (IRP).[12] Throughout the summer of 1921 the *Armagh Guardian* carried a series of reports of night-time convoys of trucks allegedly carrying arms and ammunition into Armagh from Monaghan and Louth. The newspaper claimed that while RIC officers denied any intelligence about a nationalist insurrection, a USC officer who expressed concern had been 'cribbed' by the authorities.[13] In October and November the Belfast boycott was being enforced in parts of the mid-county, while uniformed IRA volunteers conducted boycott searches in Armagh city.[14] Republican courts were held in Armagh city and elsewhere in the county, sometimes in the presence of RIC observers.[15]

To maintain the truce, communications were opened between the IRA and the Crown forces. Eoin O'Duffy was IRA liaison for all of Ulster, but in November 1921, John McCoy took on the role for Armagh alone.[16] When McCoy presented his credentials to the CI in Armagh in November 1921, he was informed that the scheme was not applicable in the six counties, where a democratically elected government was in place. Despite this initial rebuff, the CI was soon reporting breaches of the truce to McCoy, including an attempted robbery from a B Special from Tynan by armed men.[17] McCoy recalled that there was some cooperation in the pursuit of ordinary criminals, while local RIC officers and the CI referred matters to him about IRA activity. In one particular incident, the perpetrators of an ambush of an RIC patrol were found to be members of the AOH, who had used stolen IRA guns. McCoy later ascertained that this was in keeping with AOH activity in Belfast aimed at wrecking the truce.[18] He also provided weekly reports to GHQ until March 1922 and shared intelligence on specific matters, such as potential sources of arms in the USC.[19] By February 1922, McCoy's reports recorded increasing USC activity and aggression with raids on dances and shots being fired into homes in south Armagh, prompting him to ask the CI why 'those men are allowed to go around at night and terrorise peaceable people by a display of arms?'[20] As the situation deteriorated, McCoy moved his base from Armagh city to a safe house in Mullaghbawn and was relieved soon after to be recalled to divisional duties.[21] McCoy's replacement as liaison officer, Séamus Connolly, was detained by the USC on several occasions, prompting Emmet Dalton at IRA GHQ to wonder if the liaison system in Northern Ireland had now outlived its usefulness and whether the officers would be of more use in their IRA divisional duties.[22]

At the time of the truce, the 4th ND had, according to Aiken, some 1,200 men but only thirty rifles.[23] The strength of the IRA in Armagh, all of No. 3 Brigade plus the 3rd and 4th battalions, No. 1 Brigade (North Louth), in July 1921, was later (over)estimated at about 1,500.[24] The truce took Aiken by surprise, and, suspecting that it would not last, he set up training camps in Killeavy and Derrynoose in Armagh, and in Gyles' Quay, County Louth. Drilling and training camps continued into September and October at Ballymoyer, Camlough, Annahaia, Keady and Silverwood, outside Lurgan.[25] Aiken later recalled his confidence that brigade and battalion officers were well versed in guerrilla tactics by September 1921 and had hostilities resumed within two months of the truce, Britain would have got a different answer to her 'Treaty or War' threat of December 1921. He believed that as negotiations between London and Dublin continued into September and October, there was a fall-off in enthusiasm and discipline. This complaint of indiscipline was made elsewhere in the country and Aiken's observation that the IRA got too long a rest, 'became lazy, our muscles became flabby, and our nerves and spirit lost their tone', was commonplace.[26] Ernie O'Malley noted that Aiken dismissed two officers in late autumn for indiscipline and drunkenness.[27]

Within the county there were a number of other issues of great concern to the people. The post-war economic slump was sharpest in the textiles industry. By the summer of 1921, food prices were tumbling, causing problems for farmers, while manufacturing output halved. By August 1921, a quarter of textile workers in Lurgan and Portadown were believed to be unemployed and a panic set in that they would receive no benefits until November at the earliest. In response, the local councils urged the Northern government to press London for aid.[28] Around the same time the county's valuable apple crop was threatened by a fly infestation. A series of meetings and discussions were held about cures for this, including the possible use of nicotine sprays.[29] Some among the county's business leaders, many of whom were unionist in politics, argued that the new Northern Ireland parliament could be located in Armagh city. To this end, between January and August (when the news broke that the Stormont estate had been purchased for a long-term site), the Armagh Chamber of Commerce, supported by local Protestant clergy and unionist councillors, ran a publicity campaign (with brochures and press articles) and lobbied local MPs and Sir James Craig.[30] The argument was that Armagh city was an historic site, a place of public buildings and perhaps more neutral (or central) a space than Belfast. One local MP, Richard Best, was non-committal, whereas the Belfast press poked fun at the campaign. It was not helped by outbursts from a local leader, Hans Leeman, who claimed he would rather have no new parliament than see it in Belfast. He withdrew the comment and the campaign drifted into history.[31]

An open-air rally in Armagh city on Sunday 4 September 1921 was a significant political event.[32] It was organized to provide a platform for SF and their new MP, Michael Collins. He had spoken in the city before, in 1917, but was now the dominant figure on the republican side. The original idea had been to get Collins to open a fundraising event for the IRA in the south of the county, but, on hearing of these plans, Collins and Arthur Griffith asked for a much larger event to be held. After discussions between Róisín Ní Bheirne, Aiken, O'Duffy and Éamon Donnelly, plans for a meeting in Armagh city were drawn up.[33] In some ways, the day mirrored unionist rallies in 1912 and 1913. There was a procession through the city with bands, uniformed IRA and Cumann na mBan and members of the INF; a reception in the City Hall hosted by the SF members of the UDC; and, lastly, a rally in the playing fields of St Patrick's College.[34] There was clearly a measure of co-operation with the RIC to prevent clashes between those in attendance and unionists, though shots were fired as cars left afterwards and one man was wounded.[35]

A group photo at the City Hall shows a mix of leading Armagh SF members (James and Unah McGuill, Dromintee; Éamon Donnelly, Séamus O'Reilly, chair of the UDC), and visitors like Harry Boland, Joe McKelvey of Belfast, Seán Ó Murthuile, Eoin O'Duffy, George Murnaghan from Omagh, and Peter Hughes from Dundalk (see plate 12). The Civil War would take its toll on that group. Within fifteen months, three of the party – Boland, Collins and McKelvey – died violently on different sides of the conflict.

Seven speakers at the public meeting, including Collins, Boland and O'Duffy, addressed up to 10,000 nationalists and republicans. Collins was certainly the person people had come to hear; he was 'cheered to the echo' earlier in the City Hall and was greeted with extended cheering and singing of 'The Soldier's Song' when he came to the platform (see plate 13).[36] In his speech, Collins covered much of the expected ground – the memory of the dead (including Terence MacSwiney), the importance of the Irish language (he began his speech as Gaeilge) and how victory was close at hand.[37] His tone was conciliatory, speaking of concessions to unionists if they accepted 'essential unity', while assuring his audience that they would not be deserted.[38] This tone was certainly noted by the Armagh Guardian, which asked whether 'he disappointed the extreme section'. Mary MacSwiney attacked Collins as a 'compromiser' for his speech, although the Frontier Sentinel praised the greater certainty he provided.[39] By contrast, O'Duffy's speech was notably aggressive, threatening to isolate Belfast and the Northern government economically to bring both to their knees. Although he stated that he would be the last to recommend the use of force against unionists, O'Duffy asserted that they must not stand in the way of a 'march of a nation' and, if they opted for the British Empire instead of going along with the rest of the country, then republicans 'would have to put on the screw – the boycott. They would have to tighten that screw, and if necessary, they would have to use the lead against them'.[40] O'Duffy admitted immediately afterwards that he had gone too far, or as he said himself '(I) put my foot in it', though it did him no harm politically and might have been useful to Collins. The Belfast News-Letter commented that his 'threat was not a meaningless one. It was a direct intimation of carrying on the war into the Six Counties ... the Government would do well to be adequately prepared against such an emergency'.[41]

The impact of the Collins meeting on local political circumstances and, in particular, the struggle within nationalism is difficult to measure. It seems clear that members of the INF and AOH were present (even out of curiosity).[42] Some accounts point to the difficulties faced by the AOH as its members migrated to SF and sometimes wanted to take funds, halls and even band instruments with them. This caused tension and violence in the county.[43] However, SF struggled to add strength to its Ulster organization, not least because many activists were now involved in the IRA. On their way back to Dublin, Collins and Boland had stopped with Aiken at the IRA training camp in Killeavy to inspect drills and arms.[44] Within weeks of the meeting, Seán Milroy wrote that Éamon Donnelly complained about 'an atmosphere of aloofness on the part of the Volunteers and an implied attitude that the SF clubs were not serving any useful purpose'.[45]

Political matters remained uncertain as the Treaty negotiations, mentioned in passing in Armagh by Collins, commenced. Initially, the British government would not agree to these beginning unless the Irish leaders accepted allegiance to the Crown as a precondition. However, the Irish position – aiming for a republic, but prepared to accept dominion status based on the construction of a free and willing partnership between Ireland and the free countries of the British Commonwealth – became the opening negotiating position by the end of September.[46] Before then, two deputations of SF councillors from Armagh (many of whom had been in the photo with Collins a few weeks earlier) went to meet de Valera in Dublin on 16 September, one of a series of delegations from Ulster in September and October 1921. The Armagh city group protested that partition would cut off the county which was central to Ireland's history, going back to Navan Fort and the Red Branch Knights, and would ruin towns like Lurgan and Portadown economically through heavy taxation under a Belfast parliament. The south Armagh case, made by James McGuill, Aiken and others, was of their homogeneity with close connections to Newry and Dundalk, and the lack of any connection to Belfast.[47] In reply, de Valera gave little away beyond saying 'their representations would be borne in mind' and 'the nation was the unit – none other was possible'.[48] The *Armagh Guardian* poured scorn on the arguments as being cut off from reality.[49]

After lengthy negotiations a treaty was signed in London on 6 December 1921 in controversial circumstances that have been debated ever since.[50] As the terms of the Treaty were published, Aiken was attending a training camp of the 1st (North Louth) Brigade and recalled the negative reaction as 'none of the lads said much, they just exclaimed it's terrible, it's damnable, they were too crestfallen'. That evening Aiken attended a meeting in Clones of senior IRA officers, including Joe McKelvey and Seán Mac Eoin, at which O'Duffy assured them that the Treaty was just a trick. It had been signed with the approval of GHQ to get arms to continue the fight and he himself would never take the oath of fealty required of TDs to the king, nor would anyone else be required to take it. Somewhat mollified, Aiken and other senior officers of the 4th ND from this point until July 1922 accepted orders and, in time, a salary from GHQ.[51] In a later consideration of the events, Aiken showed that he was not rabidly anti-Treaty. Rather he was sympathetic to Collins's 'stepping stone' policy and conceded he might have voted for the settlement had he been elected to the Dáil.[52]

Many of Aiken's key supporters disliked the Treaty and its immediate outcome. McCoy recalled that the acceptance by the Dáil of the Treaty had a 'disappointing and disheartening effect on republican opinion in the Six County area'. He believed it also 'reinforced the authority' of the Northern Ireland government and, from February 1922, security patrols by the USC and a dusk-to-dawn curfew were re-introduced.[53] John Grant recounted that he paid no heed to debates in Dublin 'to decide the difference between tweedledum and tweedledee' and, for him, partition meant a straightforward rejection of the Treaty.[54] In north Armagh, Charles McGleenan openly denounced the Treaty at a local SF meeting in Blackwatertown in early 1922 when he believed that the meeting would accept the settlement.[55] The dangers of a split were quickly recognized and just after the Dáil narrowly voted on 7 January 1922 following a bitter debate to ratify the Treaty settlement, a SF executive meeting in mid-Armagh called on de Valera and Collins to pursue unity.[56]

Elsewhere, there was a broadly positive reaction among SF supporters and nationalists in Armagh. The *Frontier Sentinel* welcomed the Treaty, especially the Boundary Commission clause.[57] Cardinal Logue was also positive about the settlement and, before an episcopal meeting on 12 December that welcomed it, he told the press of his belief that 'the country is anxious for peace and all are anxious that the agreement should be confirmed'. While the Dáil debates on the Treaty were on recess over the Christmas period, Logue preached a sermon in Armagh Cathedral on 1 January 1922 calling for ratification of the Treaty.[58] An IRA officer, J.J. Murray, recalled that flags and bunting were hung out in nationalist areas of Lurgan in celebration of the signing of the Treaty. These received the unwanted attention of the staunchly unionist supporters of Linfield Football Club, some of whom fired shots from a passing train and which were responded to in kind by local IRA units.[59]

Outside Armagh, political and military events moved at pace in January and February 1922. In Dublin, Mulcahy, the new minister for defence in the Provisional government, and the new chief of staff, O'Duffy, called a meeting of GHQ and divisional officers on 10 January in an attempt to prevent a split in the IRA. Those opposed to the Treaty, led by Rory O'Connor and Liam Lynch, wrote to Mulcahy and demanded that an army convention be called to discuss a motion that reaffirmed the army's allegiance to the republic and to elect an executive who would control the IRA.[60] At a second meeting Mulcahy agreed to hold a convention within two months but insisted that the army must remain under the direct control of the Dáil. Aiken attended and struck a moderate tone in these discussions. He opposed the idea of holding a convention in the absence of an agreed republican constitution because without it the army had nothing to discuss apart from the terms of the Treaty, which would inevitably cause a split. He was alone in this opinion, although his position was close to that taken in the IRB Supreme Council's statement of 12 January.[61]

Beyond these debates, violence erupted in the north. On 14 January a number of senior Monaghan IRA officers, including Dan Hogan, an ally of O'Duffy, were arrested in Dromore, County Tyrone, en route to rescue two IRA men from Derry jail. In retaliation, O'Duffy ordered the kidnapping of forty-two prominent unionists and Orangemen on the night of 7/8 February 1922.[62] The USC responded by mobilizing its forces across Armagh, sealing roads from Fathom to Middletown.[63] The British government persuaded Collins and Craig to sign a pact on 21 January in an effort to halt a rise in violence. However, this quickly collapsed and Craig asked Churchill's permission to send 5,000 troops across the border to release those who had been kidnapped. Churchill refused lest it prompt the fall of the Provisional government in Dublin. A clash on

11 February at Clones train station that left four USC constables and the local IRA commander dead, spurred a serious eruption of violence in Belfast that saw thirty people killed within three days. By the end of the month, forty-three people had been killed (twenty-seven Catholics and sixteen Protestants) and 95 wounded (sixty-nine Catholics and twenty-six Protestants).[64] To diffuse the tension, Churchill ordered the release of Hogan and his men on 21 February. In response, the IRA released twenty-six of the kidnapped loyalists, the remainder being released in batches during March 1922.[65]

Tension and violence visited Armagh with seven killings in February and March, the first since the truce. On 9 February 1922, James Robinson, an unarmed IRA volunteer from Maghery, was shot and killed by unknown persons in civilian clothes not far from his home.[66] In mid-March, a 60-year-old Catholic farmer named John Garvey was shot by a USC patrol for no apparent reason, and later died.[67] Two days later a deaf man, James McGleenon, was also shot dead by the USC in Keady when he failed to respond to an order to halt.[68] In retaliation for the death of Garvey, a civilian, Robert Milligan, described as a 'well-known Orangeman', was shot and killed on 19 March while travelling to his home at Blackwatertown, and Special Constable Joseph Steenson was wounded in the same vicinity.[69] A few days later William Fleming, a Protestant farmer from Corkley near Keady, was shot and killed. It was openly speculated that this was in retaliation for the death of McGleenon. Although Fleming was not a member of the USC, his brother was a member of the patrol that fired on McGleenon and this led the police to believe that it was a case of mistaken identity and that the killers were not locals.[70] On 29 March, RIC Sergeant Patrick Early and Special Constable James Harper, who were based at Crossmaglen, were killed and Special Constable Samuel Dougall wounded in an ambush at Cullaville, planned by both Dan Hogan and Aiken and carried out apparently by an IRA patrol operating out of Carrickmacross.[71] This surge in violence abated with the second Collins–Craig pact signed on 30 March 1922.

As violence increased in the north, anti-Treaty IRA officers announced that an army convention would be held in Dublin on 26 March 1922, in defiance of a government prohibition. The convention repudiated the authority of GHQ and the Dáil, and set up an independent army executive. The convention provoked a split within the 4th ND. The divisional leadership did not approve of the convention as 'it would inevitably mean the setting up of an anti-Treaty headquarters and so divid[e] the army, but a meeting was held by the 1st (North Louth) Brigade to select delegates for the convention'.[72] There are conflicting accounts of what happened next. Either Aiken and O'Duffy turned up to dissuade them and were refused permission to address the assembly or, after the convention was held, Mulcahy and O'Duffy were refused entry to a brigade meeting.[73] In any event, no divisional officers from the 4th ND attended the convention. Afterwards the North Louth Brigade affiliated to the new anti-

Treaty IRA executive. This brigade's two Armagh-based battalions and the two other Armagh/Down-based brigades followed Aiken's line of conditional support for GHQ. McCoy was emphatic:

> We in the 4th ND remained associated with the pro-Treaty headquarters. To be consistent afterwards we remained under the old GHQ which after the convention was looked on, and did in effect, represent the pro-Treaty section of the IRA.[74]

The tensions within the 4th ND can be seen, as elsewhere in the country, in the handing over of police and army barracks.[75] Aiken was badgering GHQ for the evacuation of Dundalk army barracks as early as 21 February 1922, arguing that he needed it for training and storage. A second factor was growing concern about the security of the divisional headquarters, located in a rented house in Newry.[76] In Pádraig Quinn's version of events, GHQ was mistrustful of Aiken and planned that the Dundalk barracks would be taken over by units of the newly formed National army from Dublin. After an angry row between Aiken and Mulcahy, a secret compromise was reached, whereby Aiken would take over the barracks but would surrender it, if requested by GHQ.[77] The RIC evacuated the two police barracks in Dundalk on 29 March and these were taken over by the pro-Executive North Louth Brigade, under the command of Patrick McKenna and supported by Michael Donnelly and others.[78] When the army barracks in Dundalk was finally vacated on 13 April 1922, the new garrison, in Quinn's view, was largely made up of low-quality, recently recruited and unemployed IRA volunteers and ex-British soldiers. It was a curious mix for such an important post and one which Aiken would have cause to regret within a few months.[79]

As the divisions that would lead to Civil War in the twenty-six counties widened in the early months of 1922, Armagh was increasingly militarized and violence broke out once more. The events south of the new border were an unwelcome distraction for the 4th ND, while allowing the Northern Ireland government to increase its control over its territory. Aiken remained loyal to GHQ, if for no other reason than to keep his Armagh and Down forces intact and well supplied. However, some within GHQ may have been distrustful of Aiken because he allowed the North Louth Brigade to defy GHQ's authority. Be that as it may, Pádraig Quinn noted that Aiken always received an effusive welcome in GHQ right up to the final break in July 1922. John McCoy concurred and maintained that relations between the 4th ND and GHQ were 'very good' up to the time of disagreements in June 1922.[80] Aiken's delicate balancing act to avoid internal dissension, whether prompted by the IRA convention or by the move of the divisional headquarters to Dundalk, would continue. In a statement to his men, dated 18 April, he declared his conditional support for the Treaty:

We shall take our orders from GHQ under the Dáil Minister of Defence unless we are asked to do something which is dishonourable. ... The immediate job which is up to us here in Ulster, no matter what happens to the rest of the country, is to get Ulster to recognise [the] principle of a United Ireland. We must concentrate on our own job of keeping our units intact and preparing them for the work that is before us.[81]

8 'Something unpleasant, if not horrible': violence and civil wars in 1922–3

After the divisional reorganization of the IRA in March 1921, Louth gradually became more important to the 4th ND. This importance grew after the transfer of divisional headquarters from Newry to Dundalk in April 1922, followed soon after by active Armagh IRA units encamping just over the border in Louth and Monaghan. There was a shift in political and military focus too, at least by the divisional leadership, from a mostly local to a broader national perspective. Armagh was one of the arenas in which the strategy of the Provisional government to undermine the unionist administration in Northern Ireland played out. The poorly organized Ulster offensive by the IRA in May 1922, the mobilization by the Northern Ireland government of thousands of additional B Specials to join almost 24,000 USC already available, and the introduction of widespread internment after 22 May 1922 ended any tenuous grip the IRA had in Armagh.[1] An uneasy peace enforced by heavily armed USC and the recently formed Royal Ulster Constabulary (RUC) slowly took hold and more than one hundred men and women from Armagh were interned. Nevertheless, the IRA continued to operate from bases south of the border, especially from Louth. The period May–June 1922, in particular, was marked by acts of violence and reprisal. The campaign ended suddenly after the attack on the Four Courts in Dublin on 28 June and, although it was not recognized at the time, the start of the Civil War in the south marked the beginning of the end of the revolution in Armagh.

The year after May 1922 was marked by the continuing economic crisis, a revival in some of the activities of everyday life and changes in the leadership of the Catholic Church. In January 1922, Bishop Patrick O'Donnell of Raphoe was announced as coadjutor (or effective assistant) to the aging Cardinal Logue. He was installed in May in a grand ceremony in Armagh Cathedral. The new archbishop called for unity among Irish people in the current crisis so as to end what he referred to as anxiety and sorrow.[2] Over the next twelve months O'Donnell and Logue would regularly return to the question of conflict and civil war. Both fully supported the October 1922 pastoral that threatened to refuse sacraments to anti-treaty forces due 'to the fact of their unlawful rebellion'. While Logue was seen by other clergy as consistently pursuing a 'tactic of nagging', O'Donnell was less whole-hearted and had doubts about the policy of executions by the IFS, specifically asking for mercy for Erskine Childers in November 1922.[3] Within Armagh, in the summer of 1922, the two senior clerics were involved in a different political storm when they were repeatedly stopped by USC while driving to carry out their ministry. Logue himself brought the matter to the attention of both the local and Dublin press, infuriating Spender and Craig (who accused him of being difficult) and embarrassing the London government when the issue was raised in parliament.[4]

Unemployment continued to be a pressing concern in Armagh, especially for those in the textile mills and factories across the county and in Newry. The *Portadown News* had hoped at the start of 1922 that unionist politicians were right and that the post-war slump would end soon. By December however, the same paper was frustrated that the numbers of unemployed showed no sign of decreasing and called on the Northern Ireland government to use the 'strictest economy in [the] administration of relief'.[5] Perhaps one-third of those working in textiles (and a higher proportion of women) were unemployed during much of the year. In 1923 there were fresh hopes (this time realized) that the worst of the slump was over but the staple industries did not recover their previous levels of output while trade elsewhere was weak.[6] This sluggishness continued when the IFS introduced fiscal controls on imports on 1 April 1923 and customs posts or huts were erected on both sides of the land frontier between County Armagh and Counties Monaghan and Louth. The consequential increased cost of many consumer goods was much criticized and it spurred the growth of opportunistic smuggling in small and commercial quantities. A new classification emerged of roads that were 'approved' or 'unapproved' for cross-border traffic that imposed profound difficulties in local travel in the day-to-day lives of those who were residen in the area.[7] Retail grocers in towns such as Armagh city, Keady, Crossmaglen and Newry effectively lost customers who lived across the border and especially among those who could not travel along approved roads.[8]

In the spring of 1922, it was decided that a general IRA offensive should take place in Ulster, prompted by two factors. First, Collins, O'Duffy and Mulcahy attached greater importance to the North and destabilizing the Belfast government than they had previously. Second, an offensive offered a means of healing the split in the IRA and avoiding civil war.[9] Frank Aiken was offered the newly-created position of O/C of all the northern divisions of the IRA, but declined this in favour of the chairmanship of a committee (in some places called the 'Ulster Council' or 'Military Command'), made up of the commanders of the northern divisions.[10] His lack of enthusiasm for the commander's role has been attributed to a suspicion that he was being set up as a scapegoat in the event of failure.[11] These discussions took place as the 4th ND headquarters were moved to Dundalk army barracks and elements of the division from Armagh set up full-time training camps in Louth and Monaghan. The Mullaghbawn company, under the command of John Grant, took over a house just across the border at Dungooley, County Louth. There they underwent intensive training and, in Grant's recollection, were to be used for the defence of nationalists of south Armagh and to undertake offensive operations against Northern Ireland security forces.[12] Other camps were formed in Louth at Ravensdale (Camlough Battalion), Bridge-a-Crinn (Newtownhamilton Battalion) and in Monaghan at

Castleshane (Armagh Brigade). The idea was to form columns in each camp, in John McCoy's words, 'to use as a spearhead force in Six-County operations'.[13] They were to be supported by weapons and men from the National army and anti-Treaty IRA units in the south, coordinated by Eoin O'Duffy, and much of it channelled through the 4th ND area organized by Pádraig Quinn.[14] His memoir details that 800 rifles, 1,050 revolvers and 160,000 rounds of ammunition were requisitioned and supplied to the 2nd, 3rd and 4th Northern Divisions. These supplies came initially from those furnished to the Provisional government by its British counterpart. However, Collins and O'Duffy became concerned that they could be traced back to the Irish government if seized in Ulster. It was arranged that Liam Lynch, O/C of the anti-Treaty forces in the Four Courts, would accept arms from the Provisional government and then swap his own rifles out to units in Northern Ireland through Quinn. According to the latter, a token transfer of about 100 rifles took place when 1,200 were needed. The transfer was witnessed by senior officers from GHQ, including O'Duffy, officers from the Four Courts, Tom Morris O/C 2nd ND and Frank Aiken. It led to an open split in late April when O'Duffy publicly criticized Lynch for not keeping to his side of the deal.[15]

The initial date set for what was supposed to be a synchronized offensive or rising in Ulster was 2 May. The Belfast IRA leadership requested and were given a postponement, but the 2nd ND (Derry/Tyrone) mobilized on 2 May and made a number of unsuccessful attacks on police barracks in Tyrone. Retaliatory raids by the USC decisively ended the offensive in west Ulster.[16] The 3rd ND (Antrim/North Down) began their attacks on 19 May when Belfast IRA units tried to take over Musgrave Street barracks in Belfast with the intention of seizing all of the arms kept there. The raid was unsuccessful, but the deaths of three constables triggered a familiar bout of reprisal and counter-reprisal. Over the following six weeks, eighty-two people were killed in Belfast (fifty-two of whom were Catholic).[17] IRA units in the 3rd ND area immediately came under intense pressure from the USC, but the expected support from Aiken's 4th ND, whose offensive was due to begin on 22 May, failed to materialize for reasons that remain unclear.[18] There were certainly detailed plans for an offensive in Armagh; the Ballymacnab company in mid-Armagh had instructions to seize a local clergyman's house for use as a hospital and then to join other companies to overcome the local USC platoons and proceed towards Portadown to join an attack on that town.[19] At noon on the day of the planned offensive, Aiken instructed McCoy to give countermanding orders to the Armagh Brigade.[20] The explanation given to Patrick Casey, O/C South Down Brigade, was that 'the Armagh Brigade was not fully equipped, and for that reason [Aiken] felt justified in withdrawing his Division from [the] action'.[21]

In some recent accounts, based largely on the evidence of Casey, much responsibility for the collapse of the offensive has been attributed to Aiken's decision not to involve the 4th ND: 'He [Aiken] remained in Dundalk barracks, inactive and remote from his command and so petered out this latest, and maybe the last, rising in the Ulster area.'[22] Pádraig Quinn, who organized the logistics for the 4th ND, later recounted that the only reason the 4th ND was mobilized and in the field in the first place was to accept the handover of two or three armoured cars that the Belfast IRA expected to capture in Musgrave Street. When they were not forthcoming, the units were withdrawn.[23] John Grant, who had 150 well-armed and trained men at his disposal in Dungooley camp, recalled that he '[didn't] know much about the plans for this attack on the North', although he knew 'an expeditionary force was being put together to invade Northern Ireland from camps like ours along the border area'. This terse account concluded with 'I know that the Rising in the North was called off about the 19th May'.[24]

Diarmaid Ferriter has noted that instead of being, in the words of one Cork IRA officer, Maurice Donegan, 'fairly badly organised', the offensive was 'a fiasco and hopelessly uncoordinated'.[25] The lack of coordination can be seen in the decision to allow the offensive to go off piecemeal, instead of on the agreed date of 2 May. Indeed, it staggered on until the Belleek–Pettigo battle at the end of May. However, there are valid questions about whether the offensive had any real purpose beyond an exercise to provide a joint IRA action at a time when civil war seemed inevitable. Matthew Lewis concluded that the offensive 'was an elusive and contradictory venture from the outset and its aims were vague, perhaps deliberately so'.[26] McCoy emphasized in several different interviews that GHQ was never fully engaged in the plans, did not provide sufficient resources to support IRA units in the north, and grew less enthusiastic during the planning when it realized that the offensive would 'cause a complete smash up of all the Treaty plans with the British'. He also believed that the anti-Treaty executive and its supporters was keen on the Ulster offensive as 'the only evident means of getting the pro-Treaty forces to take a line of action that would smash up the treaty position'.[27]

The collapse of the offensive was closely followed by other events that had consequences for Armagh. The agreement of the Collins–de Valera election pact, signed on 20 May 1922, was another attempt to avoid what looked like inevitable civil war. Aiken and other Armagh SF representatives were involved in a northern delegation that tried to persuade both sides in Dublin between 16 and 19 May to avoid 'the danger of permanent partition and national disaster if the present state of affairs is allowed to continue'.[28] Immediately following the announcement of the pact, a crisis erupted over the draft IFS constitution, which the British government regarded as an 'evasion' of the Treaty. It caused a hardening of British attitudes towards the Provisional government. Troop withdrawals were suspended, there were threats that the Treaty would be abandoned and talk of 'liberty of action' in resuming powers already ceded to the Dublin government and even re-occupation of territory.[29]

In Northern Ireland, the IRA offensive gave the government cause to take further action due to the worsening security situation. In Armagh, the police reported significant arms finds near Keady, and other obvious preparations for IRA operations.[30] On 22 May, after the killing of William Twaddell, a Unionist MP, by the IRA in Belfast, the Northern government invoked the Civil Authorities (Special Powers) Act and immediately proscribed Cumann na mBan, the IRB, the IRA, and Na Fianna Éireann. That night and the next day around 200 suspects across Northern Ireland, exclusively nationalists or republicans, were rounded up, with another eighty arrested within weeks.[31] The official records show that almost 450 persons had been arrested with internment orders by the end of September 1922. Numbers peaked in June 1923. By the end of 1924, a total of 732 people had been arrested and interned at some point.[32] It is estimated that 72 people from County Armagh were interned by the Northern Ireland government.[33] By the end of 1923, a similar number of Armagh men had been interned in the IFS, arrested after the outbreak of Civil War fighting, particularly in north Louth. The cases of Séamus Connolly and Frank Hannaway are illustrative as both were targeted in the 22 May round-up. Connolly was arrested and interned on the prison ship *Argenta* from June 1922 until December 1924, where he organized a hunger strike.[34] Hannaway was not at home in May and moved to the IRA camp at Castleshane in Monaghan, where he was arrested in late August when the National army closed down the camp. He was interned in the Curragh until late 1923, where he participated in a hunger strike.[35]

The bulk of those from Armagh who were interned in Northern Ireland came from the middle and north of the county, perhaps because many from further south had moved to the camps in Louth and Monaghan. The experience of eight men arrested in Portadown on 10 June 1922 reveals the dubious intelligence involved. None of the men appear on any of the IRA membership rolls for the Portadown, Maghery or Lurgan IRA companies prepared in the 1930s, though two shared family names and a third (sometimes Foy, other times Fox) may also have done so.[36] All were Catholics with various occupations (a hotel owner, three publicans, two mill workers and two horse dealer brothers) and their arrests appear to have been carried out by soldiers and police from outside the town. The suspects were first taken to the barracks in Portadown before being transferred to Belfast.[37] Seven of the eight were officially interned nine days later, with one man struck off the detention list as he had been arrested with his brother, who seems to have been the man sought, while another may also have been quickly released. Six were sent to the *Argenta*, while one remained in Crumlin Road prison. Their files suggest a general application of 'disloyalty' to those of nationalist or republican sympathy as opposed to anything more substantial.[38]

The Portadown suspect held in Crumlin Road was J.J. O'Hanlon and his case was unusual. He had been in business in the town for almost twenty years, was Irish chess champion for nine years from 1913, and was involved in civic matters since the 1900s. Indeed, there were local (albeit denied) rumours in April 1922 that he might be made a JP.[39] O'Hanlon appealed his arrest in court and was then one of the first to appear before an advisory committee on 3 August, hastily and reluctantly established to adjudicate claims of innocence and, later, appeals for release on conditions.[40] He maintained that he had always been a supporter of the IPP, had recognized the new Northern Ireland government, even serving as a juror, and had 'been arrested on account of my religion and to injure me in business' as owner of the Queen's Hotel in Portadown. O'Hanlon believed his local prominence and leadership role in the Knights of St Columbanus were the root of his problem.[41] He also accused Attorney General Richard Best of making claims during the court hearing, including that the defendant would not recognize the court and had not asked for legal representation, that Best knew to be false.[42] Best's comments appeared designed to hurt O'Hanlon with his Protestant customers and had been carried in full in the *Portadown News*.[43] The evidence against O'Hanlon was circumstantial and pointed to the difficulties for any nationalist business-owner or civic figure who was trying to reconcile to the northern administration and retain Protestant custom.[44] O'Hanlon had supported the Belfast boycott but claimed it was due to pressure from others (perhaps from Dublin) and he admitted that he had met SF leaders in Armagh in April 1921 to appeal to them to avoid an election contest by only putting forward one candidate. Ironically, he claimed that this was at the behest of local unionists in Portadown (including Richard Best's uncle) and after a conversation with D.G. Shillington MP.[45] Initially, the advisory committee recommended that he should continue to be interned, but he was released on 10 August 1922 after a review by Colonel Topping from the ministry for home affairs.[46] Within nine months, O'Hanlon had sold the Queen's Hotel, for which he may have received an offer while in jail, and moved to Dublin where he continued in the licensed trade and as an international chess champion.[47] It is not clear whether his removal to Dublin was a condition of his release, though many of the almost 400 who appeared before the advisory committees by the winter of 1923 and the 190 who had been released agreed to leave Northern Ireland.[48]

Alongside male internees, eight or nine women were interned in Armagh gaol between May 1922 and May 1924.[49] Typically, they were held for terms of less than six months and released on the grounds of ill-health or by agreeing to conditions imposed by advisory committees, or both.[50] Róisín Ní Bheirne, Cumann na mBan leader in the county, was recommended for internment in August 1922, the local DI referring to her as a well-educated, 'bitter republican' and perhaps a spy as she worked in the office at Bessbrook Mill. However, the military adviser to the Northern Ireland government believed she should just be watched closely and her offices searched, as 'there are objections to the internment of women unless on very strong grounds'. Ní Bheirne was dismissed from her job that month, which was hardly coincidental, and she perhaps escaped arrest by going to live in Louth.[51] Nano Aiken was the only female internee from Armagh. She was interned between February 1923 and May 1924, having previously been under surveillance in the IFS.[52] She adhered to a strict policy of refusing to engage with the advisory committee and received few visitors during her period in prison except her sister, her solicitor, a dentist and two local clergy – whom she named alongside Dawson Bates as witnesses for this period in her military service pension application.[53] Her internment became a source of embarrassment after a Labour MP raised the matter at Westminster and wrote to Craig, noting that she was the only female political prisoner in Ireland at that point. The initial response was to highlight Nano's refusal to accept the normal release conditions, but then, after some discussion and a failed escape bid, she received an unconditional release on grounds of ill-health.[54] There was no doubt, at least in her brother Frank's eyes, that she was being held as a 'hostage' in his place and her internment order mentioned his and Nano's involvement in the 4th ND activities. The authorities clearly regarded her as a threat in her own right: one Home Affairs official discussing her release referred to her as a 'fanatical and dangerous lady' who would go back to her subversive activities and stated that they might need to arrest her again.[55]

The introduction of internment in Northern Ireland was followed by another intensely violent six weeks in Armagh when fourteen people lost their lives. It began on 25 May in the Jonesboro/Dromad border area between Armagh and Louth when for two days there were heavy exchanges of gunfire between the USC augmented later by the British army on one side, and the IRA from the Ravensdale camp in the IFS on the other. Two civilians and five USC constables were injured, one of whom, Herbert Martin, later died of his wounds.[56] On 1 June there was further heavy gunfire between the IRA and a combined force of USC and the British army, this time close to the camp at Dungooley. In both cases, ceasefires were agreed following negotiations, which at Jonesboro allowed for the release from custody of Cumann na mBan members.[57] These skirmishes were later portrayed as providing combat training for the IRA, but they were not repeated on the same scale, probably because of the amount of ammunition used and the negligible strategic gain. Consequently, the decision was taken to revert to organizing ambushes using columns drawn from the camps along the border.[58]

Around the same time, a dozen unionists from Northern Ireland were kidnapped by the IRA and held in Dundalk. The targets appear mainly to have been USC members, including two from the Mourne area of Down, who were off-loading their fish produce at Greenore in Louth, several more from south Armagh, and also Captain William McMorran, area commander of the USC for south Armagh, whose capture was fortuitous.[59] Questions remain about the motivation for taking hostages – whether they were supposed to protect nationalists, given the threat of reprisals, or to force the release of IRA men held in the North – and about the divisional leadership's attitude towards these kidnappings.[60] John Grant recalled receiving instructions from divisional headquarters to kidnap three specific unionists, while McCoy maintained that 'every [IRA)] camp was to make out a list of hostages and submit for approval'.[61] However, Michael O'Hanlon stated that 'Frank [Aiken] wouldn't raid for hostages. He argued when we brought back hostages that we were making the border', while Pádraig Quinn recalled that Dundalk barracks became the central place for prisoners, many of them B Specials, 'in spite of what we could do to discourage it'.[62] Whatever about the strategy, the kidnapping plans inevitably went wrong. James Woulfe Flanagan, a magistrate, was shot dead by four men when he resisted his kidnappers after leaving Mass at the Catholic cathedral in Newry on 4 June.[63] Another fatal case was that of William Frazer who was taken on 5 July near Belleeks by four armed men and, despite rumours that he was alive and being held in various places in Louth, including Dundalk army barracks, it seems likely that he died or was killed not long after his abduction and was buried near Dungooley camp.[64]

Reprisals followed. Thomas Crawley, a 30-year-old auctioneer from Lissadian, Whitecross, and 50-year-old Patrick Creegan from Bessbrook were abducted and murdered on 13 June. Creegan was playing cards at Derrymore crossroads with others when they were approached by a patrol of USC and ordered to disperse. He was later seen on the back of the USC lorry. The following morning his body was found lying in a recently excavated hole near Lislea. In another excavated hole about 150 yards away, Crawley's body was found; he was shot in the back of the skull. Crawley's bicycle was later left at a house in the vicinity by uniformed men travelling in a lorry.[65] The IRA from Dungooley had originally excavated the holes in preparation for an ambush that had not taken place.[66] Placing the bodies of Creegan and Crawley – neither of whom were active republicans – in these holes was a warning of future reprisals against the civilian population in the event of further killings by the IRA. Speaking at Thomas Crawley's funeral on 16 June, Fr Eugene Clarke had no doubt who was responsible: 'this was done with the connivance of those who were supposed to govern them'.[67] The police alleged that the two men were shot by the IRA for disclosing the location of the two landmines and, apparently, the sworn inquiry into the killings was told that the logbooks of six local USC platoons showed that none of their lorries had been on the roads that night.[68] The inquiry report when published was not a ringing endorsement of the RUC or the USC: 'I fully exonerate all the local police of any complicity in the two crimes. If they were done by police at all and not by persons disguised as police, they must have come in from some other district, presumably Co. Down or possibly Co. Louth.'[69]

On the same night that Creegan and Crawley were killed, eight men wearing USC uniforms raided a public house at Dromintee owned by James McGuill, a SF county councillor and friend of Frank Aiken. He was not present but his pregnant wife, Unah, two children, two female servants and his mother were. A detailed report, probably from Aiken, was sent to O'Duffy two days later and in turn prompted an account of events sent by Collins to Churchill.[70] According to Collins's report, 'eight disguised men reported to be 'A' Specials from Forkhill Barracks' broke into McGuill's house, 'helped themselves to drink and cash in shop but failed to open [the] money safe'. They searched the premises for men but finding none, the attack became an instance of what historians have recently cited as rape and gender-based violence.[71] The intruders 'tortured the women for the keys of the money safe. Mrs McGuill who is about to be confined was caught by two of them, thrown on the bed, abused and night clothes torn in attempt to get the keys.' In an attempt to escape 'from brutes with blackened faces, she tried to throw herself through the window but was dragged back by one of the other women.' Three of the attackers then caught one of the female servants, 'kicked her, threw her on a bed and attempted to outrage her. They failed owing to her struggle and the help of the other women.' Collins claimed that the attack lasted two hours, and that 'all the women are hysterical and one of the servants is black and blue all over the body from kicks and blows.' He also speculated that the 'object of the raid [was] presumed to be murder' and stated that the intended target was James McGuill, who had been photographed with his wife at the Armagh city meeting the previous September.[72] The police denied that the incident ever occurred. The CI claimed:

> there is no truth whatsoever in this allegation ... It is not generally believed locally that anything of such a nature occurred ... McGuill ... has lately got into money difficulties and was afraid of having his effects seized for debt and it had been known for some time that he intended moving to Dundalk.[73]

The IRA response came on the night of 17–18 June 1922. Near midnight, Aiken led an ambush on a Forkhill USC patrol, using McGuill's pub as the base. Special Constable Thomas Russell was killed, while another, S.C. Hughes, was injured.[74] According to John Grant, the USC had prior warning and tried to surprise the ambush party but having been discovered by a startled IRA scout, attacked a group who were a distance away from the main ambush site, leading to chaos among the IRA volunteers.[75] John McCoy recalled that 'Frank [Aiken] wounded an officer in a duel. But some of the (4th ND) men threw away their rifles, he had men with him who were never on jobs before ... and was going to shoot some of these men.' Patrick Casey was in command of another group and was unaware that Aiken had withdrawn and had to extricate his men under machine-gun fire to make it safely back to Dundalk.[76] Apparently, Aiken was very disappointed in the actions of some of his men and had to be persuaded not to continue with court-martial proceedings against them.[77] Subsequently, McGuill's empty premises was burnt down by the USC and on 25 June it was 'completely demolished by explosives as a work of military necessity'.[78]

Around the same time as the Dromintee ambush, IRA units attacked the house of the sole Protestant in Ballymacdermott townland, a widow called Mary Thompson, before moving on to attack six to eight farmhouses in Altnaveigh and Lisdrumliska townlands at 2:30 a.m. By the end of the attack, six people had been killed, another four wounded and at least six houses fully or partially burned down.[79] In Altnaveigh, 60-year-old Thomas Crozier and his wife Elizabeth, who was 55, were both shot dead when Thomas opened the door and appeared to recognize one of the attackers. Two of the Crozier children, Alice and David, were injured by splinters from hand grenades thrown into their house, which set furniture alight. The Little's house next door was also attacked and the family of six escaped out the back as it was set on fire, a son Joseph being shot and wounded as they fled. Two other houses in Altnaveigh – belonging to William McCullough and David McCullagh – were targeted, the former was burned down. Another group entered Lisdrumliska and attacked four adjoining farmhouses belonging to the Little, Lockhart, Heslip and Gray families. The Littles – two parents and nine children – were ordered from their home and it was set alight and their neighbours, the seven Lockharts, experienced the same treatment. After a discussion, 23-year-old James Lockhart was shot dead in front of the two families after he spoke to his mother, while his 50-year-old father, William, and Edward Little (possibly a young teenager) were also wounded. More killings occurred at the Heslip and Gray households, which were close by. Again, the raiding party ordered the occupants out of both houses before setting them on fire. John and Robert Heslip were shot and while lying prostrate were shot again, with a gunman apparently saying: 'Belfast Catholics got no mercy'. At the Gray's, the males were reportedly lined up and 20-year-old Joseph was shot dead, John Thomas, his father, was wounded. Younger sons either collapsed in fright or fled the scene. It was said that onlookers abused the attackers after the shooting, and that Joseph Gray cried out: 'Don't say that. Maybe they had to do it. I forgive them, and I hope that God will forgive them too'.[80] Although most of the party returned to the camp in Ravensdale, some attacked houses in Derrymore and Cloughrea, near Bessbrook, including those of J.N. Richardson of the spinning company and that of the former chancellor, Isaac Corry.[81]

The ambush of the USC patrol at Dromintee seems an obvious response to the attack on Unah McGuill and the other women in her house, while the motivation for the deadly attacks at Altnaveigh and Lisdrumliska is less clear.[82] It should also be noted that a third attack by men in the Bridge-a-Crinn camp took place the same evening on the houses of alleged B Special members close to Newtownhamilton.[83] For some, in the immediate aftermath and to the present day, the Protestantism of the victims was explanation enough. The president of Newry Chamber of Commerce emphasized that 'this massacre was very carefully planned and deliberately executed with a view to obliterating this small colony of Presbyterians'.[84] A later recollection stated in defence of the operation that it occurred in the Altnaveigh district because 'all of the [male] inhabitants were Orangemen and members of the B Specials … and (were) reputed to have connections with a lot of local shootings of republicans, both in pre-Truce and in 1922'.[85] John Grant was clear that the strategy of the IRA was to send columns out of the camps and into unionist areas to remind them that they were 'not immune from punishment for the misdeeds of their relatives serving in the 'B' Specials'.[86] A number of IRA pension applicants also refer to the alleged membership of the USC and of unproven involvement in the killings of four local men, John and Thomas O'Reilly, Peter McGennity and Patrick Quinn, in June 1921. However, no mention was made in contemporaneous newspaper reports or at subsequent inquests that any of the victims had a connection with the USC. Without personnel records, the claims of USC membership remain in doubt and, had such a connection existed, it is likely it would have been mentioned, particularly at the compensation stage.

The ongoing release in recent years of material by the Military Archives in Dublin has helped to clarify the horrific events that occurred. In some pension applications, the applicants refer to Altnaveigh as a 'special job' or reprisal for the more recent killings of Patrick Creegan and Thomas Crawley.[87] Those directly involved in the events were not keen to refer to them due either to a concern about implicating themselves or others, or to being haunted by what had happened there.[88] It seems clear that the orders for ambushes and reprisal attacks were given in the divisional headquarters in Dundalk. A number of witnesses in Ravensdale camp referred to orders coming down with their local commander to go to Altnaveigh and Lisdrumliska on the outskirts of Newry.[89] Perhaps eighteen men left the camp on this operation, all of them from companies with local knowledge of the target area. The main road into the townlands was also mined to prevent a police response.[90] Patrick Casey, who was at Dromintee that evening, was critical of both the killings and the orders:

> Nothing could justify this holocaust of unfortunate Protestants. Neither youth nor age was spared and some of the killings took place in the presence of their families … nothing could justify such a killing of unarmed people and I was surprised at the time that Frank Aiken had planned and authorised this.[91]

The killings at Altnaveigh and Lisdrumliska were widely reported and condemned in newspapers on both sides of the border and in Britain.[92] A three-page report in the *Illustrated London News* included drawings of the burnt-out buildings and the victims *in extremis*.[93] Political responses were more ambivalent. A press release from the publicity department of Dáil Éireann linked the USC attack on the McGuill family to what followed at Altnaveigh, and came close to justifying those events: 'It is morally certain that the tragedy enacted in south Armagh … was the direct outcome of this revolting outrage on defenceless women and children.'[94] The British and Provisional governments were in daily contact at this time, but nowhere in the archives has any reference been found to the massacre being raised as a matter of concern of either government. In Belfast, figures in the Northern government reacted to these events with a measure of opportunism. A call made by a Presbyterian minister at the funerals of the six people for better protection was quickly taken up by Wilfred Spender, cabinet secretary, who confirmed that Heath Hall, near Killeavy, was to become an army outpost.[95] Spender was also involved in cynically dealing with the discovery of a British army service revolver in one of the houses attacked in Lisdrumliska. This was identified by its serial number as one supplied by the British to the government in Dublin. Spender used the discovery to, as one home affairs official put it, 'remind the British Authorities of what the decent folk if NI have been undergoing so that they may not be too horror stricken in occasionally – as at Cushendall – the disloyal people come off worst.'[96] In the end it was decided not to raise the issue with the Dublin government 'in view of the fact that the situation in Belfast might lead to correspondence of a recriminatory nature if this question was opened'.[97]

Little changed in the area outside Newry as further reprisals and ambushes occurred in late June and July. The following week uniformed men raided and damaged the home of former RIC head constable James McQuaid in nearby Carnegat, looking for his son William who had been a target in July 1921.[98] Within days, uniformed and armed men shot dead Michael Kane in Cloughenramer, and Peter Murray, a Catholic wire-man for the Great Northern Railway, was singled out and shot at Goraghwood; both shootings were near Newry.[99] In the same week Special Constables William Mitchell and Samuel Young were killed and a 70-year-old civilian Charles Haughey was wounded during an ambush at Keady.[100] On 23 July 1922 three local girls were fired on by a British army patrol in Jonesboro as they returned from bringing food and clothes to the camp at Ravensdale; 13-year-old Margaret Moore and 18-year-old Mary Connolly were killed.[101] Another fatality occurred on 8 October 1922 when IRA volunteer Terence Watters from Monaghan was killed at an ambush in Keady.[102] In hindsight, the events at Lisdumliska and Altnaveigh might have marked the beginning of the end of the violence in Armagh, but this may have been coincidental given the shifting focus southwards from July 1922.

Robert Lynch's suggestion that Aiken ran a 'rather unique fiefdom' within the 4th ND area is questionable. By June–July 1922 it was certainly no longer the case as events turned chaotic.[103] The North Louth Brigade had split over acceptance of the Treaty, with some repudiating Aiken's command. There were disagreements over hostage-taking and the division's inaction during the May offensive. Another major source of dissatisfaction within the ranks of the 4th ND was the absence of financial support. Officers under Aiken had been paid since the banned army convention in March 1922, with a brigadier receiving £15 per month and divisional staff officers, such as McCoy and Aiken, receiving £25 per month.[104] Since April 1922, members of the 4th ND had been on full-time duty and, for the most part, living in camps in Louth or Monaghan or in Dundalk army barracks, without pay. Pádraig Quinn recalled that he and Aiken had discussed at the time whether the 100 men quartered in Dundalk barracks, many from Newry, should be attested – sworn in as soldiers in the new army being formed by the Provisional government, with a daily pay of £1 4s. 6d. Aiken decided against attestation as he feared that his ability to take independent military action would be circumscribed.[105] However, this meant that the men, who had been promised wages equivalent to National army rates, were living a hand-to-mouth existence. They were also not aware that their officers were being paid regularly, nor that £500 allocated by the Provisional government to support payments to the men sat undistributed in the barracks safe.[106]

There were a series of protests about pay in July in Dundalk barracks. After a number of men refused to take ordinary duties, McCoy paraded the entire garrison and told them that, while their clothing, boots and food were free, there were no funds for pay and anyone who wished to leave could do so. Four men left.[107] The barracks' officers then protested and on 12 July the second in command, together with four or five men, broke into the arms store to arm themselves, took a car and disappeared. McCoy caught up with them in Drogheda where they were in the custody of the National army. On being taken back to Dundalk, these men and the barrack O/C, Dominic Doherty, who was aware of the intrigue, were court-martialled. Doherty was dismissed and told to leave the area immediately while the rest were imprisoned.[108] He later asserted that he was stationed in Dundalk for four months 'without job or reward' and, after his dismissal, was sent back to Dundalk by Mulcahy and O'Duffy to 'prepare the way with some of my men who remained in the barrack'.[109]

On 16 July, General Dan Hogan of the 5th ND (Monaghan) and his men silently infiltrated Dundalk and a number of 4th ND officers opened the barrack gates. The guard was disarmed and the National army took the barracks without any opposition, finding most of the garrison, including Aiken, in bed.[110] There was also no resistance from the North Louth Brigade forces in the town, but one Armagh volunteer, John Joseph Campbell (who was working as a cook), was killed and a second man, Patrick Quigley, from Louth, was badly wounded as they attempted to escape from Anne Street barracks.[111] Hogan reported that 300 men were taken prisoner in Dundalk and given the option of enlisting in the army.[112] Aiken sent orders, dated 17 July, instructing his men, those who were arrested and those in camps along the border, not to join the Free State forces and to 'put your trust in God and keep your powder dry, and make sure you don't lose it'.[113]

Of the 300 men initially made prisoner, at least 124 agreed to join the National army, though not all would have been 4th ND members. Dominic Doherty hoped that the officers who assisted in the capture of the barracks would now receive army commissions. However, with few exceptions, they were dismissed and Doherty himself left Dundalk and went to live in Manchester.[114] The 124 enlistees were sent within a few days to the Curragh, but it did not end well for most of them as Edward Fullerton recorded. Within days they had either tired of the treatment they received and staged a mutiny, or failed to come to agreement on the terms of enlistment. They were taken back to Dundalk, unceremoniously dumped on the streets, and threatened with machine-guns when they attempted to gain access to the military barracks. The men then took over a nearby old soldiers' home, evicting the sitting tenants. Eventually, they were ordered to leave Dundalk under threat of arrest.[115] However, the army was prepared to consider enlistment applications on a case-by-case basis and to accept personal recommendations from Louth TD Peter Hughes on their behalf.[116]

Some who had been in the 4th ND successfully enlisted in the National army and remained in Dundalk. One of those was Sergeant John Lavery from Tandragee, County Armagh, who was mortally wounded while off-duty and in a pub in the town on 17 July. Lavery was an ex-British soldier who had served under Aiken in Dundalk barracks from April 1922.[117] After the shooting, a number of his former 4th ND comrades proceeded under their National army officers to search houses in the Church Street/Linenhall Street area looking for those responsible. Two officers with revolvers drawn walked down Bridge Street. One fired shots in the air, exclaiming as he did so: 'We will have blood for blood somehow'.[118] Lavery later died of his wounds on 7 August and was buried with full military honours in Dundalk on 9 August 1922.[119]

Outside Dundalk, several hundred 4th ND men, most of them from Armagh, were in camps at Castleshane, Dungooley, Ravensdale and elsewhere. Having avoided capture, John McCoy and Malachi Quinn made their way to Dungooley and found about 150 men 'in a most indignant frame of mind … to be attacked by the (Provisional) Government forces was an act of treachery they could not understand'.[120] One immediate problem for the men in the camps was provisioning. Until Aiken's capture, they had acquired provisions locally based on IOUs from Dundalk barracks. McCoy advised them to carry on as normal. Hogan reported to GHQ that after taking Dundalk he had gone to the camps and found the men at Castleshane, Ravensdale and Castleroche 'starving for a few days after we took over'. He provisioned them on 21 and 22 July, 'pending a decision by GHQ as to their futures'.[121]

The confusion cleared when many of the men in the camps took part in springing prisoners from Dundalk gaol on 23 July in the so-called 'Hole in the Wall' rescue when Aiken led a mass escape.[122] Newspaper reports referred to the escape of between 100 and 130 prisoners. However, perhaps half were quickly re-captured, while others who had been involved in the operation, including John McCoy, were themselves captured.[123] The register of prisoners committed to Dundalk gaol in the period 17–26 July 1922 records 135 entries with 41 of those linked to the 4th ND either by name or location. Of the 135 prisoners, 104 escaped and 35 of those were serving in the 4th ND, the remainder being mostly from Meath and midlands counties.[124] As there may have been up to 170 of Aiken's men initially in custody, it is clear that for whatever reason, the majority of 4th ND prisoners either initially enlisted in the National army or were unable to escape on 23 July.

Although the numbers rescued may have been small, they were enough, with those still at large, for the 4th ND men to launch an attack on Dundalk on the morning of 14 August 1922. The forces assembled in Cooley; some crossed into Dundalk by boat. Two parties, one led by Aiken, the other by Malachi Quinn, attacked the army barracks by blowing up the front and back gates. Not everything went to plan. The mines on the front gate did not work, but the early morning operation overwhelmed the garrison and Dundalk was back in the 4th ND's hands.[125] Six National army soldiers and one 4th ND officer, Patrick McKenna, were killed. Some of those who were re-captured after the previous prison break from Dundalk gaol were once more rescued, including Andy O'Hare, one of the divisional officers.[126] Over the next few days a massive store of arms and ammunition was removed to the camps and further north. With no intention of holding the town, the main body of 4th ND withdrew within days before the National army recaptured Dundalk on the evening of 16 August. Only a small force remained behind to harass the troops. In the days that followed, Hogan's forces began to move against the 4th ND camps, meeting fierce resistance at Dungooley. According to an army report, the Armagh men withdrew into Northern Ireland and the National army were prevented from pursuing them by machine-gun fire from a USC garrison in Forkhill.[127] Shortly afterwards, successful National army operations forced the closure of the camps at Ravensdale and Bridge-a-Crinn, where another skirmish occurred.[128] The camp at Castleshane in Monaghan was raided by the Free State forces, arms seized, and the camp closed on 29 August.[129] All seventy men arrested there were interned in Newbridge, County Kildare, along with perhaps another fifty from the other camps.[130]

Aiken, his officers and men were now fugitives on both sides of the border. Hogan reported that the 4th ND were billeted in houses on the northern side, and as the USC never raided these, 'it is quite safe for these Brigands to keep low there now and be always in easy striking distance of our territory'. He later claimed that Aiken was in the Jonesboro area of south Armagh 'under the shadow of the Specials barracks ... evidently he depends on the latter for his protection'.[131] This claim was repeated by Kevin O'Higgins in the Dáil in February 1923, but was based on little or no evidence.[132] The *Dundalk Democrat* may have been more accurate in reporting that by 22 August, many of Aiken's men from Down and Armagh had returned to their homes, 'complaining bitterly of the action of their officers in calling them up for the duty which they had to perform, and the nature of which they had not learned beforehand'.[133] That report received some validation some months later when there were assertions that many volunteers severed their connection with Aiken's campaign after August 1922. Tomás Ua Vadhagh, who described himself as an IRA officer from Bessbrook, wrote to the *Dundalk Democrat* that 'large portions of our Division have taken no part whatever in your little war, a war that is the outcome of egotism, jealousies, hatreds and misunderstandings' and one with 'no reasonable chance of success', a view that Cardinal Logue would have shared.[134] In an interesting analysis accompanying a roll of the Mullaghbawn company for military pensions in 1935, John Grant made the point that most of the forty men who joined the company after the truce were neutral in the Civil War, as were thirty-nine of the sixty members who had fought in the War of Independence. Only one man joined the National army, leaving perhaps twenty who fought in the Civil War.[135]

One account of the Civil War and the role of the 4th ND portrays a picture of initial reluctance to get involved hardening into violent antipathy to the National army, before the 'dump arms' order was given in May 1923.[136] The consequences for those involved were largely negative. The men who ended up in prison endured appalling conditions on both sides of the border. According to one report, 4–500 prisoners in the wooden prison hulk *Argenta* in Belfast Lough were pressed into cages in groups of fifty.[137] In Dundalk gaol, there were complaints of overcrowding, bad food, beatings and poor sanitary conditions.[138] Conditions in the Curragh were also harsh, and one young Armagh internee, Michael Bennett from Lislea, who had been active with the Drogheda IRA, was punished so severely in Mountjoy prison and also in the Glass House in the Curragh where he was 'hung up', that he contracted tuberculosis and died after release.[139] Worse followed with the establishment of military courts in October 1922 to try those 'engaged in insurrection and rebellion against the state', with powers to impose a range of penalties, including execution.[140] For a number of months after October 1922, the executions took place in Dublin. However, in January 1923 a decision was taken to localize executions and three men were executed in Dundalk gaol on 13 January 1923. One of them was John McNulty from Belleeks, County Armagh, who had been found guilty of possessing a handgun and twelve rounds of ammunition at Hackballscross, County Louth, on 9 January 1923.[141] Three more executions took place in Dundalk army barracks a week later. All were local and like McNulty were found guilty of having in their possession war materials but not of actually using them.[142] When John Grant was captured on 28 February 1923, tried and found guilty of having a loaded handgun in his possession, his prospects were not good. He was sentenced to death, but the sentence was remitted to three years' penal servitude.[143] A second Armagh man, Luke Burke from Keady, was executed in Mullingar along with Michael Geery of Athenry on 13 March 1923. The IFS government refused compensation in the case of Burke on the grounds that he was 'not killed while engaged in military service'.[144] According to newspaper reports, Burke and Geery were found guilty of taking part in an armed raid on a bank in Oldcastle, County Meath, and with having £385 in stolen money in their possession.[145] He is not usually listed among the names of republicans executed during the Civil War.

On 2 April 1923, Sergeant Martin John Daly from Ballybay, County Monaghan, and IRA Volunteer Bernard Morris, a former merchant navy sailor during the First World War from Cullaville, County Armagh, were killed when a grenade was thrown at a National army patrol in Ballybinaby, County Louth, adjacent to the south Armagh border. The final 4th ND fatality during the Civil War came after John and Pádraig Quinn, close friends of Aiken's from schooldays, were both wounded trying to evade capture at Tallanstown on 22 April 1923. John died of his wounds on 22 May, just as the Civil War was ending, while Padraig was severely wounded in the right leg.[146]

At the end of the Civil War, there were 12,000 republican prisoners in the IFS. The government refused a general amnesty, but allowed releases where individuals signed an undertaking not to take up arms against the state again. The process of releases dragged on into 1924 due to its suspension from 25 October, twelve days after the beginning of a general hunger strike.[147] By November 1923, at the height of the hunger strike, there were still 50 Armagh men in IFS custody and, of these, it was recommended that 35 should remain in detention.[148] Three of those – Eiver Monaghan, Thomas McGill and Michael Fearon – had already been released and were living in Dundalk.[149] Instructions were issued that the trio were not to be re-arrested.[150] For most, release from internment was not the end of their problems – the men from Armagh had nowhere to go as they were likely to be arrested in Northern Ireland. Army intelligence reports maintained that prisoners from Northern Ireland did not return home but 'knock[ed] around in that part of the twenty-six counties adjacent to the Border'.[151] With few prospects, the above-mentioned trio left for the US in 1925 – part of an exodus of the disaffected and unemployed who found no sanctuary on the island of Ireland.[152]

The attack on the Four Courts on 28 June 1922 marked the outbreak of Civil War in the IFS. This account has concentrated on the impact of those events on Armagh, in particular the IRA members caught up in it, as events during the

Civil War in Louth have been examined in detail in another volume of this series.[153] They were, however, central to the four different battles for control of Dundalk in July and August 1922 that marked the high point of the Civil War in Louth insofar as the 4th ND operating in large numbers was concerned. Although they carried on a guerrilla campaign for some time, when the ceasefire was called in May 1923 the strength of the 4th ND in Louth was reduced to only 50 men on the rolls, with a mere dozen operational, and 200 in prisons (perhaps 80 from Armagh) in the IFS.[154] This was the outcome long feared by Frank Aiken and the leadership of the 4th ND. Their military strength was eroded and they were now unable to operate effectively inside Northern Ireland, where the government was firmly ensconced and its security forces almost completely controlled Armagh. The only meagre hope that nationalists in Armagh could entertain was that the long-promised Boundary Commission would recognize their estrangement from the Belfast administration and allow the absorption of at least some of the county into the IFS.

9 'Carsonia' achieved: the end of the Irish Revolution in Armagh, 1923–5

By the end of 1923, the Civil War in the IFS was over and the process of releasing internees on both sides of the border had begun. Armagh unionists felt that the successful delivery of 'Carsonia' was virtually complete as the county had largely returned to peace. The name 'Carsonia' had been coined in 1913 by *Punch* magazine as a joke against unionists and became shorthand for criticism of unionist rule in Northern Ireland into the 1920s.[1] The question of the final shape of the border, which had become a customs barrier in 1923, remained uncertain as long as Article 12 of the Treaty, which promised a Boundary Commission, had not been tested. The commission began its work in December 1924 and collapsed within twelve months; the final report was shelved by the Belfast, Dublin and London governments. This left unionists in Armagh more secure, while nationalists searched for a viable strategy to reverse partition.

Attempts to develop politics beyond Orange/Green tribalism failed. The potential threat to Unionist control posed by Labour candidates in the 1920 municipal elections was extinguished.[2] The Ulster Unionist Labour Association, which had been established in 1918 to 'sound the counter-revolutionary alarm to "loyal workers" against the twin threats of socialism and republicanism', thereafter began to build branches in Lurgan and Portadown.[3] It aimed to align working-class voters to the unionist cause through concessions on housing and employment alongside a fiercely loyalist message.[4] In Portadown, David Rock and David Short, both Orangemen and the first a B Special district commander and councillor, were the leaders. A series of local government elections in 1923 highlighted near unionist hegemony and the continuing divisions within nationalism. After the January 1923 election, the Ulster Unionist Labour Association had seven councillors in Portadown alongside seven Unionists and one Independent Unionist with no Labour councillor.[5] In Lurgan, there was no contest as 15 Unionists were returned, the Labour candidates having disappeared and one Independent Labour now under a unionist banner.[6]

Nationalist control of Keady, Armagh city and Newry No. 2 councils was eliminated by legal sleight of hand in 1923. Under legislation passed in December 1921, Dawson Bates, the Northern Ireland home affairs minister, could replace an elected council by an appointed commissioner if a majority on any council would not take an oath of allegiance to the state of Northern Ireland.[7] As a consequence, the running of all three councils was handed over to an appointed commissioner in March and May 1922.[8] At the municipal elections in January 1923, nationalist candidates stood in Armagh city and Keady, in the latter only after a public meeting decided that the elections should be contested by those willing to take an oath of fealty to the Northern Ireland state.[9] Many of the councillors had been UIL councillors in the period before 1920.[10] However, there was also a smaller number who were pro-Treaty SF supporters such as Frank Short in Armagh city. Taking the oath was supported by the IFS government, the policy of non-recognition effectively ended following Collins's death in August 1922, leaving northern nationalists to choose their own path.[11] Alongside the oath came the threat from gerrymandering electoral boundaries to maximize unionist political control. The redrawing of electoral boundaries by the Leech Commission took effect in the May 1924 county council and RDC elections when nationalists were further divided about whether to contest seats.[12] The effects of gerrymandering were startling: in Newry No. 2, unionist representation increased from 4 out of 19 councillors (21 per cent) in 1923 to 12 out of 29 (41 per cent) after the elections. The other 17 seats were left unoccupied as nationalists boycotted both the elections and sitting on the council.[13] However, in Armagh city a nationalist meeting decided to nominate candidates to the local RDC and they took both the oath and their seats after the May 1924 election.[14]

Of equal importance to unionist success in achieving what the *Armagh Guardian* called a 'solid Ulster' was the implementation of stringent security policies.[15] Countering any potential or imagined revolutionary threat, be this from republicans, nationalists or labour activists, was central to unionist thinking and practice in this period.[16] This involved the UUC reviving the UVF in July 1920 and then the fledgling Northern Ireland government demanding, obtaining and arming the USC.[17] The USC was crucial to the achievement of 'Carsonia' with more than 2,800 men from Armagh, almost all Protestants, enrolled in the 'A' and B Specials and an unknown number in the reserve C Specials, all under arms and patrolling by the time of the truce.[18] The USC was once more mobilized in early 1922 to meet the threat posed to the Northern Ireland government by any IRA offensives. In Armagh, unionist enthusiasm for the USC was present from the start and remained consistent. Orange leaders urged their members in November 1920 to 'join up themselves and urge others to do so'.[19] When early A Special recruits – 'almost altogether ex-servicemen and a loyal lot' – left Armagh city and surrounding towns and villages by train for Newtownards, they were paraded to the station by supporters in scenes of enthusiasm last witnessed in 1914.[20] This support probably deepened further as USC members became targets for IRA ambushes from as early as January 1921.[21] That month, William R. Compston became the first member of the USC to be killed in an ambush near Cullyhanna. From that point until 1923, at least a dozen members of the USC were killed in Armagh. Several more from Armagh were killed on duty in Belfast and Tyrone and were buried in their home places in the county. The funeral of Compston in January 1921 was typical of the public events that would follow. Large numbers, estimated in this case at up to 1,000, attended Lisnadill church where Revd Foy preached about the menace facing his congregation.[22] Many unionists believed that the USC, especially B Specials, had played a key role in the survival of Northern Ireland in 1921–2. David Shillington proudly told the northern parliament that he had been stopped by fifteen different B Special patrols between Armagh city and Belfast one evening.[23] A church parade and service in Annaghmore in January 1923 was attended by 500 B Specials from the Portadown district and was addressed by local Protestant ministers, including Revd Edward Stack of Loughgall, who used the text, 'He who is not with us is against us'.[24] A similar service in May 1923 in Armagh city for local USC members was addressed by Archbishop Frederick D'Arcy, Crozier's successor as Church of Ireland archbishop of Armagh, who told the congregation that 'the order they had restored to them in this part of Ireland was very largely due to the work of the B Specials'.[25]

When the Boundary Commission held hearings in Armagh in March 1925, fear of the USC caused several nationalist witnesses to state their community's desire to be transferred from Northern Ireland.[26] The story of the commission is important as the hope that large parts of the county would be transferred into the IFS inspired many Armagh nationalists and republicans to support the Treaty in 1921.[27] Certainly, Michael Collins, briefly an Armagh MP until his death in August 1922, believed that unity would occur once the commission transferred large parts of Northern Ireland into the IFS.[28] The debates on the Treaty in Dáil Éireann, when they addressed partition at all, may have revealed little understanding of just how any Boundary Commission would work, but the assumption that it would either make Northern Ireland unviable or persuade unionists to reopen a discussion about future unity was largely uncontested. Only Seán MacEntee raised the awkward question about transfers of territory from the Free State to Northern Ireland. The possibility that a Northern Ireland government could opt out of the IFS (which they did in December 1922) was ignored.[29]

For almost three years after the Treaty was ratified, the Northern Ireland government refused to appoint a commissioner and was barely pressed to do so by successive governments in London, which sought to avoid the issue.[30] When Carson was proposed by the Labour government as the Northern Ireland commissioner in September 1924, strong opposition from within the northern cabinet was led by Richard Best, Armagh MP and attorney general.[31] The commission, when finally appointed, was comprised of Eoin MacNeill, representing the IFS; J.R. Fisher, nominated by the British government to represent Northern Ireland; and Richard Feetham, a British-born judge in South Africa, who was chairman. It began its investigations in November 1924. The appointment of Fisher, the former editor of the *Northern Whig* newspaper and a close friend of Carson and Craig, was hailed by the unionist press to highlight how 'fearless' a unionist advocate he would be.[32] However, opposition to the Boundary Commission's work was prevalent on both sides of the political divide. When the commissioners planned to visit Armagh in December 1924, there were reports that Archbishop D'Arcy refused to give them an audience.[33] Unionist recalcitrance was accompanied by announcements in border areas by Craig and other leading unionist politicians that no transfer of territory would be countenanced. This message was given to a Black Preceptory meeting in Newry in September 1924 by J.H. Andrews and Best, who stated that the Northern Ireland government would have nothing to do with the commission.[34] When Best and Shillington won two Armagh seats in the April 1925 'boundary election' on a large 60 per cent vote share, Shillington claimed that the result showed 'what Co[unty] Armagh thought of the Border question. Their motto was "Not an Inch"'.[35]

Behind the scenes, however, the UUC officials worked with local unionist-controlled councils and other bodies in Armagh to prepare submissions to the commission.[36] The North-East Boundary Bureau (NEBB) and its northern agents, including J.H. Collins who covered Armagh and south Down from his Newry base as a solicitor, did likewise for the Dublin government from October 1922. Both sides gathered a significant volume of statistical and economic data, while the NEBB also explored ways in which local plebiscites might be held.[37]

The NEBB had maps drawn for minimum and maximum claims in May 1923: at a minimum, one-third of the area of Armagh would be transferred to the IFS, including the towns of Keady, Newtownhamilton and Crossmaglen. In the maximum claim, half of the area of the county, to include the east of the county and Armagh city, would be transferred (see map 4). It was understood that this may not have been in line with economic and geographic conditions, but it had the logic of leaving Northern Ireland as a 'solid block of territory whose inhabitants were unwilling to come into the Free State'.[38] As time passed and delays mounted, by December 1924 the NEBB found that nationalists in Armagh appeared divided and disinterested over the whole issue of the commission.[39] A poor showing in the 1924 Westminster election, where Dr James McKee (interned and standing as an anti-Treaty SF candidate) came a distant second to W.J. Allen, the sitting Unionist MP for Armagh, hardly helped. SF struggled to get an election committee together and provoked the *Frontier Sentinel* to editorialize: 'The Six County question is but a stone in the catapult of a political party, and it is no wonder that many people are sick of politics'.[40] Prominent SF leaders denounced any commission as 'fruit of the poisoned tree of the Treaty' and declared that they would not be satisfied with any finding.[41] Others were sceptical that even large-scale boundary changes would make Northern Ireland unviable and that they would primarily only affect south Armagh, leaving nationalists in the rest of the county within Northern Ireland. John D. Nugent was a noted sceptic and told an AOH meeting in Armagh city

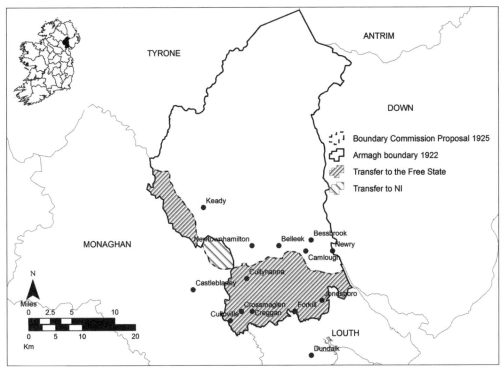

4 Boundary Commission's final proposals for boundary changes, November 1925

in May 1923 that Article 12 of the Treaty was 'merely eyewash for a deluded people'. He also argued against the endless waiting for a commission, claiming that the 'policy of drift has to come to an end'.[42] In August 1924 he questioned whether the position of northern nationalists would be worse in a more solid state, where negotiations might wring concessions from Craig in return for dropping the commission.[43] However, these musings may have cost him his seat in the 1925 elections when Éamon Donnelly and J.H. Collins took two of the Armagh seats and Nugent lost out.

The fiasco in 1925 may ultimately have proven Nugent right. The commissioners returned to Armagh city in March 1925 and over the next two weeks (between sittings there and Rostrevor, County Down) heard from more than sixty individual or groups of witnesses, including some representing local government, boards of public bodies (such as Camlough waterworks) and delegations or business organizations.[44] The hearings took place as an alternative to organizing local plebiscites, and presumably confirmed the commissioners in what they already believed.[45] The Boundary Commission's proposal in October 1925 was little more than a tweaking of the existing border, something Feetham had made quite clear in his questioning of witnesses and then in his deliberations.[46] Much of south Armagh and an area around Middletown (comprising 16,000 people) would be transferred to the IFS, while a small portion around Glaslough (comprising about 1,000 people) would transfer north from County Monaghan.[47] In 1922, Fisher had advised Craig that a two-way transfer could create a 'solid ethnographic and strategic frontier to the South'. Now, as one of the commissioners, he told his friend Carson 'no centre of even secondary importance goes over, and with Derry, Strabane, Enniskillen, Newtownbutler, Keady and Newry in safe keeping your handiwork will survive'.[48] On 7 November 1925, the Tory-supporting *Morning Post* carried a forecast of the commission's report, probably leaked by Fisher. W.T. Cosgrave, president of the executive council, was politically embarrassed at how ineffective Eoin MacNeill had proven to be. With the agreement of the British government, the report was suppressed and a compact was signed on 3 December 1925 that gave permanent recognition to the boundaries as established by the 1920 Government of Ireland Act. Cosgrave failed to secure any concessions for the rights of the nationalist minority in Northern Ireland, dismissing such guarantees as 'scraps of paper' and suggested that the best hope for the minority lay in future bipartite meetings between himself and Craig.[49] Such meetings never took place.

In Portadown, the UDC passed a resolution to congratulate Craig on the settlement and the Good Templars were told that goodwill had broken out not only in the Pact of Locarno and between the 'classes and the masses', but also in Ireland.[50] In contrast, the *Frontier Sentinel* articulated the disappointed hopes not only in the commission but in the Treaty settlement:

> It is now coolly asserted that time can be depended on to heal the difference between Belfast and the rest of Ireland. That argument could have been brought forward when the Treaty was new, but if it had been the debates on the merits of the Treaty would have been gloriously short. It is brought forward now as the straw at which drowning men grasp.[51]

By the end of 1925, unionism had much to be content about and held a day of thanksgiving on Sunday 6 December to mark what looked like a strong and solid settlement. At one service in Newtownhamilton, the congregation heard the settlement compared to the deliverance of the Israelites through a providential hand.[52] The creation of a consensus around Craig's government was identified as the goal for all responsible unionists. The case of Thomas Shillington showed that the new consensus even co-opted old foes. He had been a leading Ulster Liberal and a Gladstonian home ruler since the 1880s, but when he died in January 1925, his past was treated as a sort of relic. Obituaries stressed his contributions as a leading businessman and local civic philanthropist in

Portadown, and his recent accession to the Northern Ireland privy council.[53] For the *Northern Whig*, Shillington had embraced the economic opportunity associated with a new Northern Ireland.[54] Thus, someone who opposed Carson's anti-home rule campaigns and who spoke against partition in June 1916 was co-opted by the new state. His earlier politics would belong to a lost world, forgotten by both unionists and nationalists.[55]

The opportunities associated with Northern Ireland seemed precarious in the aftermath of partition. Trade had begun to recover in 1924, driven by higher prices for agricultural produce, but industry lagged badly and unemployment for those in textiles and engineering works remained high right into the 1930s. Other everyday activities, such as sports and other forms of socializing, also saw a resurgence in 1923 with GAA and soccer leagues taking place across the county. The *Armagh Guardian* was driven to bemoan that the city had fallen far behind Lurgan and Portadown in almost all the sports leagues (football, hockey, rugby) and, while the Armagh Musical Society had folded, Portadown now had a Musical Festival Association holding an annual competition in April 1923.[56] This civic pessimism could also be seen, for a different reason, in the *Frontier Sentinel*, which lamented the difficulties of reorganizing the GAA in Armagh and Down in a hostile environment where David Shillington MP could refer to a GAA match in Lurgan as a threat to public order.[57]

Any later tension among Ulster unionists, between those committed to a populist and exclusive form of Northern Ireland and those aiming at a more moderate version that could include nationalists, did not exist at this point.[58] The views of imperial civil servant, S.G. Tallents, sent by Churchill to look at the state of Northern Ireland in 1922, that too many ministers were incompetent or were 'too close to their followers and cannot treat their supporters from a distance', were borne out in a protest by an Armagh B Special commander about proposed reductions to the USC in 1925:

> Any voluntary force like the 'B' force is a delicate instrument needing to be played skilfully and not banged on, and whatever their shortcomings, they don't like to be told they are no good and must either be swept or completely reorganized, officers and all.[59]

In the event, the B Specials were fully retained while the other two classes were reduced.[60]

For many Armagh nationalists the end of the revolutionary period raised the key question of how to operate politically within Northern Ireland. Elected councillors, after 1923, took their seats and controlled the levers of local government in Keady, Armagh city and Newry No. 2. However, when it came to the northern parliament, their representatives were generally abstentionist, taking their seats for only a short period in the late 1920s before walking out again.[61] Debates in 1927 over the issue saw J.H. Collins in favour of entering parliament, but abdicating any responsibility for it.[62] For Éamon Donnelly, who could not enter Northern Ireland from 1924 until 1939, a convention of republicans in Armagh confirmed that he would continue as an abstentionist MP.[63] The declining AOH was consistently in favour of taking seats but was unable to shape the debate.[64] Those active in the revolutionary events, especially members of the Irish Volunteers, the IRA and Cumann na mBan, largely rejected the Northern Ireland state and looked south, where they could apply for military pensions from the IFS. After 1934, this widened to include a larger number of applicants from Armagh who had opposed the Treaty.

The applications and associated papers showed the extent to which many of those who had been IRA members in the period lived outside the county. Only a third of one south Armagh company and a quarter of divisional staff in July 1922 lived in Northern Ireland after that date. Some emigrated to the United States, Canada or England but most started over in the Free State.[65] Some, like Charles McGleenan, Eddie Boyle, Nano Aiken and Jack McElhaw, returned to their homes in Armagh from prison or having been on the run, but ran the risk of being subject to police surveillance, or being charged with offences, or being interned.[66] They could apply for military service pensions in the IFS but the process proved difficult and disappointing for many. Plate 15 in this book captures seven 4th Northern Division volunteers who were interned during the Civil War and had been involved in the IRA since 1919. Peter Boyle, one of the seven, was furious that his application for a wound suffered during the War of Independence was initially denied as having being received in service; Frank Monaghan, who had moved to British Columbia, lost touch with the process and found it impossible to prove service or a serious disablement while Peadar Murney denounced the whole process as flawed and resigned from any role in processing applications in Northern Ireland.[67]

The disappointments of the decade were made worse for members of Cumann na mBan as demonstrating military service was particularly difficult. In 1939 John McCoy, then a member of the advisory committee adjudicating on pensions, outlined the dilemma as he saw it:

> It would be unwise to adopt a standard of service for the women less exacting than what will be applied to the men who are classed as 'key men'. On the other hand, it would be most ridiculous to expect women to have taken part under arms in engagement with enemy forces.[68]

While this argument had been made in the Dáil by Frank Aiken, as minister for defence, in 1934, McCoy stressed the value of those who carried dispatches, provided safe houses and took charge of arms and dumps.[69] In Armagh this meant that one applicant who provided safekeeping for IRA and arms could prove military service, while another, a leading officer in Cumann na mBan, could not for the same years, a decision described by Róisín Ní Bheirne as 'galling'.[70] Likewise, the mothers of the two girls, Mary Connolly and Margaret Moore, who were shot by soldiers at Edenappa in July 1922 were unsuccessful as they had no military service, but a sister, Mary Connolly, got a wound pension of £30 per annum as a despatch carrier for the Dromintee IRA company.[71] Unsurprisingly, Aiken was equally exacting when it came to men proving service. With regard to the Adavoyle ambush, he was insistent that only six men were involved, not eleven as listed by the Camlough O/C, nor another four whose presence nobody could recall.[72]

The deaths and killings, whether at Adavoyle, Altnaveigh, Mullaghbawn or of Armagh natives living outside the county, were a result of the violence that was central to the revolutionary decade, a period in which the belief in a vindication through use of arms was strong locally, nationally and on a global scale. Richard Mulcahy's point in the Treaty debates, that the capacity of the IRA was such that they were unable to remove their enemy from anything more than a 'fairly good sized police barracks', was rhetorical but it also pointed to the limitations of armed revolution in Armagh.[73] Set-piece confrontations were few, the violence perpetrated by both sides was generally more personal and localized where victims were more often known and targeted by their killers. Thirty years later, John McCoy would question whether the use of violence had not 'a persistent habit of recoiling on the user', especially in the north. Aiken was somewhat more circumspect. He pointed out that Eoin O'Duffy could not be blamed alone for the pogroms worsening due to his aggressive approach as liaison officer in Belfast in 1921 since 'his attitude was merely representative of the whole Army. We were great believers then in the power of the gun alone to cure all our evils'.[74]

In 1912 Armagh was on edge, not just because of the 'normal' deep division along sectarian lines due to the near parity of ethno-religious groups or because, even without the political temperature of the home rule crisis, sectarian violence could regularly break out in both industrial towns and rural areas. Within the county, unionists and nationalists had a highly evolved sense of the uniqueness of their own identity with an impressive organizational infrastructure, ranging from relatively benign cultural and sports clubs to the quasi-religious/political Orange Order and AOH, which had the strength in numbers and the willingness to take the fight to each other. The debate over the third home rule bill was distinguished by a readiness on both sides to arm themselves for the avowed purpose of defeating or supporting the proposals. Despite many efforts, no compromise could be reached between the aspirations of the nationalist majority for a government with severely limited powers in Dublin, content to live as part of the United Kingdom with the British monarch as head of state, and the unionist minority who regarded such proposals as an unacceptable threat to their political and religious freedom. In 1914, Ireland came close to civil war, only to be 'saved' by the outbreak of war in Europe. What emerged as a constitutional settlement in 1920–1 was a solution unsought by most in Armagh in 1914 – a partitioned island with a six-county home rule government in Belfast, and a government in Dublin that was soon to show that it was, to all intents and purposes, completely independent of Britain, but cut off politically also from Northern Ireland. That Armagh fell under the jurisdiction of Belfast and not Dublin in 1922 was a failure of unionist objectives of 1912 to oppose home rule for all of Ireland, and of nationalist and republican aims to establish a government for all of the island of Ireland in Dublin. Partition meant that for fifty years, the two governments in Ireland only had to deal with each other at administrative arm's length, storing up rather than solving problems created and effectively smothered generations before.

Appendix: Signatories of the Ulster Covenant in County Armagh, 1912

North Armagh

District	No. of signing places	No. of males	No. of females	Agent(s)
Portadown	2	2,880	3,167	W.K. Bright
Loughgall	9	1,097	1,030	Joseph Jackson George Magowan
Lurgan	21	3,450	4,285	H.C. Malcolm N. Armstrong
Tartaraghan	3	220	220	James J. Brownlee
Clonmakate	1	109	130	Robert Brennan
Milltown	3	235	233	W.B. Allinar
Drumcree	1	410	356	Revd Fred Hallahan
Seagoe	2	373	714	T.J. Atkinson
Knocknamuckly	1	138	0	Revd G.H. Daunt
Montiaghs	2	11	20	Revd R. Dixon Patterson
Drumsill	1	0	99	Revd Fred Hallahan
Gilford	2	0	73	N. Armstrong
Ernecash	1	0	35	Revd Owane
Dobbin	1	207	173	J.N.A. Wilson
Totals	**50**	**9,130**	**10,535**	

Mid Armagh

District	No. of signing places	No. of males	No. of females	Agent(s)
Keady	2	681	670	W.J. Greer
Markethill	2	379	349	W.J. Greer
Richhill	4	768	796	W.J. Greer
Middletown	1	213	185	W.J. Greer
Tanderagee	2	1,261	1,519	W.J. Greer
Armaghbrague	1	147	171	George Kane
Armagh City	4	1,966	1,829	J. Patterson Best
Ballyards	1	0	234	J. Patterson Best
Aghavilly	1	0	10	J. Patterson Best
Lisnadill	1	0	150	J. Patterson Best
Redrock	1	0	9	J. Patterson Best
Charlemont	1	165	240	
Killyleagh	1	732	637	J. Patterson Best
Mullabrack	2	437	499	Sgt James McMullan, etc.
Kildarton	1	112	124	W.J. Greer
Not recorded		16	4	W.J. Greer
Totals	**25**	**6,877**	**7,446**	

South Armagh

District	No. of signing places	No. of males	No. of females	Agent(s)
Killeavy	1	14	17	
Jonesboro	1	10	0	Revd R. McCracken
Bessbrook	1	567	663	Alex Ardis
Tullyhappy & Mullaghglass	4	231	238	Robert L. Rantin John Lambe
Newtown	4	687	540	Alex Ardis John Magill
Poyntzpass	6	368	355	Revd W.L. Jonston Revd E.A. Nelson William Laverty
Markethill	4	312	221	W.J. Greer John Acheson
Kingsmill	2	116	98	John King John Samuel Robb
Redrock	2	111	102	W.T. Williamson Mrs J.T. Roulston
Mountnorris	1	97	83	John Wallace
Totals	**26**	**2,713**	**2,317**	

Overall Totals

District	No. of signing places	No. of males	No. of females	Totals
North Armagh	50	9,130	10,535	19,665
Mid Armagh	25	6,877	7,446	14,323
South Armagh	26	2,713	2,317	5,030
Total	**101**	**18,720**	**20,298**	**39,018**

Notes

CHAPTER ONE *Armagh in 1912*

1 Cormac Bourke, *Patrick: the archaeology of a saint* (Dublin, 1993).

2 See Henry A. Jefferies, *Priests and prelates of Armagh in the age of reformations, 1518–1558* (Dublin, 1997), p. 63.

3 R.J. Hunter, 'County Armagh: a map of plantation, *c*.1610' in A.J. Hughes and William Nolan (eds), *Armagh: history and society. Interdisciplinary essays on the history of an Irish county* (Dublin, 2001), pp 265–94.

4 *Census of Ireland, 1911: province of Ulster, county of Armagh, Table XXIX, Religious professions and sexes of the inhabitants*, House of Commons, 1912 (Cd. 6051), p. 73.

5 For more on this localized census population data, see the Irish Historical Mapping Tool for County Armagh at http://airo.maynoothuniversity.ie (accessed 31 May 2022).

6 *Armagh Guardian (AG)*, 26 July, 2 Aug. 1912.

7 Cormac Ó Gráda, 'Economic status, religion and demography in an Ulster town [Lurgan] in the early twentieth century', *Journal of the History of the Family*, 13:4 (2008), 350–2.

8 L.A. Clarkson, 'Armagh town in the eighteenth century' in Brenda Collins, Philip Ollerenshaw & Trevor Parkhill (eds), *Industry, trade and people in Ireland, 1650–1950: essays in honour of W.H. Crawford* (Newtownards, 2005), p. 65; W.H. Crawford, 'Evolution of towns in County Armagh' in Hughes & Nolan (eds), *Armagh: history and society*, p. 877.

9 Alvin Jackson, 'Unionist politics and Protestant society in Edwardian Ireland', *Historical Journal*, 33:4 (1990), 840.

10 *Census of Ireland, 1911, Armagh, Table XIX, Occupations of males and females*, pp 40–66.

11 Department of Agriculture and Technical Instruction for Ireland, *Agricultural statistics 1913* (Dublin, 1913), pp 22–3, 28–31.

12 John Bateman, *Great landowners of Great Britain and Ireland* (1876, reprinted Leicester, 1971), analysis of Armagh estates.

13 Maura Cronin, *Agrarian protest in Ireland, 1750–1960* (Dundalk, 2012), pp 28–9, 36–43.

14 Patrick John Cosgrove, 'The Wyndham Land Act, 1903: a final solution to the Irish land question?' (PhD, NUI Maynooth, 2008), pp 19, 61; Alvin Jackson, 'Irish unionism and the Russellite threat, 1894–1906', *Irish Historical Studies*, 100:25 (1987), 376–404.

15 Cosgrove, 'Wyndham Land Act', pp 371–4.

16 See County Inspector (CI) Armagh, Feb., May, Nov. 1912 (TNA, CO 904/86, 87, 88).

17 John Bradley, 'The Richardsons of Bessbrook: a Quaker linen family', *Seanchas Ard Mhacha*, 22:2 (2009), 159–91.

18 *Census of Ireland, 1911, Armagh, Table XIX, Occupations of males and females*, pp 40–66.

19 *Royal Irish Constabulary and Dublin Metropolitan Police, Report of the Committee of Enquiry 1914*, Appendix VIII (London, 1914) (Cd. 7421), p. 341.

20 *Royal Irish Constabulary list and directory*, Jan. 1914 (Dublin, 1914), p. 99.

21 http://www.census.nationalarchives.ie/pages/1911/Armagh/Armagh_E__Urban/Barrack_Hill/326932/ (accessed 12 June 2023).

22 *Kerry Sentinel*, 21 Mar. 1900.

23 Donal Hall, 'The Louth Militia mutiny of 1900', *Journal of the County Louth Archaeological and Historical Society*, 24:2 (Dundalk, 1998), 281–95.

24 P.J. Jupp and Eoin Magennis, 'Introduction' in idem (eds), *Crowds in Ireland, 1720–1920* (Basingstoke, 2000), p. 33.

25 CI Armagh, June 1902 (TNA, CO 904/70); *Portadown News (PN)*, 14 June 1902.

26 *Thirty-Fourth report of the General Prisons Board, Ireland, 1911–1912* (Dublin, 1912), pp 18, 2., 25, 28, 32, 35, 37; Elaine Farrell, *Women, crime and punishment in Ireland: life in the nineteenth-century convict prison* (Cambridge, 2020), p. 95.

27 *Freeman's Journal (FJ)*, 8 Apr. 1918.

28 *Seventy-seventh report of the Commissioners of National Education in Ireland, 1910–1911: section 3* (Dublin, 1912), pp 28–37.

29 *Appendix to the seventy-eighth report of the Commissioners of National Education in Ireland, 1912– 13* (Dublin, 1914), pp 136–7, 138, 140, 143, 146.

30 Desmond McCabe, 'Trimble, William' and 'Trimble, Samuel Delmege', *Dictionary of Irish biography (DIB)*, DOI: https://doi.org/10.3318/dib.008657.v1.

31 John Rouse, 'Connellan, Joseph', *DIB*, DOI: https://doi.org/10.3318/dib.001945.v1; report of seditious literature at a meeting at Slieve Gullion, 5 Aug. 1906 (TNA, CO 904/161, ff 128– 55).

32 Pádraigín Ní Uallacháin, *A hidden Ulster: people songs and traditions of Oriel* (Dublin, 2003), p. 28.

33 *Census of Ireland, 1911, Armagh, Table XXXVII, Comparison between 1901 and 1911, the number and ages of persons who spoke Irish only*, p. 97.

34 *AG*, 2 Aug. 1912.

35 *Frontier Sentinel (FS)*, 2 Mar., 7 Sept. 1912; *AG*, 6 Sept. 1912; CI Armagh, Feb. 1910, Mar. 1911, Mar., June 1912 (TNA, CO 904/80, 83, 86–7).

36 CI Armagh, Dec. 1909, Feb. 1910, Feb. 1912 (TNA, CO 904/79, 80, 86).

37 Phil McGinn, *Armagh Harps GFC: celebrating 120 years* (Armagh, 2008), pp 10–28; Tom Hunt, 'The diverse origins and activities of early GAA clubs' in Dónal McAnallen, David Hassan and Roddy Hegarty (eds), *The evolution of the GAA: Ulaidh, Éire agus eile* (Armagh, 2009), pp 89–90.

38 *Lurgan Times (LT)*, 26 Nov. 1912.

39 Eric Villiers, 'Commemorative postcards celebrate penalty king', *History Armagh*, 4 (2007), 4–5.

40 Paul Rouse, *Sport and Ireland: a history* (Oxford, 2015), pp 124, 282–4.

41 *Belfast News-Letter (BNL)*, 9 Sept. 1893; *Lurgan Mail (LM)*, 6 Nov. 1915.

42 Brian Weir, 'Armagh Cricket Club', *History Armagh*, 4:2 (2018), 31–3.

43 British political historian John Vincent quoted in Jackson, 'Unionist politics and Protestant society', 858.

44 *AG*, 20 Sept. 1912.

45 *PN*, 20 Feb. 1912; Peter Geraghty, 'John James O'Hanlon: a forgotten Irish sporting hero', *Seanchas Ard Mhacha*, 26:1 (2016), 170–1.

46 Frank Thompson, 'The Armagh elections of 1885–6', *Seanchas Ard Mhacha*, 8:2 (1977), 360–85.

47 B.M. Walker, *Parliamentary election results in Ireland, 1801–1922* (Dublin, 1978), pp 122, 130, 383.

48 Paul Bew, *Ideology and the Irish question: Ulster unionism and Irish nationalism, 1912–1916* (Oxford, 1994), p. 19.

49 Brian M. Walker, 'Actions and views: J.B. Lonsdale, Unionist MP, 1900–1918 and party leader, 1916–1918' in D. George Boyce and Alan O'Day (eds), *The Ulster crisis, 1885–1921* (Basingstoke, 2006), pp 128–45; Jackson, 'Unionist politics and Protestant society', 842–3, 847–8.

50 Bridget Hourican, 'Moore, Sir William', *DIB*, DOI: https://doi.org/10.3318/dib.005949.v1; Alvin Jackson, *Colonel Edward Saunderson: land and loyalty in Victorian Ireland* (Oxford, 1995), pp 211–12; David Burnett, 'The modernisation of Ulster unionism, 1892–1914' in Richard English and Graham Walker (eds), *Unionism in modern Ireland* (Dublin, 1997), pp 41–62.

51 See index in *Census of Ireland, 1901: General topographical index* (Cd. 2071), (Dublin, 1904), pp 1040–2.

52 *Irish Times (IT)*, 19, 24 Jan. 1911.

53 *PN*, 14, 21 Jan. 1911.

54 *LT*, 14 Jan. 1911.

55 Jackson, 'Unionist politics and Protestant society', 866; *Ulster Gazette* (*UG*), 19 Oct. 1912.

56 The figures are estimated from County Armagh Grand Orange Lodge, *Annual Report*, 1911, pp 14–20 (with thanks to Dr Allan Blackstock for this source); David Fitzpatrick, *Descendancy: Irish Protestant histories since 1795* (Cambridge, 2014), Table 6.2, p. 244; CI Armagh, Mar. 1916 (TNA, CO 904/99).

57 CI Armagh, Sept. 1910, July 1911 (TNA, CO 904/82, 85).

58 For examples see *FJ*, 10 Apr. 1912; *FS*, 7 Sept. 1912.

59 David Fitzpatrick, 'The Orange Order and the border', *Irish Historical Studies*, 33:129 (2002), 61; Alvin Jackson, 'Origins, culture and politics of Irish unionism' in Thomas Bartlett (ed.), *The Cambridge history of Ireland. Volume iv: 1800 to the present* (Cambridge, 2018), 93–5.

60 For these figures see CI Armagh, Feb. 1912 (TNA, CO 904/86).

61 John Privilege, *Michael Logue and the Catholic Church in Ireland, 1879–1925* (Manchester, 2009), pp 87–8; CI Armagh, Oct. 1909 (TNA, CO 904/82).

62 *FS*, 13 Jan., 13 Apr. 1912.

63 John McCoy (BMH, WS 492, p. 6); Daniel McCurdy, 'The Ancient Order of Hibernians in Ulster, 1905–1918' (PhD, Ulster University, 2019), p. iii.

64 Owen McGee, *The Irish Republican Brotherhood from the Land League to Sinn Féin* (Dublin, 2005), p. 324.

65 Crime Special Branch (CSB) précis, June 1911 (TNA, CO 904/13).

66 Andrew R. Holmes, 'Presbyterians, loyalty and Orangeism in nineteenth-century Ulster' in Allan Blackstock and Frank O'Gorman (eds), *Loyalism and the formation of the British world* (Woodbridge, 2014), pp 141–5.

67 Alvin Jackson, *The Ulster Party: Irish unionists in the House of Commons, 1884–1911* (Oxford, 1989), p. 234; Jackson, 'Unionist politics and Protestant society', *Historical Journal* (1990), 845–8.

68 *UG*, 13 Jan. 1912.

69 Burnett, 'Modernisation of Ulster unionism', pp 49–53, 56–7.

70 Jackson, *Ulster Party*, p. 313.

71 Ibid., pp 311–13; Burnett, 'Modernisation', pp 49–55.

72 Alex Fisher to Dawson Bates, 10 Oct. 1910; Joseph Dealey to Dawson Bates, 18 Mar. 1911, 20 Apr. 1912 (Public Record Office of Northern Ireland (PRONI), UUC papers, D/1327/23/1A/16). Over time, however, this machinery weakened and was said to be non-existent by the end of the war; see Revd W.F. Johnston to Dawson Bates, 23 Mar. 1919 (PRONI, D/1327/18/18/3).

73 Jackson, 'Unionist politics and Protestant society', 849.

74 Olwen Purdue, *The MacGeough Bonds of the Argory: an Ulster gentry family, 1850–1950* (Dublin, 2005), p. 35.

75 Charles Townshend, *The partition: Ireland divided, 1885–1921* (London, 2021), p. 36 (citing Thomas MacKnight, editor of the *Northern Whig*, in 1893).

76 James Loughlin, 'Creating "a social and geographical fact": regional identity and the Ulster question', *Past & Present*, 195 (2007), 159–96; Gillian McIntosh, *The force of culture: unionist identities in twentieth-century Ireland* (Cork, 1999), pp 6–31.

77 *AG*, 29 Mar., 24 May 1912.

78 James McConnel, *The Irish Parliamentary Party and the third home rule crisis* (Dublin, 2013), pp 94–180; Fergal McCluskey, *Fenians and ribbonmen: the development of republican politics in east Tyrone, 1898–1918* (Manchester, 2011), p. 87.

79 Privilege, *Michael Logue*, pp 88–9; Donal Hall, 'Violence and political factionalism in north Louth, 1874–1943' (PhD, NUI Maynooth, 2009), pp 23–9; Frank Callinan, *T.M. Healy* (Cork, 1996), p. 474; *Irish Independent* (*II*), 17 July 1911.

80 *FS*, 10 Dec. 1910.

81 UIL National Directory minutes, 18 Jan. 1911 (NLI, MS 708, UIL Minute Book, 1904–8).

82 McCluskey, *Fenians and ribbonmen*, pp 61–82.

83 McGee, *Irish Republican Brotherhood*, pp 253, 312; Matthew J. Kelly, *The Fenian ideal and Irish nationalists, 1882–1916* (Woodbridge, 2006), pp 141–4.

84 CSB précis, Feb. 1911 (TNA, CO 904/13).

85 CI Armagh, June 1915 (TNA, CO 904/97).

86 Patrick Beagan (BMH, WS 612, p. 1); Frank Donnelly (BMH, WS 941, pp 1–3); Eugene Loughran (BMH, WS 526, p. 1).

87 Mats Greiff, 'Industrial struggles and trades unions among female linen workers in Belfast and Lurgan, 1872–1910', *Saothar*, 22 (1997), 29–44.

88 Emmet O'Connor, *Derry Labour in the age of agitation, 1889–1923: Larkinism and syndicalism* (Dublin, 2016), p. 11.

89 Diane Urquhart, *Women in Ulster politics, 1890–1940* (Dublin, 2000), pp 8–12.

90 *Irish Citizen*, 18 Apr. 1914.

91 *AG*, 20 Sept. 1912; *Irish Citizen*, 30 Nov. 1912.

92 Mary McVeigh, 'Votes for women: the Armagh campaign', *History Armagh*, 1:2 (2005), 21–4.

93 *AG*, 12 Jan., 12 June, 3 Sept. 1912; *UG*, 5 Oct. 1912.

94 *AG*, 19 Jan., 5 July 1912.

95 Senia Pašeta, *Irish nationalist women, 1900–1918* (Oxford, 2013), p. 91; Urquhart, *Women in Ulster politics*, p. 21.

96 Urquhart, *Women in Ulster politics*, p. 102.

CHAPTER TWO *Enemies and adherents of home rule in 1912*

1 Margaret O'Callaghan, 'Democratisation and polarisation in Ireland: the Covenant and the third home rule bill', unpublished conference paper for Institute of British-Irish Studies, 22 Sept. 2012.

2 *FJ*, 31 Jan. 1912.

3 Thomas Bartlett, 'When histories collide: the third home rule bill for Ireland' in Gabriel Doherty (ed.), *The home rule crisis, 1912–1914* (Cork, 2014), pp 24, 27; Kelly, *The Fenian ideal*, pp 200–4; John O'Donovan, 'The All-for-Ireland League and the home rule debate, 1910–1914' in Doherty (ed.), *Home rule crisis*, pp 138–63.

4 *FJ*, 25 Mar. 1912.

5 *AG*, 29 Mar. 1912.

6 Jackson, 'Unionist politics and Protestant society', 839–66.

7 See also Fergal McCluskey, *Tyrone: the Irish Revolution, 1912–23* (Dublin, 2014), p. 26 and *AG*, 28 May 1912 reports on 'Empire Day' in Tynan.

8 CI Armagh, Jan. 1911 (TNA, CO 904/83).

9 Ibid., Mar., May, Oct. 1911 (TNA, CO 904/84–5).

10 *LT*, 6 May 1911.

11 Patrick Maume, 'Unionists and patriots: James Whiteside and the dilemmas of the Protestant nation in Victorian Ireland' in Blackstock & O'Gorman (eds), *Loyalism*, p. 160.

12 *UG*, 2 Sept. 1911; *IT*, 28 Aug. 1911.

13 Report by Assistant IG Edward Pearson, Sept. 1911 (TNA, CO 904/28).

14 *Northern Whig* (*NW*), 1 Dec. 1911.

15 RIC inspector general (IG), 'Report on drilling in Ulster', 23 Feb. 1912 (TNA, CO 904/86).

16 CI Armagh, 'Report on drilling from county Armagh', 13 Feb. 1913 (TNA, CO 904/89).

17 Ibid., Jan. 1913 (ibid.).

18 Ibid., Feb., Mar. 1912 (TNA, CO 904/86).

19 *II*, 2 Feb. 1912.

20 CI Armagh, Jan. 1912 (TNA, CO 904/86).

21 *II*, 15 Jan. 1912.

22 *AG*, 12 Apr. 1912.

23   IG report, Mar. 1912 (TNA, CO 904/86).

24   *AG*, 27 Sept. 1912. The government also looked at the case again in 1912 and the file includes some press coverage from 1886 (TNA, CO 908/182).

25   *AG*, 1 Mar. 1912.

26   Michael Wheatley, *Nationalism and the Irish Party: provincial Ireland, 1910–1916* (Oxford, 2005), pp 166–7.

27   For more on this see Patrick Maume, 'The *Irish Independent* and the Ulster crisis, 1912–1921' in Boyce & O'Day (eds), *The Ulster crisis*, pp 202–28.

28   *IT*, 22, 26 Sept. 1911; *II*, 22 Sept. 1911.

29   *FS*, 30 Mar. 1912.

30   *FJ*, 23 May 1912.

31   *AG*, 24 May 1912.

32   Ibid., 14 June 1912.

33   Commons speeches on 3 and 4 Dec. 1912 cited in Thomas Hennessey, *Dividing Ireland: World War 1 and partition* (New York, 1998), p. 10.

34   *FJ*, 10 Apr. 1912; *AG*, 12 Apr. 1912.

35   CI Armagh, June 1912 (TNA, CO 904/87).

36   For these events see Jonathan Bardon, '"Grotesque proceedings?": localised responses to the home rule question in Ulster' in Doherty (ed.), *Home rule crisis*, pp 286–92.

37   For the bitter aftermath of the events see Bew, *Ideology and the Irish question*, pp 56–62.

38   *FS*, 13 July 1912.

39   *AG*, 5 July 1912.

40   Ibid., 12 July 1912.

41   Ibid., 9 Aug. 1913.

42   Ibid., 23 Aug. 1912.

43   CI Armagh, July 1912; IG, July 1912 (TNA, CO 904/87).

44   CI Armagh, Sept. 1912 (TNA, CO 904/88).

45   *AG*, 12 July 1912; *II*, 9 July 1912; *FS*, 20 July 1912.

46   Ibid., 19 July 1912.

47   *IT*, 13 Aug. 1912.

48   *AG*, 19 July 1912.

49   CI Armagh, Aug. 1912 (TNA, CO 904/87).

50   *AG*, 6 Sept. 1912.

51   CI Armagh, Sept. 1912 (TNA, CO 904/88); *AG*, 6 Sept. 1912.

52   Report dated 26 Sept. 1912, cited in Alan Parkinson, *Friends in high places: Ulster's resistance to Irish home rule, 1912–1914* (Belfast, 2012), p. 124.

53   *IT*, 25 Sept. 1912.

54   *AG*, 20 Sept. 1912.

55   *II*, 30 Sept. 1912; *IT*, 30 Sept. 1912.

56   *AG*, 4 Oct. 1912.

57   *UG*, 5 Oct. 1912.

58   https://www.nidirect.gov.uk/articles/about-ulster-covenant (accessed 9 Aug. 2019).

59   David Fitzpatrick, 'Ulster Covenanters' in idem, *Descendancy: Irish Protestant histories since 1795* (Cambridge, 2014), p. 108.

60   Ibid., p. 110.

61   Urquhart, *Women in Ulster politics*, p. 62.

62   CI Armagh, Sept. 1912 (TNA, CO 904/88).

63   *FS*, 23, 30 Sept., 5 Oct. 1912.

64   *UG*, 5 Oct. 1912.

65   *IT*, 12, 17 Sept. 1912.

66   CI Armagh, Sept., Oct., Dec. 1912 (TNA, CO 904/88).

67 *II*, 25 Sept. 1912.
68 CI Armagh, Oct. 1912 (TNA, CO 904/88).
69 Ibid.

CHAPTER THREE *'Prepared to begin the fight': the deepening home rule crisis, 1913–14*

 1 *IT*, 23 Jan. 1913.
 2 *II*, 30 Jan. 1913.
 3 *BNL*, 3 Jan. 1913.
 4 CI Armagh, Feb. 1913 (TNA, CO 904/89).
 5 *BNL*, 14, 18, 20 Jan., 13 Feb. 1913; *AG*, 14 Feb. 1913.
 6 *IT*, 8 Feb. 1913.
 7 *AG*, 21 Feb. 1913.
 8 CI Armagh, Apr., June 1913 (TNA, CO 904/89, 90).
 9 Letter from P.F. Downey, Armagh, in *Irish Worker*, 22 Mar. 1913.
10 CI Armagh, Sept. 1913 (TNA, CO 904/91); *Irish Worker*, 30 Aug. 1913.
11 Marie Coleman, 'Nugent, John Dillon', *DIB*, DOI: https://doi.org/10.3318/dib.006252.v2.
12 CI Armagh, Nov. 1913 (TNA, CO 904/91).
13 Ibid., Jan. 1913 (TNA, CO 904/89).
14 *II*, 13 Jan. 1913; *UG*, 22 Jan. 1913.
15 Ibid., Jan. 1913 (TNA, CO 904/89).
16 Ibid., June, Aug. 1913 (TNA, CO 904/90).
17 Ibid., July 1913 (ibid.).
18 CI Armagh, Mar. 1913 (TNA, CO 904/89); *FJ*, 29 Jan., 12, 19 Feb., 11, 21 Mar., 3, 10 Apr. 1913.
19 *II*, 10 Feb. 1913.
20 *FJ*, 22 Apr. 1913.
21 CI Armagh, Sept. 1913 (TNA, CO 904/91); *IT*, 11 Nov. 1913.
22 *FJ*, 7 Jan. 1914.
23 *II*, 18 Mar. 1913; CI Armagh, Oct. 1913 (TNA, CO 904/91).
24 *Irish Freedom*, 1 Mar., 1 Apr. 1913.
25 *IT*, 17 Jan. 1913.
26 Ibid., 11 Mar. 1913.
27 *BNL*, 27 Mar. 1913.
28 *II*, 5 Apr. 1913.
29 *AG*, 23 Apr. 1913.
30 Timothy Bowman, 'The North began … but when?: the formation of the Ulster Volunteer Force', *History Ireland* (Mar./Apr. 2013), 28–9.
31 Bowman, *Carson's army*, pp 21, 78–9.
32 *IT*, 16 Apr. 1913; *FJ*, 2 May 1913.
33 CI Armagh, Jan., Apr. 1913 (TNA, CO 904/89).
34 IG, Jan. 1913 (ibid.).
35 CI Armagh, Feb., Mar., Apr. 1913 (TNA, CO 904/89).
36 IG, Feb. 1913 (TNA, CO 904/89).
37 CI Armagh, Feb. 1913; IG, Apr. 1913 (TNA, CO 904/89).
38 Bowman, *Carson's army*, p. 23.
39 CI Armagh, July 1913 (TNA, CO 904/90).
40 *IT*, 14 Mar. 1913; CI Armagh, Mar. 1913 (TNA, CO 904/89).
41 Jackson, 'Unionist politics', p. 860; 1st Battalion, Armagh regiment UVF, 1913 (Armagh County Museum (ACM), UVF papers, MS 56,1960).
42 Special report for IG on Ulster movement, July 1913 (TNA, CO 904/27).

43 CI Armagh, July 1913 (TNA, CO 904/90).

44 IG, July 1913 (TNA, CO 904/90).

45 Benjamin Grob-Fitzgibbon, 'Neglected intelligence: how the British government failed to quell the Ulster Volunteer Force, 1912–1914', *Journal of Intelligence History*, 6:1 (2006), 1–24.

46 Memo by Under-Secretary J.B. Dougherty, 13 Mar. 1913 (TNA, CO 903/27/3).

47 Ronan Fanning, *Fatal path: British government and Irish Revolution, 1910–1922* (London, 2013), p. 76.

48 Armagh County Museum (ACM, UVF papers, MS 56,1960) and www.census.nationalarchives.ie (accessed 4 Sept. 2021).

49 Colin Cousins, *Armagh and the Great War* (Dublin, 2010), p. 230, n.25.

50 Bowman, *Carson's army*, p. 79.

51 Cited in ibid., pp 78, 86.

52 CI Armagh, Sept. 1913 (TNA, CO 904/91).

53 Printed programme, 4 Oct. 1913 (PRONI, Leslie papers, D/1855/1).

54 CI Armagh, Oct. 1913 (TNA, CO 904/91).

55 *IT*, 6 Oct. 1913.

56 *BNL*, 10 Jan. 1914.

57 *FS*, 11 Oct. 1913.

58 *FJ*, 6 Oct. 1913.

59 *II*, 6 Oct. 1913.

60 *FJ*, 6 Oct. 1913.

61 Alvin Jackson, *Home rule*, p. 124; *FS*, 18 Oct. 1913.

62 Fanning, *Fatal path*, pp 79–80.

63 See for instance articles in *The Times* in October and November 1913 by Claud Lovat Fraser, cited by Parkinson, *Friends*, pp 211–13 and reproduced as *Lovat Fraser's tour of Ireland in 1913: an event within the home rule conflict* (Belfast, 1992).

64 Lonsdale to Armstrong, 13 Dec. 1913 (PRONI, H.B. Armstrong papers, D3727/E/46/12).

65 Memo by David Harrel, 7 Jan. 1914, cited in Bowman, *Carson's army*, p. 85. For Harrel see Patrick Long, 'Harrel, Sir David Alfred', *DIB*, DOI: https://doi.org/10.3318/dib.003814.v1.

66 CI Armagh, Feb. 1914 (TNA, CO 904/92).

67 Lonsdale to Armstrong, 17 Feb. 1914 (PRONI, Armstrong papers, D3727/E/46/14).

68 CI Armagh, Jan., Feb., Mar. 1913 (TNA, CO 904/92).

69 Olwen Purdue, *The Big House in the north of Ireland, 1878–1960* (Dublin, 2009), pp 184–5.

70 CSB, report on the UVF, Mar. 1914 (TNA, CO 904/14).

71 CI Armagh, Feb. 1914 (TNA, CO 904/92).

72 Bowman, *Carson's army*, p. 126; CI Armagh, Apr. 1913 (TNA, CO 904/93).

73 *AG*, 16 Apr. 1914.

74 *II*, 4 June 1914.

75 CSB, report on the UVF, May 1914 (TNA, CO 904/14).

76 Detail from the *Armagh Guardian* is carried in James Kane, 'The arms raid on the Cope family residence at Drumilly, Loughgall in August 1919', *Dúiche Néill*, 23 (2016), 235.

77 Bowman, *Carson's army*, p. 124.

78 R.J. Adgey, *Arming the Ulster Volunteers 1914* (Belfast, n.d.), pp 22–3.

79 Weekly report by CI Armagh, 28 Mar. 1914 (TNA, CO 903/27(3)).

80 The story is best told in A.T.Q. Stewart, *The Ulster crisis, 1912–1914* (London, 1967).

81 *II*, 27 Apr. 1914.

82 Ibid., 1, 12 May 1914.

83 'Returns of arms in the possession of Irish, National and Ulster volunteers', 28 Feb. 1917 (TNA, CO 904/29(2)).

84 Bowman, *Carson's army*, p. 106.

85 Ibid., p. 145.

86 Alvin Jackson, 'The Larne gun running of 1914', *History Ireland*, 1:1 (1993), 38.

87 Wheatley, *Irish Party*, pp 178–9; Fanning, *Fatal path*, p. 79.

88 *DD*, 15 Oct. 1913; Michael Wheatley, '"Ireland is out for blood and murder": nationalist opinion and the Ulster crisis in provincial Ireland, 1913–1914' in Boyce & O'Day (eds), *The Ulster crisis*, pp 182–201.

89 For these see F.X. Martin (ed.), *The Irish Volunteers, 1913–1915* (Dublin, 1963), pp 57–60, 98–101.

90 McCluskey, *Tyrone*, p. 45 refers to three.

91 Joost Augusteijn, *From public defiance to guerrilla warfare: the experience of ordinary volunteers in the Irish War of Independence, 1916–1921* (Dublin, 1996), p. 43; Kelly, *Fenian ideal*, p. 205.

92 CI Armagh, Dec. 1913 (TNA, CO 904/91).

93 Marnie Hay, 'The foundation and development of Na Fianna Éireann, 1909–1916', *Irish Historical Studies*, 36:141 (2008), 62.

94 'Report on Irish National Boy Scouts', Jan. 1914 (TNA, CO 904/120 (1)).

95 Noted in CI Armagh, Feb. 1914 (TNA, CO 904/92) and a report on the IRB in Newry/south Armagh, Feb. 1914 (TNA, CO 904/120 (1)).

96 Charles McGleenan (BMH, WS 829, p. 1); John Southwell (BMH, WS 230, p. 5).

97 Report on AOH (Board of Erin), Apr. 1914 (TNA, CO 904/120 (1)); CI Armagh, Apr. 1914 (TNA, CO 904/93).

98 *FS*, 24 Mar. 1914; *FJ*, 7, 8 Apr. 1914.

99 *II*, 15 Apr. 1914.

100 CI Armagh, Apr. 1914 (TNA, CO 904/93); Memorandum from J.D. Nugent, 9 May 1914 (NLI, Éamonn Ceannt papers, MS 13,070/9); report on Irish Volunteers, May 1914 (TNA, CO 904/14/2).

101 CI Armagh, May 1914 (TNA, CO 904/93).

102 This is in contrast to open clerical support from January 1914 in County Monaghan; see Terence Dooley, *Monaghan: the Irish Revolution, 1912–23* (Dublin, 2016), p. 27.

103 CI Armagh, June 1914 (CO 904/93); *FJ*, 25, 26 May 1914; *II*, 27 May 1914.

104 *FJ*, 26 May, 2 June, 6 July 1914.

105 *II*, 27 May, 15 June 1914.

106 *FJ*, 2, 10 June 1914.

107 Report on Irish Volunteers, May 1914 (TNA, CO 904/14(2)).

108 CI Armagh, June, July 1914 (TNA, CO 904/93, 94).

109 John McCoy (BMH, WS 492, p. 10).

110 Report on Irish Volunteers, July 1914 (TNA, CO 904/14(2)).

111 'Returns of arms in the possession of Irish, National and Ulster volunteers', 28 Feb. 1917 (TNA, CO 904/29(2)).

112 CI Armagh, June 1914 (TNA, CO 904/93); John McCoy (BMH, WS 492, p. 9).

113 *FJ*, 26 May 1914; CI Armagh, May 1914 (TNA, CO 904/93).

114 Dooley, *Monaghan*, pp 27–8.

115 *FJ*, 8 June 1914; *II*, 9 June 1914.

116 *FJ*, 17, 18, 19 June, 6 July 1914.

117 CI Armagh, May 1914 (TNA, CO 904/93).

118 Eamon Phoenix, *Northern nationalism: nationalist politics, partition and the Catholic minority in Northern Ireland, 1890–1940* (Belfast, 1994), pp 11–15; Fanning, *Fatal path*, pp 122–3.

119 *II*, 23 June 1914.

120 John Morley cited in Fanning, *Fatal path*, p. 123.

121 CI Armagh, June 1914 (TNA, CO 904/93).

122 *II*, 10 July 1914.

123 Ibid., 13 July 1914.

124 Reports on the UVF, July, Aug. 1914 (TNA, CO 904/14(2)).

125 *II*, 21 July 1914.

126 *BNL*, 27 July 1914.

127 *II*, 31 July 1914.

128 *FS*, 29 Aug. 1914.

CHAPTER FOUR *War and distant rebellion, 1914–16*

1 Quoted in Jackson, *Judging Redmond and Carson* (Dublin, 2017), p. 121.

2 CI Armagh, July 1914 (TNA, CO 904/94).

3 Geoffrey Lewis, *Carson: the man who divided Ireland* (London, 2006), p. 166.

4 CI Armagh, Aug. 1914 (TNA, CO 904/94).

5 *BNL*, 14 Sept. 1914. UVF membership was probably overestimated by the CI and may have been about 5–5,500 with 500 recruits enlisting in the army; see Breandán Mac Giolla Choille, 'Strength of Ulster Volunteer Force, 1915', also 'Return of Recruits who joined the Army between 15 December 1914 and 15 December 1916' in Breandán Mac Giolla Choille (ed.), *Intelligence notes, 1913–16* (Dublin, 1966), pp 177, 181.

6 Timothy Bowman, William Butler and Michael Wheatley, *The disparity of sacrifice: Irish recruitment to the British armed forces* (Manchester, 2020), pp 88–90.

7 CI Armagh, Sept. 1914 (TNA, CO 904/94).

8 *BNL*, 22 Sept. 1914.

9 CI Armagh, Sept. 1914 (TNA, CO/904/94).

10 *II*, 24 Aug. 1914.

11 CI Armagh, Sept. 1914 (TNA, CO 904/94).

12 Daithí Ó Corráin, '"A most public-spirited and unselfish man": the career and contribution of Colonel Maurice Moore, 1854–1939', *Studia Hibernica*, 40 (2014), 98–9.

13 CI Armagh, Oct. 1914 (TNA, CO 904/94).

14 Reports of meetings in Keady and Armagh city, *FJ*, 3 Oct. 1914 and *BNL*, 30 Oct. 1914.

15 John McCoy (BMH, WS 492, pp 12–15).

16 Ibid., p. 15.

17 CI Armagh, Nov. 1914 (TNA, CO 904/95).

18 Ibid., Apr. 1915 (TNA, CO 904/96); *AG*, 5, 12 Feb. 1915; *IT*, 22 Mar., 3 May 1915.

19 *Dundalk Democrat (DD)*, 6 Nov. 1915; McConnel, *Irish Parliamentary Party*, pp 297–311.

20 *Statement giving particulars regarding men of military age in Ireland* (HMSO, CD 8390, 1916). Numbers serving in the Royal Flying Corps/Royal Air Force (260), Royal Navy (30) and the Mercantile Navy (100) cover the full 1914–18 period; see Findmypast.com, accessed February 2022.

21 Absent Voters Lists for the constituencies of South Armagh, Mid Armagh and North Armagh, Sept. 1918 (PRONI, ARM/5/3/2/1A, 1B and 1C).

22 Comprising of 986 'west of the Bann', Joe Center, *Armagh war dead in the Great War* (Armagh, 2018), and 395 from the Lurgan and Portadown district: http://www.lurganancestry.com/ ww1/worldwar1.htm (accessed 12 June 2023). This is comparable to the other counties within the Royal Irish Fusiliers depot area: Co. Louth (820), Donal Hall, *Louth: the Irish Revolution, 1912–23* (Dublin, 2019), p. 57; Co. Cavan (655) Cavan Co. Council, *Roll of Honour, County Cavan's World War 1 dead.* (Cavan, 2012), p. 2; and Co. Monaghan (539), Kevin Cullen, *Book of honour for County Monaghan* (Monaghan, 2010), p. 4. Total estimated fatalities for the four counties in the RIF depot area, 3,395.

23 Mac Giolla Choille (ed.), *Intelligence notes*, pp 181–2.

24 With the names and addresses of many of those who served now known, it would be possible to derive more accurate estimates of the religious breakdown of recruits.

25 CI Armagh, Report on the state of the counties, 1916 (TNA, CO 904/120).

26 CI Armagh, Dec. 1917 (TNA, CO 904/104).

27   Ibid., Apr., June 1918 (TNA, CO 904/105, 106).
28   Hall, *Louth*, pp 25–6.
29   Andrew Scholes, *The Church of Ireland and the third home rule bill* (Dublin, 2010), pp 90–1; *II*, 22 Sept. 1914; *BNL*, 30 Oct. 1914.
30   Cousins, *Armagh and the Great War*, pp 88–9.
31   *AG*, 11 Feb. 1916.
32   Revd David Millar in Armagh, *AG*, 18 Sept. 1914; Rev. Joseph Linahan in Portadown, *PN*, 14 Nov. 1914.
33   Jérôme aan de Wiel, *The Catholic Church in Ireland, 1914–1918: war and politics* (Dublin, 2003), p. 42.
34   Privilege, *Michael Logue*, pp 100, 110; Oliver P. Rafferty, 'Catholic chaplains to the British forces in the First World War' in Oliver P. Rafferty, *Violence, politics and Catholicism in Ireland* (Dublin, 2016), pp 144, 157.
35   aan de Wiel, *Catholic Church*, p. 53; Privilege, *Michael Logue*, p. 110.
36   Lenten pastoral letter, 1916 (CÓFLA, Logue papers).
37   Cousins, *Armagh and the Great War*, pp 101–6, 116–21.
38   Ibid., p. 128.
39   *IT*, 9 Aug. 1915.
40   Lonsdale to Armstrong [late 1915] (PRONI, Armstrong papers, D3727/E/46/82).
41   *FS*, 8 Apr. 1916, which criticized William Coote (South Tyrone Unionist MP) for his attack on farm profits before admitting it was true.
42   Ibid., 3 Mar. 1916.
43   CI Armagh, Feb. 1917 (TNA, CO 904/102).
44   *FJ*, 13 Aug. 1917; *AG*, 8 Sept. 1917.
45   Cousins, *Armagh and the Great War*, p. 115; CI Armagh, Jan. 1917 (TNA, CO 904/102).
46   Cousins, *Armagh and the Great War*, pp 117–18.
47   CI Armagh, July, Sept., Oct., Nov. 1917 (TNA, CO 904/103, 104).
48   *BNL*, 2 Apr. 1918.
49   CI Armagh, Jan., Mar., Apr. 1918 (TNA, CO 904/105).
50   *IT*, 21 Mar. 1918; *AG*, 22, 29 Mar. 1918; *II*, 9 Apr. 1918; Ciaran Mulholland and Anton McCabe, 'Red flag over the asylum: the story of the Monaghan soviet, 1919' in Pauline Prior (ed.), *Asylums, mental health care and the Irish, 1800–2010* (Dublin, 2012), pp 108–22.
51   Esmonde to Moore, 29 Oct. 1914 (NLI, Moore papers, MS 10547(2)); reported in *National Volunteer*, 21 Nov. 1914.
52   CI Armagh, Mar. 1916 (TNA, CO 904/99).
53   *FJ*, 7 Apr. 1916; *FS*, 8 Apr. 1916.
54   *FJ*, 20 Aug. 1915.
55   *IT*, 20, 21 Aug. 1915.
56   *FJ*, 11 Sept. 1915.
57   William J. Kelly (BMH, WS 893, pp 11–15); Leonard obituary, *Irish Press*, 23 Apr. 1947; McCluskey, *Tyrone*, pp 90–1.
58   Charles Townshend, *Easter 1916: the Irish rebellion* (London, 2015), pp 68–70.
59   CI Armagh, Dec. 1914 (TNA, CO 904/95).
60   John McCoy (BMH, WS 492, pp 9–12); *FS*, 30 Oct. 1914; CSB précis of information, Oct. 1914 (TNA, CO 904/120(1), p. 123).
61   CI Armagh, Feb. 1915 (TNA, CO 904/96); *FJ*, 5 Apr. 1915; *II*, 6 Apr. 1916.
62   J.C. O'Reilly to Moore, 20 Feb., 5 May 1015; O'Reilly to Diarmaid Coffey, 1 Sept., 5 Oct. 1915 (NLI, Moore papers, MS 10547(2)).
63   CSB précis of information, Oct. 1914 (TNA, CO 904/120/2, p. 42).
64   Charles McGleenan (BMH, WS 839, p. 2); CI Armagh, Nov. 1914, Feb. 1915 (TNA, CO 904/95, 96).

65 CI Armagh, June 1915 (TNA, CO 904/97). On Pim see Patrick Maume, 'Pim, Herbert Moore', *DIB*.

66 CI Armagh, Feb./Mar. 1916 (TNA, CO 904/99).

67 CSB précis of secret societies reports, 1914 (TNA, CO 904/14(2), p. 150).

68 John Southwell (BMH, WS 230, pp 2, 5).

69 Townshend, *Easter 1916*, p. 225.

70 James McCullough (BMH, WS 529, pp 2–3).

71 Charles McGleenan interview, Sept. 1964 (CÓFLA, Louis O'Kane collection, LOK/IV/47D).

72 Donal O'Hannigan (BMH, WS 161, pp 9, 16).

73 Pádraig Quinn interview, Aug. 1971 (CÓFLA, O'Kane collection, LOK/IV/A/86C).

74 *PN*, 29 Apr. 1916; *Ulster Herald*, 27 May 1916. According to folk memory, Éamon Donnelly was also arrested but there is no official record of this.

75 Patrick McHugh (BMH, WS 677, Addendum 1, p. 3); Kevin Murphy, 'Michael Donnelly of Carnally: a revolutionary journey', *Creggan*, 18 (2018), 41–58.

76 Michael Donnelly interview (UCDA, O'Malley papers, P17b/116/43). A 'large number' of arrests in counties Armagh, Derry, Tyrone and Monaghan were reported, but there are no further details.

77 John Garvey (BMH, WS 178, p. 3).

78 *PN*, 29 Apr. 1916.

79 Ibid.

80 CI Armagh, Apr. 1916 (TNA, CO 904/99); *FS*, 6 May 1916. Something similar occurred in Louth – see Hall, *Louth*, p. 42.

81 Neil Richardson, *According to their lights: stories of Irishmen in the British army, Easter 1916* (Cork, 2015), pp 148–9.

82 *PN*, 6 May 1916.

83 Richardson, *According to their lights*, p. 149; *BNL*, 5 June 1916.

84 Townshend, *Easter 1916*, pp 162–3; *IT*, 6 May 1916.

85 Edward Costello (IMA, MSPC, 1D261). His widow, Annie, who lived in Lurgan, was awarded a widow's pension of £90 p.a.

86 *UG*, 6 May 1916.

87 *PN*, 6 May 1916; Peel to Lonsdale, 9 May 1916 (PRONI, J.E. Peel papers, D889/3/1D, f. 956).

88 *PN*, 15 July 1916.

89 Dooley, *Monaghan*, pp 54–6; Hall, *Louth*, pp 43–4.

90 John McCoy (BMH, WS 492, p. 17).

91 *FS*, 6 May 1916.

92 Ibid., 13 May 1916.

93 Ibid.

94 Ibid.

95 *BNL*, 6 June 1916.

96 CI Armagh, June 1916 (TNA, CO 904/100).

97 Oliver P. Rafferty, 'Catholic Church and the Easter Rising', *Studies*, 105:417 (2016), 52.

98 *BNL*, 28 Apr. 1916.

99 *II*, 26 Apr., 4 May 1916.

100 *Evening Herald*, 21 June 1916.

101 Privilege, *Michael Logue*, p. 114.

102 Jackson, *Home rule*, pp 184–5.

103 Patrick Buckland, *Irish unionism II: Ulster unionism and the origins of Northern Ireland* (Dublin, 1972), p. 106; Townshend, *The partition*, pp 99–102.

104 *PN*, 10 June 1916.

105 *BNL*, 10 June 1916.

106 *AG*, 16 June 1916; *LT*, 17 June 1916; *PN*, 17 June 1916.

107 Jackson, 'Irish unionism, 1870–1922' in D. George Boyce and Alan O'Day (eds), *Defenders of the Union* (London, 2001), p. 132.

108 Scholes, *Church of Ireland*, pp 120–1.

109 CI Armagh, June 1916 (TNA, CO 904/100).

110 *FJ*, 17 June 1916.

111 *UG*, 24 June 1916.

112 Phoenix, *Northern nationalism*, p. 26.

113 Privilege, *Michael Logue*, p. 115.

114 Dillon to O'Connor, 17 June 1916 (Trinity College Dublin (TCD), John Dillon papers, DP 6741/320).

115 McCluskey, *Tyrone*, pp 82–3.

116 *II*, 9, 14 June 1916; *FS*, 8 July 1916.

117 A.C. Hepburn, *Catholic Belfast and nationalist Ireland in the era of Joe Devlin, 1871–1934* (Oxford, 2008), p. 179; 'Printed report on Lloyd George's proposals, Belfast Convention', 23 June 1916 (Newry & Mourne Museum, Éamon Donnelly papers, NMM.2011.29.2.3).

118 *FJ*, 21 June 1916.

119 Report of UIL National Directory, 3 July 1916 (NLI, MS 708).

120 Jackson, *Home rule*, pp 172–7.

121 *Hansard (Lords)*, 11 July 1916, vol. 22, cols 645–9; M.C. Rast, 'Ulster unionists "on Velvet", home rule and partition in the Lloyd George proposals', *American Journal of Irish studies*, 14 (2017), 129–31.

122 McCluskey, *Tyrone*, pp 62–3; Adrian Grant, *Derry: the Irish Revolution, 1912–23* (Dublin, 2018), pp 73–7; Brian Feeney, *Antrim: the Irish Revolution, 1912–23* (Dublin, 2021), pp 45–6; *UG*, 23 Sept. 1916.

123 CI Armagh, June 1916 (TNA, CO 904/100).

124 *UG*, 30 Sept. 1916.

125 *FJ*, 25 Sept. 1916; Bernard O'Neill, Armagh, Mar. 1896 (TNA, Register of suspects (Home), 1890–1898, CO 904/18).

126 CI Armagh, Sept. 1916 (TNA, CO 904/101).

127 *UG*, 9, 16, 23 Sept. 1916; *FJ*, 13, 23, 25 Sept. 1916.

128 CI Armagh, Sept. 1916 (TNA, CO 904/101).

129 Jackson, *Judging Redmond and Carson*, p. 200.

130 Michael Laffan, *The resurrection of Ireland: the Sinn Féin party, 1916–23* (Cambridge, 1999), p. 64.

131 McCluskey, *Tyrone*, pp 63–6; Grant, *Derry*, pp 74–6; CI Armagh, Oct. 1916 (TNA, CO 904/101).

132 F.J. O'Connor to George Gavan Duffy, 18 Oct. 1916 (NLI, G.G. Duffy papers, MS 5,581/81).

133 Caoimhe Nic Dháibhéid, 'The Irish National Aid Association and the radicalisation of public opinion in Ireland, 1916–1918', *Historical Journal*, 55:3 (2012), 709.

134 *FS*, 8 July 1916; *II*, 13 July 1916; CI Armagh, June 1916 (TNA, CO 904/100).

135 CI Armagh, Aug. 1916 (TNA, CO 904/100); *II*, 19 Aug. 1916.

136 *FS*, 14 Oct. 1916.

137 CI Armagh, Report on the state of the counties, 1916 (TNA, CO 904/120).

138 Ibid., Dec. 1916 (TNA, CO 904/101).

139 *IT*, 2, 27 Oct. 1916; *II*, 3 Oct. 1916.

140 *UG*, 18 Nov. 1916.

141 Stronge to Montgomery, 26, 29 Dec. 1916 (PRONI, Fellenberg Montgomery papers, D/627/429/86, 90).

CHAPTER FIVE *An altering political situation?: Armagh in 1917–18*

1 Elaine Callinan, *Electioneering and propaganda in Ireland, 1917–1921* (Dublin, 2020), pp 32–8.

2 Laffan, *Resurrection*, p. 115.

3 Ibid., p. 121.

4 Jackson, *Home rule*, p. 179.

5 CI Armagh, Jan., Dec. 1917 (TNA, CO 904/102, 107); the higher number can be found in Seán Milroy report on SF clubs, 12 Dec. 1917 (NLI, Count Plunkett papers, MS 11,405/2).

6 *FS*, 10 June 1917; *FJ*, 25 July 1917; Collins to Miss Annie Kielty, Armagh, 23 Aug. 1917 (NLI, INA & VDF papers, MS 23,466).

7 CI Armagh, June 1917 (TNA, CO 904/103).

8 Ibid., July 1917 (Ibid.).

9 Chief Inspector Dublic Metropolitan Police to CI Armagh, 14 Aug. 1917 (TNA, CO 904/196/65); Anne Dolan and William Murphy, *Michael Collins: the man and the revolution* (Cork, 2018), pp 72–3.

10 Frank Donnelly (BMH, WS 941, pp 1–2); Charles McGleenan (BMH, WS 829, p. 3); *FS*, 29 July 1916; Patrick Rankin (BMH, WS 671, p. 1).

11 McCluskey, *Fenians and ribbonmen*, pp 213–16.

12 IG, Sept. 1917, CI Armagh, Sept., Nov. 1917 (TNA, CO 904/104); *II*, 14 Sept. 1917.

13 *AG*, 26 Oct., 18 Nov. 1917.

14 CI Armagh, Dec. 1917 (TNA, CO 904/104); Éamonn Ó hUallacháin, 'Sinn Féin in Cullyhanna (1916–1921)', *Creggan*, 18 (2018), 59–65.

15 CI Armagh, Nov. 1917 (TNA, CO, 904/104).

16 *II*, 16, 17 Aug. 1917; *FJ*, 16 Aug. 1917; *UG*, 18 Aug. 1917.

17 *AG*, 24 Nov. 1917; CI Armagh, Nov. 1917 (TNA, CO 904/104).

18 CI Armagh, Sept. 1917 (TNA, CO 904/104).

19 *FJ*, 3, 10, 24 Oct., 7, 21 Nov. 1917; *II*, 15, 20 Sept., 6 Nov. 1917.

20 Lonsdale to Armstrong, 24 Mar. 1918 (PRONI, Armstrong papers, D3727/E/46/40).

21 R.B. McDowell, *The Irish Convention, 1917–18* (London, 1970), p. 77.

22 Adam Duffin to Olive Duffin, 14 June 1917 (PRONI, Adam Duffin papers, MIC127/21); Minute book of the Ulster delegation to the Irish Convention, 10 Oct. 1917 (PRONI, UUC papers, D1327/2/17).

23 Montgomery to Stronge, 18 May 1917; Stronge to Montgomery, 1 May 1917 (PRONI, Montgomery papers, D627/431/26, 27).

24 *PN*, 16 June 1917.

25 CI Armagh, May 1917 (TNA, CO 904/103); Lonsdale to Armstrong, 5 Aug. 1917 (PRONI, Armstrong papers, D3727/E/46/30).

26 Scholes, *Church of Ireland*, pp 134–40.

27 Ibid.; Unpublished Irish Convention memorandum [1918] (PRONI, Armstrong papers, D3727/E/45/181); Montgomery to H.T. Barrie, 21 Jan. 1918 (PRONI, Fellenberg-Montgomery papers, D627/433/11).

28 Minute book of the Ulster Unionist delegation to the Irish Convention (PRONI, UUC papers, D1327/2/17).

29 McDowell, *Irish Convention*, pp 79–81; Duffin to Armstrong, 28 Aug. 1917; Armstrong to Charles Johnston, 30 July, 11 Oct. 1917 (PRONI, Armstrong papers, D3727/E/45/174).

30 Notes and papers on the Irish Convention (PRONI, Armstrong papers, D3727/E/45/19, 215).

31 Walker, 'Lonsdale', p. 141; *AG*, 1 Nov. 1917.

32 *II*, 31 Oct., 6 Nov. 1917.

33 *FJ*, 8 Jan. 1918; *IT*, 16 Jan. 1918; circular letter of James Lonsdale, 16 Jan. 1918 (PRONI, Armstrong papers, D3727/E/46/37).

34 *Irish Catholic Directory 1918*, p. 538; *FJ*, 26 Nov. 1917.

35 *DI*, 1 Dec. 1917; *FS*, 1 Dec. 1917.

36 Privilege, *Michael Logue*, p. 118.

37 CI Armagh, Nov. 1917 (TNA, CO 904/104).

38 Siobhán McGuinness, 'The February 1918 by-election in south Armagh', *Creggan*, 6 (1992), 59–79; Erica Doherty, '"The party hack, and tool of the British government": T.P. O'Connor,

America and Irish Party resilience in the February 1918 South Armagh by-election',
Parliamentary History, 34:3 (2015), 339–64.

39 *II*, 15 Jan. 1918; *AG*, 18 Jan. 1918; Report by Seán Milroy to SF Standing Committee, 17 Jan.
1918 (NLI, SF standing committee minutes, 1918–22).

40 Dillon to T.P. O'Connor, 23 Jan. 1918 (TCD, Dillon papers, MS 6742/441).

41 *FJ*, 23 Jan. 1918.

42 *II*, 23 Jan. 1918.

43 Kevin O'Shiel (BMH, WS 1770, pp 741–51); MacCurtain to Seán Ó hÉigeartaigh, 27 Jan.
[1918] (Cork Public Museum, Tomás MacCurtain papers, L1955).

44 *IT*, 26 Jan. 1918; *AG*, 1 Feb. 1918.

45 *NR*, 21 Jan. 1918; Damian Woods, 'Dr Patrick McCartan of Carrickmore and Easter 1916 in
County Tyrone', *Seanchas Ard Mhacha*, 26: 1 (2016), 1–43; Marie Coleman, 'McCartan,
Patrick', *DIB*, DOI: https://doi.org/10.3318/dib.005575.v1.

46 *II*, 23 Jan. 1918. Donnelly had strong clerical support (see McConnel, *Irish Parliamentary
Party*, p. 58).

47 *FJ*, 21 Jan. 1918.

48 Ibid., 25 Jan. 1918; *DD*, 2 Feb. 1918; *NR*, 2 Feb. 1918.

49 *AG*, 25 Jan. 1918; *II*, 26 Jan., 1 Feb. 1918.

50 Pašeta, *Irish nationalist women*, pp 220–3; Diarmaid Ferriter, *A nation and not a rabble: the Irish
Revolution, 1912–23* (London, 2015), pp 81–2.

51 *NR*, 29 Jan. 1918; *II*, 30 Jan. 1918; *IT*, 1 Feb. 1918.

52 John McCoy (BMH, WS 492, p. 25); *DD*, 2 Feb. 1918.

53 *AG*, 1 Feb. 1918; *FJ*, 28 Jan. 1918; John McCoy (BMH, WS 492, p. 26); 'Master' Devlin to Dr
Con Short, 13 Feb. 1959 (in private collection) notes de Valera's injury and the AOH division
in Glassdrummond being responsible.

54 *II*, 31 Jan. 1918; *FJ*, 1 Feb. 1918. For the concept see McConnell, *Irish Parliamentary Party*,
p. 137 and Patrick Maume, *The long gestation: Irish nationalist life, 1891–1918* (Dublin, 1999),
p. 97 on the North Leitrim by-election of 1907.

55 John Grant (BMH, WS 658, p. 2).

56 *DD*, 2 Feb. 1918.

57 James Short (BMH, WS 534, pp 2–3).

58 *AG*, 25 Jan. 1918.

59 *FS*, 26 Jan. 1918; *NR*, 26 Jan. 1918.

60 *IT*, 29, 30 Jan. 1918; *FS*, 26 Jan. 1918.

61 Charles McGleenan (BMH, WS 829, pp 3–4); James McGuill (BMH, WS 353, p. 30).

62 John Cosgrove (BMH, WS 605, pp 2–3).

63 *Nationality*, 8 Feb. 1918; CI Armagh, Jan. 1918 (TNA, CO 904/105); *AG*, 1 Feb. 1918.

64 Kevin O'Shiel (BMH, WS 1,770, p. 752); *FJ*, 11 Feb. 1918.

65 *IT*, 9 Feb. 1918.

66 *II*, 26, 28 Jan. 1918; *Irish News (IN)*, 28 Jan. 1918; *FJ*, 31 Jan. 1918; John Bowman, *De Valera
and the Ulster question, 1917–1973* (Oxford, 1982), p. 35.

67 *NR*, 2 Feb. 1918.

68 *FJ*, 21 Jan. 1918; *II*, 29 Jan. 1918.

69 *FS*, 26 Jan. 1918.

70 Ibid., 2 Feb. 1918.

71 John McCoy (BMH, WS 492, pp 20, 30–1).

72 James Short (BMH, WS 534, p. 1); Jack McElhaw (BMH, WS 634, p. 1).

73 James McGuill (BMH, WS 353, pp 29–30).

74 John McCoy (BMH, WS 492, pp 24–5).

75 Augusteijn, *Public defiance to guerrilla warfare*, pp 67–9.

76 CI Armagh, Mar. 1918 (TNA, CO 904/105).

77 *FJ*, 4 Apr. 1918.

78 *II*, 1 Apr. 1918; *BNL*, 1, 4 Apr. 1918; *IT*, 15 Apr. 1918.

79 *FS*, 20 Apr. 1918.

80 CI Armagh, Apr. 1918 (TNA, CO 904/105).

81 Mathew Lewis, 'The Newry Brigade and the War of Independence, 1919–1921', *Irish Sword*, 108 (2010), 225–6.

82 Lonsdale to Armstrong, 19 Nov. 1915 (PRONI, Armstrong papers, D3727/E/46/24).

83 Alan J. Ward, 'Lloyd George and the 1918 Irish conscription crisis', *Historical Journal*, 17:1 (1974), 107–9.

84 *DD*, 13 Apr. 1918.

85 *II*, 13 Apr. 1918.

86 Ibid., 15, 16 Apr. 1918.

87 Pauric Travers, 'The conscription crisis and the general election of 1918' in John Crowley, Donal Ó Drisceoil, Mick Murphy and John Borgonovo (eds), *Atlas of the Irish Revolution* (Cork, 2017), pp 323–7.

88 CI Armagh, Apr. 1918 (TNA, CO 904/105).

89 See for instance aan de Wiel, *Catholic Church*, pp 203–55.

90 Privilege, *Michael Logue*, pp 122–4; Pauric Travers, 'The priests in politics: the case of conscription' in Oliver MacDonagh, W.F. Mandle and Pauric Travers (eds), *Irish culture and nationalism, 1750–1950* (Dublin, 1983), p. 161.

91 Reports from *FJ*, 19, 20, 25, 30 Apr., 7 May 1918; *FS*, 20, 27 Apr. 1918.

92 CI, Armagh, Apr. 1918 (TNA, CO 904/105).

93 *II*, 18 June 1918.

94 Hepburn, *Catholic Belfast*, p. 195.

95 *PN*, 13 Apr. 1918; *Hansard (Commons)*, 9 Apr. 1918, vol. 10, 4 col. 1444.

96 *II*, 11 Apr. 1918.

97 *BNL*, 4 May 1918.

98 CI Armagh, May 1918 (TNA, CO 904/106).

99 Laffan, *Resurrection*, pp 143–4.

100 John McCoy (BMH, WS 492, p. 36); CI Armagh, June 1918 (TNA, CO 904/106); *FS*, 22 June 1918.

101 *FS*, 29 June 1918; *AG*, 22 Aug. 1918.

102 CI Armagh, Aug. 1918 (TNA, CO 904/107).

103 *BNL*, 25 May 1918.

104 CI Armagh, June 1918 (TNA, CO 904/106).

105 *AG*, 13 July 1918.

106 Cousins, *Armagh and the Great War*, pp 52–3; *IT*, 4 Nov. 1918.

107 CI Down, Aug. 1918 (TNA, CO 904/107); *FS*, 8 Feb. 1919.

108 IG, Nov. 1918 (TNA, CO 904/107).

109 *FJ*, 28 Nov. 1918.

110 Letter to the editor of *An tÓglach*, 29 Nov. 1918 (NLI, Piaras Béaslaí papers, MS 33,912/13); Dolan & Murphy, *Michael Collins*, p. 134.

111 Logue to Bishop MacRory, 9 Dec. 1918 (CÓFLA, Michael Logue papers).

112 Walker (ed.), *Parliamentary election results*, p. 383.

113 John McCoy (BMH, WS 492).

114 Devlin to Dillon, 28 Nov. 1918 (TCD, Dillon papers, DP6730/201); quote from Donnelly to T.J. Hanna, 29 Nov. 1918 (ibid., DP6763/197).

115 *FS*, 7 Dec. 1918.

116 *IT*, 9, 11 Dec. 1918; *FS*, 14 Dec. 1918.

117 *IT*, 2 Jan. 1919; Phoenix, *Northern nationalism*, p. 62.

118 CI Armagh, Nov. 1918 (TNA, CO 904/107).

119 Walker, *Parliamentary election results*, p. 186; *FJ*, 13 Dec. 1918.
120 Walker, *Parliamentary election results*, p. 383.
121 *II*, 4 Dec. 1918.
122 *FJ*, 27 Nov. 1918.
123 CI Armagh, Dec. 1918 (TNA, CO 904/107).
124 Tom Garvin, *The evolution of Irish nationalist politics* (Dublin, 2005 [1981]), p. 134; Alan de
      Bromhead, Alan Fernihough and Enda Hargaden, 'Representation of the people: franchise
      extension and the "Sinn Féin Election" in 1918', *Journal of Economic History*, 80:3 (2020),
      886–925.
125 David Fitzpatrick, *The two Irelands, 1912–1939* (Oxford, 1998), p. 76.
126 *Church of Ireland Gazette*, 29 Nov. 1918, cited in Scholes, *Church of Ireland*, p. 156.

CHAPTER SIX *Armagh and the War of Independence, 1919–21*

  1 David Fitzpatrick, 'The geography of the War of Independence' in Crowley et al. (eds), *Atlas
      of the Irish Revolution*, pp 534–43.
  2 Michael Hopkinson, *The Irish War of Independence* (Dublin, 2002), p. 201.
  3 Charles Townshend, 'The Irish Republican Army and the development of guerrilla warfare,
      1916–21', *English Historical Review*, 94:371 (1979), 318–45.
  4 Authors' estimate.
  5 John McCoy (BMH, WS 492 p. 34); Frank Aiken, 23 Dec. 1936 (IMA, MSPC, REF59339).
  6 'Records supplied by Mr Andrew O'Hare', 4th Northern Division GHQ (IMA, MSPC,
      RO423).
  7 CI Armagh, July 1921 (TNA, CO 904/116).
  8 Frank Aiken memoir (UCDA, O'Malley papers, P19b/93).
  9 Establishment of IRA strength, 11 July 1921, 4th Northern Division (IMA, MSPC, RO-609
      p. 7); 4th Northern Division, North Louth Battalion, 11 July 1921 (IMA, MSPC, RO424, pp
      66, 68).
 10 Louise Ryan, 'Splendidly silent: representing Irish republican women, 1919–1923' in Ann-
      Marie Gallagher, Cathy Lubelska and Louise Ryan (eds), *Re-presenting the past: women in
      history* (Abingdon and New York, 2001), pp 23–43; Marie Coleman, 'Compensating Irish
      female revolutionaries, 1916–1923', *Women's History Review*, 26:6 (2016), 915–34.
 11 Eveline Devlin interview, 23 July 1940 (IMA, MSPC, 34REF20486).
 12 Alice Cashel (BMH, WS 366, p. 2), Dooley, *Monaghan*, p. 64; Hall, *Louth*, p. 19, McCluskey,
      Tyrone, p. 64.
 13 South Armagh District Council (IMA, MSPC, CMB59); Mid Armagh District Council (IMA,
      MSPC, CMB55).
 14 Cal McCarthy, *Cumann na mBan and the Irish Revolution* (Cork, 2014), pp 119–32; Marie
      Coleman, 'Cumann na mBan in the War of Independence' in Crowley et al. (eds), *Atlas of the
      Irish Revolution*, pp 400–8.
 15 For an excellent account see Elizabeth Marner's (née McInerney) hand-written memoir as part
      of her pension application (IMA, MSPC, 34REF47220, pp 24–31); Jennie Hanratty (née
      Garvey) interview, 25 Sept. 1939 (IMA, MSPC, 34REF42875).
 16 Sarah Carroll interview, 19 July 1940 (IMA, MSPC, 34REF59091).
 17 John Grant (BMH, WS 658, p. 4).
 18 John Grant to referees, 2 Aug. 1939 in Mary Ann McCreesh pension application (IMA, MSPC,
      34REF48841).
 19 Two other applicants were awarded medical allowances rather than full pensions; details from
      a search of released applications, MSPC online catalogue (Aug. 2023).
 20 Róisín Ní Bheirne (Rose Beirne) (IMA, MSPC, 34REF2848).
 21 Ibid., p. 36; Róisín O'Beirne internment file (PRONI, Home Affairs files, HA/5/2108).

22 Nano Magennis (née Aiken) interview, 2 Feb. 1938 (IMA, MSPC, 34D1754, pp 25–9); Eoin Magennis and Lesa Ní Mhunghaile, 'Class and gender in the Irish Revolution in the north east: the case of Nano Aiken', unpublished conference paper, NUI Galway, Nov. 2019.

23 Róisín Ní Bheirne to the referees, 3 Oct. 1939 (IMA, MSPC, 34REF2848, p. 48).

24 CI Armagh, June 1920 (TNA, CO 904/113).

25 Jack McElhaw (BMH, WS 634, p. 3); *NR*, 8 July, 14 Aug., 10 Oct. 1919.

26 For example, *NR*, 6 Apr. 1920; *AG*, 9 Apr. 1920; *DD*, 10 Apr. 1920.

27 Charles Townshend, *The Republic: the fight for Irish independence* (London, 2013), pp 78–80.

28 Dooley, *Monaghan*, p. 82.

29 John McCoy (BMH, WS 492, p. 38).

30 John Borgonovo, '"Army without banners": the Irish Republican Army, 1920–1921' in Crowley et al. (eds), *Atlas of the Irish Revolution*, pp 394–6.

31 Charles McGleenan interview, 18 Aug. 1964 (CÓFLA, O'Kane collection, LOK/IA/A/47D).

32 'Return of arms in possession of Irish, National and Ulster volunteers', 1917 (TNA, CO 904/29(2)).

33 *NR*, 16 Jan., 3 May 1919.

34 Eddie Boyle interview, 8 Aug. 1963 (CÓFLA, O'Kane collection, LOK/IV/A/49A).

35 Michael Collins to James McGuill, 12 Aug. 1919 (IMA, Collins papers, IE/MA/CP/03/09). Constable McKeefry apparently survived the period unscathed.

36 Patrick Casey (BMH, WS 1148, p. 3).

37 Hall, *Louth*, p. 64.

38 *AG*, 15 Aug. 1919; Charles McGleenan (BMH, WS 829, pp 8–9); John Cosgrove (BMH, WS 605, p. 2). The statements disagree over whether arms were missed because the search was hurried, or if they had been removed beforehand as letters from Mrs Cope suggest; see Kane, 'The arms raid on the Cope residence', 229–40.

39 Rev. Foy compensation claim, 1920 (PRONI, Best and Gillespie papers, D1616/14/9); Patrick Rankin to Michael Collins, 7 Nov. 1919 (IMA, Collins papers, A/0304 VIII (I)); *AG*, 7, 14 Nov. 1919; CI Armagh, Nov. 1919 (TNA, CO 904/110).

40 Murphy, 'Michael Donnelly', pp 45–6.

41 John McCoy (BMH, WS 492, p. 59).

42 Michael Donnelly interview (UCDA, O'Malley notebooks, P17b/116, p. 43).

43 *DD*, 12 June 1920.

44 John McCoy (BMH, WS 492, p. 90).

45 *AG*, 28 Jan. 1921. Louth National Volunteers also had an arsenal of forty modern rifles which were voluntarily surrendered during the 1916 Rising, returned by the RIC in 1917 and remained untouched by the IRA; Comerford to Eckersby, 3 Jan. 1917 (NLI, Moore papers, MS 10,549/7).

46 Frank Aiken memoir (UCDA, O'Malley papers, P19b/93).

47 CI Armagh, Nov. 1919 (TNA, CO 904/110).

48 *BNL*, 4, 6 Apr. 1920; *NR*, 7 Apr. 1920.

49 CI Armagh, Jan. 1921 (TNA, CO 904/114).

50 John McCoy (BMH, WS 492, p. 96).

51 Stronge to Montgomery, 10 [May] 1918 (PRONI, Montgomery-De Fellenberg papers, D627/434/11).

52 McCluskey, *Tyrone*, p. 88; Fitzpatrick, 'The Orange Order and the border', 54.

53 Stronge to Montgomery, 12 Mar. 1920 (PRONI, Montgomery-De Fellenberg papers, D627/435/9).

54 Same to same, 5, 22 Apr., 4, 30 May 1920 (ibid., D627/435/19, 48, 71, 94).

55 Bates to J. Patterson Best, 4 May 1920; same to James Johnston, 18 May 1920 (PRONI, UUC papers, D1327/18/29/2, 18).

56 *AG*, 29 May 1920; Lonsdale to Armstrong, 10 May 1920 (PRONI, Armstrong papers, D3727/E/46/49).

57 Bridget Hourican, 'Moore, Sir William (1864–1944)', *DIB*.

58 Stronge to Montgomery, 30 May 1920 (PRONI, Montgomery-De Fellenberg papers, D627/435/94).

59 Townshend, *The Republic*, pp 175–6.

60 *FS*, 31 July 1920.

61 Robert Lynch, *The northern IRA and the early years of partition, 1920–1922* (Dublin, 2006), pp 28–9, 35.

62 Richard Abbott, *Police casualties in Ireland* (Cork, 2000), pp 114–15.

63 Christopher Magill, *Political conflict in east Ulster: revolution and reprisal, 1920–1922* (Woodbridge, 2020), pp 39–46; Feeney, *Antrim*, pp 70–6.

64 *AG*, 20, 27 Aug. 1920; *LM*, 21 Aug. 1920.

65 CI Armagh, June, July, Aug. 1920 (TNA, CO 904/113).

66 'Typescript re. formation of the USC in Armagh', *c.*1961 (PRONI, Webster papers, D1290/6).

67 Seán Bernard Newman, 'For God, Ulster and the B-men: the Ulsterian revolution, the foundation of Northern Ireland and the creation of the Ulster Special Constabulary, 1910–1927' (PhD, University of London, 2020), p. 173.

68 *AG*, 10 Sept. 1920; *Lisburn Standard*, 22 Oct. 1920.

69 Bowman, *Carson's army*, pp 190–2, 195; Bryan A. Follis, *A state under siege: the establishment of Northern Ireland, 1920–1925* (Oxford, 1995), p. 4.

70 Magill, *Political conflict in east Ulster*, p. 118.

71 *PN*, 20 Nov. 1920.

72 USC weekly recruiting returns, Nov. 1920 to Mar. 1921, Apr. 1921 to Sept. 1921 (PRONI, Ministry of Finance papers, FIN18/1/8, 10).

73 *Belfast Telegraph*, 2 Dec. 1920.

74 *FS*, 4 Dec. 1920.

75 For various contributions to this debate see Michael Farrell, *Arming the Protestants: the formation of the Ulster Special Constabulary and the Royal Ulster Constabulary, 1920–27* (London, 1983), pp 48–52; Follis, *State under siege*, pp 16–17; Newman, 'For God, Ulster and the B-men', pp 181–5.

76 *Londonderry Sentinel*, 13 Nov. 1920.

77 *Lisburn Standard*, 22 Oct. 1920.

78 Committee of Catholic magistrates in Lurgan to Clark, 18 Nov. 1920; Clark to Armaghdale, 20 Nov. 1920 (PRONI, Sir Ernest Clark papers, D/1022/2/9).

79 Michael Hopkinson, 'The Collins-Craig pacts of 1922: two attempted reforms of the Northern Ireland government', *Irish Historical Studies*, 27:106 (1990), 151.

80 Magill, *Political conflict in east Ulster*, p. 124. A similar sample of 852 recruits was provided for Armagh in 2016 to one of the authors but permission to use the anonymized data from personnel files has proven impossible to attain.

81 *FS*, 18 Sept. 1920.

82 CI Armagh, Oct./Nov. 1920 (TNA, CO 904/113).

83 *FS*, 4 Dec. 1920.

84 'Protest against Special Constabulary in County Armagh' [Dec.] 1920 (PRONI, FIN/18/1/92).

85 *DD*, 1 Jan. 1921; *FS*, 8 Jan. 1921; Privilege, *Michael Logue*, pp 180–3.

86 John Grant (BMH, WS 658 p. 11); *NR*, 30 Dec. 1920, 1 Jan. 1921.

87 Lewis, *Frank Aiken's war*, pp 78–80; Tim Wilson, *Frontiers of violence: conflict and identity in Ulster and Upper Silesia, 1918–1922* (Oxford, 2010), pp 107–9; for example, see file relating to the shooting of James McGleenan, 17 Mar. 1922 (PRONI, Home Affairs files, HA/5/184).

88 *Dáil Éireann debates*, vol. 1, cols 192–3, 6 Aug. 1920.

89 Ibid.

90 Robert Lynch, *The partition of Ireland, 1918–25* (Cambridge, 2019), p. 123.

91 Patrick Beagan (BMH, WS 561, pp 2–3).

92 *NR*, 21 Aug. 1920.

93 *AG*, 7 Feb. 1921.

94 J.J. Murray (BMH, WS 1096, p. 7).

95 Terence Dooley, *The plight of Monaghan Protestants, 1912–1926* (Dublin, 2000), p. 45; idem, *Monaghan*, pp 96–7.

96 *DD*, 13 Nov. 1920.

97 Conor Kostick, *Revolution in Ireland, 1917–1923* (London, 1996), pp 120–30.

98 Martin Maguire, 'Labour in County Louth, 1912–1923' in Donal Hall and Martin Maguire (eds), *County Louth, and the Irish Revolution, 1912–1923* (Newbridge, 2017), pp 73–4.

99 *DD*, 24 July 1920; *NR*, 10 Aug. 1920, *AG*, 17 Sept. 1920.

100 *AG*, 12 Nov. 1920.

101 *North Down Herald and County Down Independent*, 15 Jan. 1921.

102 *NR*, 8 Feb. 1921.

103 *FS*, 19 Mar. 1921.

104 Linda Connolly, 'Towards a further understanding of the sexual and gender-based violence women experienced in the Irish Revolution' in Linda Connolly (ed.), *Women in the Irish Revolution* (Newbridge, 2020), pp 103–28.

105 John McCoy (BMH, WS 492, p. 113).

106 John Cosgrove (BMH, WS 605, pp 1–2).

107 *NR*, 10 Nov. 1921.

108 Eddie Boyle interview [1963] (CÓFLA, O'Kane collection, LOK/IV/A/42).

109 John 'Ned' Quinn interview, 8 May 1966 (CÓFLA, O'Kane collection, LOK/IV/A/47/A); Eddie Boyle interview, 8 Aug. 1963 (CÓFLA, O'Kane collection, LOK/IV/A/49/A). An ex-soldier, John McCabe, was taken from Crossmaglen to Carrickmacross in April 1921, and shot with a notice pinned to him, but he survived; *NR*, 19 Apr. 1921. For the killing of John Cosgrove, a cousin of Hugh O'Hanlon and also living near Camlough, on 13 June 1921, see *NR*, 14 Mar. 1922; John Cosgrove (TNA, WO 35/148/32).

110 Dooley, *Monaghan*, pp 87–92.

111 Brian Hughes, *Defying the IRA? Intimidation, coercion and communities during the Irish Revolution* (Liverpool, 2016), p. 125.

112 David M. Leeson, 'Reprisals' in Crowley et al. (eds), *Atlas of the Irish Revolution*, p. 384.

113 Andy O'Hare, 'List of activities in 4th Northern divisional area', 1918–23 (IMA, MSPC, A/51/2, pp 13–14); Jack McElhaw (BMH, WS 634, pp 10–13) for a detailed account.

114 Séamus Kavanagh (BMH, WS 1,053, p. 14); *NR*, 10 Feb. 1920.

115 John McCoy (BMH, WS 492, pp 46–7); Joseph Lawless (BMH, WS 1,043, p. 241).

116 John McCoy (BMH, WS 492, pp 54–5).

117 Jack McElhaw (BMH, WS 634, pp 22–3).

118 Brigid McDermott (née McCoy) (IMA, MSPC, 34REF48466, p. 13).

119 *AG*, 9, 23 Jan. 1920; *NR*, 12 June 1920.

120 *PN*, 11 Dec. 1920.

121 Lewis, *Frank Aiken's war*, p. 224.

122 Figures from Gary Evans, 'The raising of the first internal Dáil Éireann loan and the British responses to it' (MLitt, NUI Maynooth, 2012), p. 154.

123 John McCoy (BMH WS 492, pp 50–3).

124 Lewis, *Frank Aiken's war*, p. 88.

125 Hall, *Louth*, pp 77–8; 1st Northern Louth Brigade, 4th Northern Division (IMA, MSPC, A/51(1) encl.51).

126 Patrick Casey (BMH, WS 1,148, p. 11). Casey's recollection of the details was faulty, as he believed it happened in February 1921 and at another location.

127 Thomas McCrave (BMH, WS 695, pp 19–21); *IT*, 11 Apr. 1921.

128 James Rogan (BMH, WS 598, p. 8).

129   Ibid.; John McCoy (BMH, WS 492, p. 91).
130   CI Armagh, Apr. 1921 (TNA, CO 904/115).
131   Frank Donnelly (BMH, WS 941, p. 8).
132   *AG*, 24 June 1921.
133   Ibid., 1 July 1921.
134   Townshend, *The Republic*, pp 228–9. According to Townshend, at least thirty officially approved reprisal actions were taken every month in areas under martial law.
135   Further details in Eunan O'Halpin and Daithí Ó Corráin, *The dead of the Irish Revolution* (New Haven and London, 2020), pp 265, 272, 507–8.
136   John Doran, 13 Jan. 1921 (TNA, Courts of Inquiry files WO 35/149A/37); *NR*, 14 Jan. 1921; John Doran (IMA, MSPC, DP788). The application to the Irish Free State for a gratuity was unsuccessful as £150 in compensation had been paid in 1922.
137   John McCoy (BMH, WS 492, p. 80).
138   *IT*, 24 June 1921.
139   *NR*, 25 June 1921. A report for *An tÓglach*, probably from Aiken, claimed that more than 25 soldiers had been killed but this was not confirmed anywhere else (NLI, Béaslaí papers, MS 33,911/3).
140   *II*, 27 June 1921; *NR*, 27 June 1921.
141   For varying accounts of the failure to attack these trains see Jack Plunkett (BMH, WS 865, pp 50–1) and Eugene Kavanagh, 'South Louth, No. 9 Brigade 1st Eastern Division IRA', 17 May 1938 (IMA, MSPC, /A/63).
142   For differing accounts see John Grant (BMH, WS 658, pp 15–17); Francis Gallagher (TNA, WO 35/150/54).
143   For details of the Hazlehatch ambush see James Crenegan (BMH, WS 1,395, pp 20–4); Seán Boylan (BMH, WS 1,715, pp 36–8); David Hall (BMH, WS 1,539, pp 14–16); Séamus Finn (BMH, WS 1,060, pp 52–6).
144   Pathé News carried a film reel and the attack was reported in full (often with photographs) in *Pall Mall Gazette*, 24, 25 June 1921; *Daily Mirror*, 25, 27 June 1921; *Sunday Mirror*, 26 June 1921; and eighteen other regional English and Scottish papers.
145   *DD*, 2 July 1921; *FS*, 9 July 1921.
146   *NR*, 7 July 1921; Patrick Quinn, John & Thomas O'Reilly; Peter McGennity (TNA, WO 35/158/15).
147   List of dead and executed men of the IRA (UCDA, Twomey papers, P69/35(42–3)); John Grant (BMH, WS 658, p. 15).
148   *NR*, 14 July 1921.
149   John Grant (BMH, WS 658, pp 16–17).
150   De Valera to Collins, 13 Jan. 1921; De Valera to O'Keeffe, 8 Mar. 1921; De Valera to Stack, 7 Mar. 1921 (UCDA, de Valera papers, P150/1381).
151   Phoenix, *Northern nationalism*, pp 107–9; *FS*, 5, 26 Feb. 1921.
152   Phoenix, *Northern nationalism*, p. 126.
153   Devlin to Dillon, 22 Apr. 1921 (TCD, Dillon papers, MS 6730/294).
154   O'Keeffe to de Valera, 5 Apr. 1921 (UCDA, de Valera papers, P150/1381).
155   Lewis, *Frank Aiken's war*, p. 70.
156   Laffan, *Resurrection*, p. 340; Keiko Inoue, 'Sinn Féin propaganda and the "partition election", 1921', *Studia Hibernica*, 30 (1998/1999), 47–61.
157   Follis, *State under siege*, p. 196.

CHAPTER SEVEN *'A dirty type of peace': truce and Treaty, 1921–2*

1   Under the terms of the Anglo-Irish Treaty signed on 6 December 1921, the Irish Free State (IFS) did not legally come into existence until 6 December 1922. For ease of reference the term IFS will be used to cover the twenty-six-county area from January 1922 onwards.

2 *NR*, 12 July 1921; *AG*, 15 July 1921.

3 J.J. Murray (BMH, WS 1,096, p. 12); *DD*, 16 July 1921.

4 *DD*, 16 July 1921; J.J. Murray (BMH, WS 1,096, p. 12).

5 *AG*, 15 July 1921.

6 *BNL*, 13 July 1921.

7 Ibid.

8 *NR*, 21 July 1921.

9 *AG*, 15 July 1921.

10 *DD*, 23 July 1921.

11 Cabinet conclusions, 28 Nov., 1 Dec. 1921 (PRONI, CAB 4/27/11, 28/4).

12 *AG*, 5 Aug. 1921; *NR*, 20 Sept. 1921.

13 *AG*, 19, 26 Aug., 2 Sept. 1921; Trimble to CI, 19 Aug. 1921 (TNA, CO 904/151).

14 *AG*, 18 Nov. 1921.

15 Ibid., 26 Oct. 1921; CI Armagh to IG, 30 Oct. (Keady); DI McFarland to CI, 9 Nov. (Camlough), 12 Nov. 1921 (Adavoyle) (TNA, CO 904/151).

16 Col. Wickham to Spender, 8 Sept. 1921 (TNA, CO 904/151); Éamonn Duggan to Emmet Dalton, 30 Nov. 1921 (IMA, Northern Liaison papers, LE4/16/A).

17 CI Armagh to IG, 23 Nov. 1921 (TNA, CO 904/151).

18 John McCoy (BMH, WS 492, pp 109–17).

19 McCoy to Dalton, 28 Nov. 1921, 23 Jan., 1, 8, 15 Mar. 1922 (IMA, Northern Liaison papers, LE4/16/A).

20 Same to same, 6 Feb. 1922 (ibid., LE4/16/A).

21 John McCoy interview, 9 June 1966 (CÓFLA, O'Kane collection, LOK/IV/A/131); Dalton to McCoy, 22 Feb. 1922 (IMA, LE4/16/A).

22 Frank Donnelly (BMH, WS 941, p. 14); Dalton to Mulcahy, 27 Mar. 1922 (IMA, LE4/16/A).

23 Frank Aiken memoir (UCDA, Aiken papers, P104/1305, p. 1).

24 4th Northern Division GHQ rolls (IMA, MSP/RO/434/4 ND/3); 1 Brigade, 3rd Battalion (Camlough) rolls (IMA, MSP/RO/ 428/4 ND); 1 Brigade, 4th Battalion (Newtownhamilton), rolls (IMA, MSP/RO/ 429/4 ND).

25 'Breaches of the truce by Sinn Féin' (PRONI, Home Affairs files, HA/32/1/4).

26 Frank Aiken memoir, *c.*1925 (UCDA, Aiken papers, P104/1305, pp 1–3); Townshend, *The Republic*, pp 318–21.

27 'Notes' of Frank Aiken (UCDA, O'Malley notebooks, P17b/93, p. 2).

28 *PN*, 13 Aug. 1921.

29 *NW*, 4 Aug. 1921.

30 Printed (illustrated) copy of resolution from Armagh Chamber of Commerce, Mar. 1921 (PRONI, D/2567/8).

31 *AG*, 14, 21 Jan., 18 Mar., 15 July, 5, 26 Aug. 1921; *PN*, 30 July 1921.

32 David Fitzpatrick, *Harry Boland's Irish Revolution* (Cork, 2004), pp 229–32.

33 Róisín Ní Bheirne interview with Advisory Board, 13 June 1937 (IMA, MSPC, 34REF2848, p. 27); file on SF meeting in Armagh city, Sept. 1921 (National Archives of Ireland (hereafter NAI), Dáil Éireann secretariat files, DE 2/274).

34 For the details see Des Fitzgerald, 'Michael Collins in Armagh', *History Armagh*, 7 (2013), 7–11.

35 Ibid., p. 10.

36 *UG*, 9 Sept. 1921.

37 *FJ*, 5 Sept. 1921.

38 Eamonn Phoenix, 'Michael Collins and the Northern question, 1916–22' in Gabriel Doherty and Dermot Keogh (eds), *Michael Collins and the making of the Irish state* (Cork, 1998), pp 95–6.

39 *AG*, 9 Sept. 1921; MacSwiney to Boland, quoted in Fitzpatrick, *Harry Boland*, pp 231–2; *FS*, 10 Sept. 1921.

40 *BNL*, 5 Sept. 1921.

41 Liam Gaynor interview, 1964 (CÓFLA, O'Kane collection, LOK/IV/61A); Fearghal McGarry, *Eoin O'Duffy: a self-made hero* (Oxford, 2005), pp 80–2; *BNL*, 5 Sept. 1921.

42 *UG*, 9 Sept. 1921.

43 Phoenix, *Northern nationalism*, pp 143–4.

44 Jack McElhaw (BMH, WS 634, p. 28).

45 Milroy to Mulcahy, 22 Sept. 1921 (UCDA, Mulcahy papers, P7A/36 (171)).

46 Townshend, *The Republic*, pp 331–2.

47 *NR*, 20 Sept. 1921.

48 *FS*, 24 Sept. 1921.

49 *AG*, 30 Sept. 1921.

50 Mícheál Ó Fathartaigh and Liam Weeks, *Birth of a state, the Anglo-Irish Treaty* (Newbridge, 2021), pp 54–61.

51 Frank Aiken memoir, *c.*1925 (UCDA, Aiken papers, P104/1308, pp 7–8).

52 'Notes' of Frank Aiken (UCDA, O'Malley notebooks, P17b/93, p. 3).

53 John McCoy (BMH, WS 492, p. 112).

54 John Grant (BMH, WS 658, p. 12).

55 Charles McGleenan interview (CÓFLA, O'Kane collection, LOK/IV/A/47D).

56 *AG*, 12 Jan. 1922.

57 *FS*, 10, 31 Dec. 1921.

58 *FJ*, 12 Dec., 1921; *AG*, 5 Jan. 1922.

59 J.J. Murray (BMH, WS 1,096, pp 13–15).

60 Maryann Gialanella Valiulis, *Portrait of a revolutionary: General Richard Mulcahy and the founding of the Irish Free State* (Newbridge, 1992), p. 124.

61 Townshend, *The Republic*, pp 390–2; Patrick Taaffe, 'Richard Mulcahy and the genesis of the Civil War', *Irish Sword*, 118 (2014), 442.

62 Lynch, *Northern IRA*, p. 104.

63 *AG*, 17 Feb. 1922.

64 Alan Parkinson, *A difficult birth, the early years of Northern Ireland, 1920–25* (Dublin, 2020), pp 192–6; see also McGarry, *Eoin O'Duffy*, pp 99–100.

65 Lynch, *Northern IRA*, pp 115–16; Hopkinson, 'The Collins–Craig pacts of 1922', 145–6.

66 J.J. Murray (BMH, WS 1,096, pp 15–16), *Northern Whig*, 13 Feb. 1922. Murray recalled that a retaliatory ambush took place at Derrytrasna which resulted in a number of USC being wounded but details of this have not been found. James Robinson is listed among 4th ND fatalities (UCDA, Twomey papers, P69/35/42–3).

67 *FS*, 25 Mar. 1923.

68 *AG*, 24 Mar. 1922; Patrick Beagan (BMH, WS 612, pp 5–6).

69 *BNL*, 23 Mar. 1922.

70 *AG*, 31 Mar. 1922; Patrick Beagan (BMH, WS 612, pp 5–6); 'Wm Fleming wounded by unknown men, 28.3.23' (PRONI, Home Affairs papers, HA/5/195).

71 *NW*, 27 Mar. 1922; *DD*, 1 Apr. 1922; RIC bi-monthly report, 31 Mar. 1922 (PRONI, HA/5/152); McGarry, *Eoin O'Duffy*, p. 100.

72 John McCoy (BMH, WS 492, p. 137).

73 Pádraig Quinn memoir (Kilmainham Gaol Archive); Michael Donnelly interview (UCDA, O'Malley notebooks, P17b/116, p. 2). Mulcahy had gone to a 1st Southern Division meeting uninvited on 20 March to try and persuade them to postpone the convention; see Pádraig Ó Caoimh, *Richard Mulcahy: from the politics of war to the politics of peace, 1913–1924* (Newbridge, 2019), p. 105.

74 John McCoy (BMH, WS 492). Aiken was to emphasize repeatedly over the years that it was only when attacked by the National army that the 4th ND took the anti-Treaty side in the Civil War.

75 Hopkinson, *Green against green: the Irish Civil War* (Dublin, 1988), pp 60–6.

76 Aiken to adjutant-general, 21 Feb. 1922 (IMA, O'Sullivan papers); Aiken to Dalton, 8 Mar. 1922 (IMA, Liaison papers, LE/4/16A).
77 Lewis, *Frank Aiken's war*, p. 127.
78 Michael Donnelly interview (UCDA, O'Malley notebooks, P17b/116, p. 3).
79 Pádraig Quinn memoir (Kilmainham Gaol Archive).
80 Ibid.; John McCoy interview, 26 Apr. 1967 (CÓFLA, O'Kane collection, LOK IV/A/53A).
81 Memorandum, 18 Apr. 1922 (UCDA, Aiken papers, P104/1237(2); *AG*, 23 June 1922.

CHAPTER EIGHT *'Something unpleasant, if not horrible': violence and civil wars, in 1922–3*

1 Follis, *A state under siege*, pp 100–1.
2 *NR*, 17 Jan. 1922; *FS*, 7 May 1922.
3 Privilege, *Michael Logue*, pp 167, 169.
4 *DD*, 10, 17, 24 June 1922; *II*, 22 June 1922; Privilege, *Michael Logue*, pp 180–3.
5 *PN*, 7 Jan., 23 Dec. 1922.
6 *FS*, 27 Jan. 1923.
7 For more see Peter Leary, *Unapproved routes: histories of the Irish border, 1922–1972* (Oxford, 2016), pp 125–63.
8 The details can be found in Catherine Nash, Lorraine Dennis and Brian Graham, 'Putting the border in place: customs regulation in the making of the Irish border, 1921–1945', *Journal of Historical Geography*, 36:4 (2010), 421–31.
9 Lynch, *Northern IRA*, pp 134–5; Hopkinson, *Green against green*, p. 88; Phoenix, 'Collins and the Northern question', p. 114; Seán MacBride interview in Uinseann Mac Eoin, *Survivors* (Dublin, 1980), p. 117.
10 Lynch, *Northern IRA*, p. 100.
11 Pádraig Quinn memoir (Kilmainham Gaol Archive); Michael O'Hanlon interview (UCDA, O'Malley notebooks, 17b/106/76).
12 John Grant (BMH, WS 658, p. 19).
13 John McCoy (BMH, WS 492, p. 121).
14 Patrick Casey (BMH, WS 1148, p. 28); Lynch, *Northern IRA*, pp 136–9.
15 Pádraig Quinn memoir (Kilmainham Gaol Archive); Lynch, *Northern IRA*, p. 138; Ó Caoimh, *Richard Mulcahy*, pp 115–19.
16 McCluskey, *Tyrone*, pp 121–4.
17 Lynch, *Northern IRA*, pp 143–4.
18 Matthew Lewis, 'The Fourth Northern Division and the joint-IRA offensive, April–July 1922', *War in History*, 21:3 (2013), 1–20.
19 John Cosgrove (BMH, WS 605, p. 8).
20 John McCoy interview (UCDA, O'Malley notebooks, P17b/94/98).
21 Patrick Casey (BMH, WS 1148, p. 33).
22 Ibid.; *Frank Aiken: from gunman to statesman* (Mint Productions 'Hidden History' documentary for RTÉ Television, 2006).
23 Pádraig Quinn memoir (Kilmainham Gaol Archive).
24 John Grant (BMH, WS 658, p. 20).
25 Diarmaid Ferriter, *Between two hells: the Irish Civil War* (London, 2022), p. 29.
26 Lewis, 'The joint-IRA offensive', 19.
27 John McCoy (BMH, WS 492, p. 123); John McCoy interview (O'Malley notebooks, P17b/116/15); John McCoy interview, June 1966 (CÓFLA, O'Kane collection, LOK/IV/A/131).
28 Circular from Aiken and Pat Lavery, 12 May 1922 (UCDA, Mulcahy papers, P7a/145).
29 Winston Churchill, *Hansard (Commons)*, 22 May 1922, vol. 154, cols 800; Townshend, *The Republic*, pp 397–8; Hopkinson, *Green against green*, p. 106; Lloyd George, *Hansard (Commons)*, 31 May 1922, vol. 154, cols 2128.

30 RIC bi-monthly report, 16 May 1922 (PRONI, Home Affairs papers, HA/5/152); *AG*, 19 May 1922.

31 Seán McConville, *Irish political prisoners, 1920–62: pilgrimage of desolation* (London, 2014), p. 327.

32 Fortnightly returns of prisoners detained under Regulation 23, Special Powers Act, 1922–1924 (PRONI, HA/5/2592). Denise Kleinrichert, *Republican internment and the prison ship* Argenta, *1922* (Dublin, 2001), pp 335–68, names more than 900 men and women and includes those on whom orders were issued but not able to be served.

33 The number comes from Kleinrichert, *Argenta*, pp 335–68; McConville, *Irish political prisoners*, p. 328; and a review of the internment files at PRONI, HA/5/940–2400.

34 *AG*, 27 May 1922; Kleinrichert, *Argenta*, pp 226, 340.

35 Frank Hannaway (IMA, MSPC, 34REF1488, pp 37, 46). In the 1930s Hannaway was living in Dublin and employed as a labourer in the Army Corps of Engineers for £2 15s. per week.

36 Membership rolls, 3rd Battalion, 3rd Brigade, 4th Northern Division (IMA, MSPC/RO/437, pp 22–30).

37 *FS*, 17 June 1922.

38 For the files see Richard Brophy (PRONI, HA/5/1903); Patrick Lappin (PRONI, HA/5/1901); Patrick Lynch (PRONI, HA/5/1900); Thomas Foy [Fox] (PRONI, HA/5/959D); Henry Sharkey (PRONI, HA/5/959C). There are no Home Affairs internment files for John Sharkey and Peter Connolly who are mentioned in Kleinrichert, *Argenta*, pp 340, 366.

39 W.T. Church to Dawson Bates [Apr. 1922] and reply, 21 Apr. 1922 (PRONI, Commissions of the Peace, Co Armagh, HA/5/37(12–13)).

40 Phoenix, *Northern nationalism*, p. 238; Kleinrichert, *Argenta*, pp 176–88.

41 Notes of J.J. O'Hanlon's appearance to advisory committee, 3 Aug. 1922 (PRONI, HA/5/959).

42 O'Hanlon to secretary, ministry of home affairs, 11 July 1922; correspondence between home affairs officials and prison governor, 14, 16 July 1922 (PRONI, HA/5/959).

43 *PN*, 22 July 1922.

44 Adding to the circumstantial evidence is the fact that three men in the Portadown IRA company of the 3rd Battalion worked and lived in the Queen's Hotel (IMA, MSPC, RO/437, p. 27).

45 Minute sheet, 2 Aug. 1922; O'Hanlon to Colonel Topping, 23 June 1922 (PRONI, HA/5/959).

46 Vera O'Hanlon to Colonel Topping, 11 Aug. 1922 (ibid.).

47 Geraghty, 'J.J. O'Hanlon', pp 175–88.

48 Return of internees, 30 Nov. 1923 (PRONI, HA/5/2290).

49 Kleinrichert, *Argenta*, p. 293 to which should be added Alice Mallon; see Fergal McCluskey, 'Alice Mallon: "a very bad type of woman"' in McAnallen (ed.), *Reflections on the revolution in Ulster*, pp 84–100.

50 Rose Black, Feb.–June 1923 (PRONI, HA/2/2321); Winifred Carney, July–Aug. 1922 (PRONI, HA/5/2069); Lizzie Keown, Sept. 1923–Mar. 1924 (PRONI, HA/5/2463); Mary Kerr, June–Nov. 1922 (PRONI, HA/5/1887); Alice Mallon, Apr.–Aug. 1923 (PRONI, HA/5/2342); Maureen Watson, Aug.–Sept. 1923 (PRONI, HA/5/2454); Katherine Williams, Mar.–June 1923 (PRONI, HA/5/2333). Alice O'Rourke was sentenced to six months in Armagh gaol in June 1922 for possession of arms (PRONI, HA/5/2524) and Annie Keelan was arrested in Omagh in February 1923 and remanded in Armagh until June 1923 when she was deported to Dundalk (Annie Maguire, IMA, MSPC, 34REF56373).

51 DI McFarland to CI, 3 Aug. 1922; Solly-Flood to Topping, 10 Aug. 1922; McFarland to CI, 4 Sept. 1922 (Róisín O'Beirne file, PRONI, HA/5/2108).

52 *Iris an Airm*, 29 Sept. 1922. See Eoin Magennis and Lesa Ní Mhunghaile, 'Gender, class and violence in the Irish border region, 1918–1924: the case of Nano Aiken' (unpublished conference paper, University of Galway, 16 Nov. 2019).

53 Nano Aiken (PRONI, HA/5/2303); Nano Magennis (née Aiken) (IMA, MSPC, 34/D/1754, p. 9).

54 John Scurr MP to Craig, 22 Mar. 1924; Samuel Watt to Capt Poynting, 29 Mar. 1924; Spender to IG RUC, 6 May 1924 (PRONI, HA/5/2303). For the planned escape which it appears Nano Aiken herself did not go along with, see Patrick Beagan (BMH, WS 612, pp 8–10); Charles McGleenan and John McCoy interview, Sept. 1968 (CÓFLA, O'Kane collection, LOK/IV/50A).

55 Frank Aiken to Molly Childers, 10 Mar. 1924 (TCD, Erskine Childers papers, MS 7847/13); notes on Wilfred Spender to Captain Poynting, 15 Apr. 1924 (PRONI, HA/5/2303).

56 *FS*, 3 June 1922.

57 Elizabeth Marner (née McInerney), 'An account of my activities in Cumann na mBan', undated (IMA, MSPC, 34REF47720, p. 5); Jack McElhaw (BMH, WS 634, pp 36, 38).

58 John McCoy interview, 27 Feb. 1949 (UCDA, O'Malley notebooks, P17b/94/96).

59 'NI residents unlawfully detained in Irish State' (NAI, TSCH/3/S1317). According to the British list, another fifteen hostages were allegedly held in Athlone, the headquarters of the prominent pro-Treatyite General Seán Mac Eoin.

60 Lewis, *Frank Aiken's war*, pp 147–8.

61 John Grant (BMH, WS 658, p. 21); John McCoy interview (UCDA, O'Malley papers, 17b/94 p. 100).

62 Michael O'Hanlon (UCDA, O'Malley papers, P17b/106, pp 75–9); Pádraig Quinn memoir (Kilmainham Gaol Archives).

63 Edward Fullerton (IMA, MSPC, 24SP8177).

64 *NR*, 6 July 1922; 'William Frazer, kidnapped at Newtownhamilton, Carrowmannon by armed men 6/7/22' (PRONI, HA 5/253); handwritten note on transcript of John 'Ned' Quinn interview, 8 May 1966 (CÓFLA, O'Kane collection, LOK/IV/A/47A).

65 *FS*, 17 June 1922; *NR*, 1 July 1922.

66 John Grant (BMH, WS 658, pp 22–3).

67 *FS*, 24 June 1922.

68 *NR*, 1 July 1922.

69 File relating to the murders of Paddy Cruddan (*sic*) and Thomas Crawley (PRONI, HA/5/239).

70 Aiken to O'Duffy, 'Report of outrage by disguised A Specials from Forkhill barracks on the night of the 13th and the morning of the 14 June', 15 June 1922 (NAI, NI Outrages, Jan.-Oct. 1922, TSCH/S5462).

71 See Robert Lynch, 'Explaining the Altnaveigh massacre', *Éire-Ireland*, 45:3&4 (2010), 184–210 which has been drawn on in Linda Connolly, 'Sexual violence in the Irish Civil War: a forgotten war crime?', *Women's History Review*, 30:1 (2021), 126–43; Mary McAuliffe, 'Gendered violence against women' in Darragh Gannon and Fearghal McGarry (eds), *Ireland 1922* (Dublin, 2022), pp 136–41.

72 Collins to Churchill, telegram, 20 June 1922 (NAI, TSCH/S5462).

73 File relating to alleged raid on house of James McGuill (PRONI, HA/5/249).

74 *DD*, 24 June 1922.

75 John Grant (BMH, WS 658, p. 26).

76 Patrick Casey (BMH, WS 1,148, pp 30–1); John McCoy (UCDA, O'Malley papers, P17b/94, p. 100).

77 John McCoy interview, 9 June 1966 (CÓFLA, O'Kane collection, LOK/IV/A/131).

78 *DD*, 24 June 1922; *IT*, 26 June 1922.

79 *AG*, 23 June 1922.

80 *NR*, 20 June 1922; *IT*, 19 June 1922; *II*, 19 June 1922; *DD*, 24 June 1922.

81 *NR*, 20 June 1922.

82 For three different approaches to the events see Lynch, 'Explaining the Altnaveigh massacre'; Matthew Lewis, 'Sectarianism and Irish republican violence on the south-east Ulster frontier, 1919–1922', *Contemporary European History*, 26:1 (2017), 1–21; Tim Wilson, '"The widening

gyre": the Altnaveigh killings in context', unpublished paper delivered to Louth County Council 'Border 100' seminar series, 27 Oct. 2021.

83 Edward Boyle (BMH, WS 647, pp 23–4).

84 *FS*, 24 June 1922.

85 Jack McElhaw (BMH, WS 634, pp 39–40).

86 John Grant (BMH, WS 658, p. 21).

87 Thomas Woods (IMA, MSPC, 34REF3916); Patrick Loughran (IMA, MSPC, 34REF11586); James Marron (IMA, MSPC, 34REF318); John McEnerney (IMA, MSPC, 34REF41141); James Murphy (IMA, MSPC, 34REF62652).

88 James Fearon (IMA, MSPC, 34REF57139); James Marron (IMA, MSPC, 34REF318).

89 James Marron (IMA, MSPC, 34REF318); Edward Fearon (IMA, MSPC, 34REF2873).

90 Terence McGivern (IMA MSPC, 34REF54461).

91 Patrick Casey (BMH, WS 1,148, p. 31).

92 For example, *Pall Mall Gazette*, 17 June 1922; *The Scotsman*, 19 June 1922; *Daily News* (London), 19 June 1922.

93 *Illustrated London News*, 24 June 1922.

94 *Cork Examiner*, 22 June 1922.

95 *NR*, 26 June 1922.

96 Note by Harold Topping to Samuel Watt, 13 Sept. 1922 (PRONI, HA 5/250). The mention of Cushendall is a reference to the killing of three Catholics by the USC in disputed circumstances on 23 June 1922, which the nationalist press believed was an unprovoked attack by the USC on civilians; *II*, 26 June 1922; Magill, *Political conflict in east Ulster*, ch. 5.

97 Spender to secretary ministry of home affairs, 25 Sept. 1922 (PRONI, HA 5/250).

98 *NR*, 22 June 1922.

99 *DD*, 24 June 1922.

100 *AG*, 23 June 1922.

101 Ibid., 4 Aug. 1922.

102 *DD*, 14 Oct. 1922.

103 Lynch, *Northern IRA*, p. 49.

104 John McCoy interview, 26 Apr. 1967 (CÓFLA O'Kane collection, LOK/IV/A/53A).

105 Pádraig Quinn memoir (Kilmainham Gaol Archives).

106 John McCoy interview, 26 Apr. 1967 (CÓFLA O'Kane collection, LOK/IV/A/53A).

107 John McCoy (BMH, WS 492, pp 142–3).

108 Ibid.

109 Pension application of Dominic Doherty, 3 May 1926 (IMA, MSPC, 24SP6707).

110 Doherty letter, 12 June 1925 (ibid.).

111 *NR*, 18 July 1922; John Joseph Campbell (IMA, MSPC, DP562).

112 Phone message, 17 July 1922 (UCDA, Mulcahy papers, P/7/B/109/272).

113 Frank Aiken, 'Position of the Fourth Northern Division from January 1922 to 17th July 1922, 3 p.m.' (IMA, MSPC, A/51(2), p. 2).

114 Dominic Doherty letter, 12 June 1925 (IMA, MSPC, 24SP6707).

115 Edward Fullerton (BMH, WS 890, pp 28–9).

116 'Re the 124 Recruits returned to Dundalk', 10 Aug. 1922 (UCDA, Mulcahy papers, B7/B/59/117).

117 Application for dependants pension for Mrs Annie Matthews, mother of Sgt John Lavery, 4 Dec. 1923 (IMA, MSPC, WD186).

118 Owen Keegan papers (County Louth Archaeological and Historical Society).

119 *DD*, 12 Aug. 1922.

120 John McCoy (BMH, WS 492, p. 148).

121 Dan Hogan, 'Report from Headquarters 5th ND, Military Barracks, Clones. 24 July 1922 to Adjutant General' (UCDA, Mulcahy papers, P/7/B/109/158).

122 Details of this can be found in interviews with Eddie Boyle, Eiver Monaghan and Charlie McGleenan, May 1971 (CÓFLA, O'Kane collection, LOK/IV/86A).

123 *FS*, 5 Aug. 1922.

124 Donal Hall and Lorraine McCann, *'Hole in the Wall': Dundalk jail during the Civil War* (Dundalk, 2022); 'Dundalk general register of prisoners (NAI, PRIS/1/16/1) – Transcript of Escaped Prisoners 27th July 1922'. https://www.louthcoco.ie/en/services/archives/louth-1916–1923/dundalk-jail-1916–1923.html (accessed 12 June 2023).

125 'Report of the capture of Dundalk town, *c*.13 Aug. 1922' (NLI, IRA Executive papers, MS 43,123).

126 Andrew J. O'Hare (IMA, MSPC, 34REF4567); Eddie Boyle interview [1963] (CÓFLA, O'Kane collection, LOK/IV/42A).

127 'Report of action at Dungooley, 18 Aug. 1922' (UCDA, Mulcahy papers, B7/B/59/48); Eiver Monaghan (IMA, MSPC, 34REF4051); John Grant (IMA, MSPC, 34REF1738, pp 24–5).

128 Eddie Boyle interview [1963] (CÓFLA, O'Kane collection, LOK/A/42).

129 *DD*, 2 Sept. 1922; Charles McGleenan (BMH, WS 829, p. 32).

130 Eugene Loughran (BMH, WS 526, p. 10); Charles McGleenan (BMH, WS 829, p. 30).

131 5th Northern Division Operational reports, 23, 25 Aug. 1922 (UCDA, Mulcahy papers, B7/B/59/33, 26).

132 *NW*, 8 Feb. 1923.

133 *DD*, 26 Aug. 1922.

134 Ibid., 6 Jan. 1923. There is no information on Tomás Ua Vadhagh. He does not appear on Divisional rolls.

135 John Grant to Secretary to the Referee, 11 June 1935 (IMA, MSPC, RO/428, pp 64–72).

136 Lewis, *Frank Aiken's war*, pp 183–97.

137 *FH*, 21 July 1922.

138 *Éire: the Irish nation*, 30 June, 7 July, 18 Aug. 1923.

139 Evidence of Thomas Clarke, 17 Apr. 1933 in Michael Bennett (IMA, MSPC, 2RB190), p. 9. In 1933 his family was awarded £112 10s. in compensation; Michael Bennett (IMA, MSPC, 52AP894).

140 Eunan O'Halpin, *Defending Ireland* (Oxford, 1999), p. 30.

141 He gave a false name and address – Joseph Murphy of Newry – at the time of his arrest and was published as such when the execution was announced, only to be corrected shortly afterwards (*DD*, 20 Jan. 1923). The 'Murphy' name was the one remembered in later recollections, including interview with Eddie Boyle, Eiver Monaghan and Charlie McGleenan, May 1971 (CÓFLA, O'Kane collection, LOK/IV/86A).

142 Hall & McCann, *'Hole in the Wall'*, pp 28–9.

143 Trials by Military Courts, Dec. 1923 (IMA, CW/P/02/02/18).

144 Dept. of Defence to Francis Burke, 20 Dec. 1937 (IMA, DP903, application for Luke Burke).

145 *Meath Chronicle*, 17 Mar. 1923.

146 *NR*, 24 Apr. 1923; *DD*, 26 May 1923; Pádraig Quinn (IMA, MSPC, 34REF10216 and DP3362/1, pp 156–62).

147 *FJ*, 26 Oct. 1923.

148 Residents of north-east Ulster imprisoned by Saorstát, 15 Nov. 1923 (IMA, CW/P/02/02/18, box 33).

149 Military Customs Brigade Headquarters, Dundalk to Director of Intelligence, 16 Nov. 1923, 'NE Ulster ex-prisoners activities in Dundalk' (IMA, CW/P/02/01/11, Box 31).

150 Director of Intelligence to Intelligence Officer, Border, 19 Nov. 1923 (IMA, CW/P/02/01/11, box 31).

151 Director of Intelligence to Minister for Defence and Chief of General Staff, 8 Nov. 1923 (ibid.).

152 Eiver Monaghan (IMA, MSPC, 34REF4051); Foster, *Irish Civil War and society*, pp 203–21.

153 Hall, *Louth*, pp 105–10.
154 D/O 4th ND to C/S, 21 July 1923 (UCDA, Twomey papers, P69/35(207–209)).

CHAPTER NINE *'Carsonia' achieved: the end of the Irish Revolution in Armagh, 1923–5*

 1 *II*, 25 June 1913; *FS*, 12 Mar., 11, 18 June, 12 Nov. 1921, 4 Feb., 6 Oct. 1928.
 2 *LM*, 23 Jan. 1920; *PN*, 24 Jan. 1920.
 3 Paul Bew, Peter Gibbon and Henry Patterson, *Northern Ireland, 1921–2001: political forces and social classes* (London, 2002 ed.), p. 17.
 4 Austen Morgan, *Labour and partition* (London, 1991), pp 215–28.
 5 *PN*, 12 Jan. 1923.
 6 *AG*, 12 Jan. 1923.
 7 Phoenix, *Northern nationalism*, pp 153–5.
 8 *FS*, 25 Mar., 13 May 1922; *PN*, 6 May 1922.
 9 Phoenix, *Northern nationalism*, p. 269; *PN*, 23 Jan. 1923.
10 For example, Peter Lenagh and James Mone had been councillors in Keady UDC since 1908; *UG*, 11 Jan. 1908.
11 Kevin O'Shiel to J.H. Collins, 12 Jan. 1923; Robert Kelly to Collins, 1 Jan. 1923 (PRONI, J.H. Collins papers, D/921/2/3/3). For the IFS policy see Ernest Blythe, 'Memorandum on policy relating to the north east', 9 Aug. 1922 (UCDA, Blythe papers, P24/70).
12 Phoenix, *Northern nationalism*, pp 300–2.
13 *AG*, 18 May 1924; *FS*, 7 June 1924.
14 *NW*, 29 Apr., 14 May 1924.
15 *AG*, 29 May 1920.
16 Anne Dolan, 'The British culture of paramilitary violence in the Irish War of Independence' in Robert Gerwarth and John Horne (eds), *War in peace: paramilitary violence in Europe after the Great War* (Oxford, 2012), pp 213–15.
17 Parkinson, *A difficult birth*, pp 16–60; Bowman, *Carson's army*, pp 190–2, 195; Follis, *State under siege*, p. 4.
18 USC weekly recruiting returns, Apr. 1921 to Sept. 1921 (PRONI, Ministry of Finance papers, FIN18/1/10).
19 Cited in Fitzpatrick, 'The Orange Order and the border', 55, n. 14.
20 *AG*, 10 Dec. 1920.
21 Lewis, *Frank Aiken's war*, p. 74.
22 *AG*, 21 Jan. 1921.
23 *LM*, 25 Feb. 1922; Notes on kidnap and arrests, June 1922 (PRONI, J.H. Collins papers, D921/2/2(3)); *Parliamentary debates* (House of Commons), ii, 23 May 1922, col. 617.
24 *PN*, 27 Jan. 1923.
25 *AG*, 25 May 1923.
26 Submission of inhabitants of Ballymacnab and adjoining districts (TNA, Irish Boundary Commission papers, CAB 61/26, pp 8–9).
27 K.J. Rankin, 'County Armagh and the Boundary Commission' in Hughes & Nolan (eds), *Armagh*, pp 947–90; Paul Murray, *The Irish Boundary Commission and its origins, 1886–1925* (Dublin, 2011); James A. Cousins, *Without a dog's chance: the nationalists of Northern Ireland and the Irish Boundary Commission, 1920–25* (Newbridge, 2020).
28 Michael Collins, *The path to freedom* (Cork, 2011 ed.), p. 82.
29 Ó Fathartaigh & Weeks, *Treaty*, pp 120, 189.
30 Kevin Matthews, *Fatal influence: the impact of Ireland on British politics, 1920–1925* (Dublin, 2004), pp 89, 112–15.
31 Follis, *State under siege*, p. 162.

32 *PT*, 24 Oct. 1924.
33 Geoffrey Hand, 'MacNeill and the Boundary Commission' in F.X. Martin and F.J. Byrne (eds), *The scholar revolutionary: Eoin MacNeill and the making of the new Ireland, 1867–1945* (Shannon, 1973), p. 233; *AG*, 13 Dec. 1924; *UG*, 20 Dec. 1924.
34 *FS*, 6 Sept. 1924.
35 *PN*, 11 Apr. 1925; *PT*, 24 Apr. 1925.
36 File of Boundary Commission correspondence, Feb.–Dec. 1925 (PRONI, UUC papers, D1327/24/3).
37 Murray, *Boundary Commission*, pp 140–9.
38 Rankin, 'County Armagh', pp 954–5 for the detail of Armagh maps and NEBB memorandum, 23 May 1922.
39 E.M. Stephens memorandum, 22 Dec. 1924 (NAI, NEBB files, TSCH S1801).
40 *PN*, 31 Oct. 1924; *UG*, 1 Nov. 1924; *FS*, 25 Oct. 1924.
41 *FS*, 25 Oct. 1924 (addresses by Mary MacSwiney and Dr J.W. McKee in Derrymacash).
42 Ibid., 12 May 1923; *IN*, 11 May 1923.
43 T.P. O'Connor to Dillon, 14 Aug. 1924 (TCD, Dillon papers, MS 6744/960).
44 The archive of twenty-one submissions and transcripts of evidence sessions from Armagh can be found in TNA, CAB 61 – see https://discovery.nationalarchives.gov.uk/browse/r/h/C386694/last/C386723 (accessed 28 Aug. 2022).
45 Geoffrey Hand (ed.), *Report of the Irish Boundary Commission, 1925* (Shannon, 1969), pp 12, 140–4; K.J. Rankin, 'The role of the Irish boundary commission in the entrenchment of the Irish border: from tactical panacea to political liability', *Journal of Historical Geography*, 34:3 (2008), 430–3.
46 Murray, *Irish Boundary Commission*, pp 134, 202–3.
47 Hand, *Irish Boundary Commission*, p. 146; Rankin, 'Armagh', p. 982.
48 Fisher to Craig, cited in Follis, *State under siege*, p. 164; Fisher to Carson, 18 Oct. 1925, reproduced in Hand, 'MacNeill and the Boundary Commission', p. 274, n. 36.
49 *Dáil Éireann debates*, 7 Dec. 1925, vol. XII, cols 1306–9.
50 *PN*, 11 Dec. 1925.
51 *FS*, 5 Dec. 1925.
52 *BNL*, 8 Dec. 1925.
53 Conor Morrissey, '"Rotten Protestants": Protestant home rulers and the Ulster Liberal Association, 1910–1918', *Historical Journal*, 81:3 (2018), 747, 754; James Loughlin, 'The Irish Protestant Home Rule Association and nationalist politics, 1886–1893', *Irish Historical Studies*, 24:95 (1985), 343–5; *PN*, 7 Feb. 1925; *AG*, 4 May 1923; D.G. Shillington to Craig, 12 Mar. 1922 (PRONI, PM1/55/8990).
54 *NW*, 26 Jan. 1925.
55 CI Armagh, July 1913 (TNA, CO 904/90); *FS*, 23 June 1916.
56 *AG*, 24 Feb. 1923; *PT*, 2 Mar. 1923.
57 *FS*, 31 Mar. 1923.
58 Bew, Gibbon & Patterson, *Northern Ireland 1921–2001*, p. 6.
59 S.G. Tallents, Private notes and diary on Northern Ireland, 1 July 1922 (TNA, CO906/24); Commander, Loughgall B Specials to Spender, 14 Dec. 1925 (PRONI, CAB9/G/26/12).
60 Cabinet conclusions, 17 Dec. 1925 (PRONI, CAB4/157/20); Farrell, *Arming the Protestants*, pp 253–4.
61 Phoenix, *Northern nationalism*, pp 337–61.
62 *FS*, 8 Oct. 1927.
63 Eamon Phoenix, 'Éamon Donnelly (1877–1944): Republican politician and lifelong anti-partitionist' in Newry, Mourne & Down Museum, *The legacy: Newry, 1920–1930* (Newry, 2022), pp 10–15; *FS*, 22 Oct. 1922.

64 Martin O'Donoghue, 'Faith and fatherland?: the Ancient Order of Hibernians, northern nationalism and the partition of Ireland', *Irish Historical Studies*, 169 (2022), 93–7.

65 For the Meigh company see Lewis, *Frank Aiken's war*, p. 199; for the divisional staff see 4th Northern Division HQ (IMA, MSPC, A/51(2), p. 5).

66 File relating to arrest of Jack McIlhaw, 1925 (PRONI, Home Affairs papers, HA5/2558); file relating to Newry IRPDF fund-raising, 1924 (PRONI, Home Affairs secret files, HA/31/ 1/432); Eoin Magennis, 'Sedition in isolation?: Charlie McGleenan and the experience of revolution in north Armagh' in McAnallen (ed.), *Reflections on the revolution in Ulster*, pp 63–4; Kevin Murphy, 'Old men were once young', ibid., p. 116.

67 Peter Boyle (IMA, MSPC, 34REF2016); Frank Monaghan (IMA, MSPC, 34REF17746); Peter Murney to Peadar Barry, 10 Jan. 1939 (IMA, MSPC, RO430). Eiver Monaghan successfully applied (IMA, MSPC, 34REF4051), but, at time of writing, no record has been released relating to Jimmy Goodfellow, Martin O'Donnell or Willie Lawless.

68 John McCoy, Memorandum on interpreting qualifying service, 11 June 1939 (IMA, MSPC, CNM163) cited in Ferriter, *Between two hells*, pp 178–9.

69 Quoted in Coleman, 'Compensating Irish female revolutionaries', 928.

70 Mary Ann McCreesh (IMA, MSPC, 34REF48841); Róisín Ní Bheirne to John McCoy, 28 Nov. 1939 (IMA, MSPC, 34REF2848, pp 73–8).

71 Application of Catherine Moore (IMA, MSPC, DP23924); application of Kate Connolly (IMA, MSPC, DP122); application of Mary Nugent (née Connolly) (IMA, MSPC, DP7503).

72 Letter to the secretary to the referee, 8 Mar. 1941 (IMA, MSPC, A/51/1/1, p. 22); Michael Fearon to same, 6 May 1940 (IMA, MSPC, A/51/2/4, pp 2–3).

73 Cited in Ó Caoimh, *Richard Mulcahy*, p. 90.

74 Aiken to Molly Childers, 18 Apr. 1924 (TCD, Childers papers, MS 7487/14).

Select bibliography

PRIMARY SOURCES

MANUSCRIPTS

Armagh
Cardinal Tomás Ó Fiaich Memorial Library and Archive
Michael Logue papers
Patrick O'Donnell papers
Louis O'Kane recorded interviews

Armagh County Museum
Ulster Volunteer Force, County Armagh regiment papers

Belfast
Public Record Office of Northern Ireland
Absent Voters Lists for Armagh Constituencies, 1918
H.B. Armstrong papers
Best & Gillespie Solicitors papers
Cabinet papers
Sir Edward Carson papers
Sir Ernest Clark papers
J.H. Collins papers
Adam Duffin papers
Cahir Healy papers
Sir Shane Leslie papers
Ministry of Finance papers
Ministry of Home Affairs papers
Ministry of Home Affairs, secret series
Montgomery-De Fellenburg papers
J.E. Peel papers
Prime Ministers' papers
Ulster Unionist Council papers
Ulster Volunteer Force, 1st Battalion Armagh papers
John Webster papers

Cork
Cork Public Museum
Tomás MacCurtain papers

Dublin

Irish Military Archives
BMH Contemporary documents
BMH Witness statements
Brigade activity reports
Civil War prisoners series
Michael Collins papers
Cumann na mBan nominal rolls
Evacuation papers
Liaison papers
IRA nominal rolls
Military Service Pensions Collection

Kilmainham Gaol Archives
McCann Cell collection
Pádraig Quinn memoir

National Archives of Ireland
Chief Secretary's Office Registered Papers
Dáil Éireann records
Department of the Taoiseach records
North-Eastern Boundary Bureau files

National Library of Ireland
Robert Barton papers
Piaras Béaslaí papers
Éamonn Ceannt papers
George Gavan Duffy papers
Irish National Aid & Volunteer Dependants' Fund papers
Maurice Moore papers
Florrie O'Donoghue papers
Count Plunkett papers
John Redmond papers
Sinn Féin Standing Committee minute book
United Irish League National Directory minute book

Trinity College, Dublin
Ernest & Molly Childers papers
John Dillon papers

UCD Archives
Frank Aiken papers
Ernest Blythe papers
Éamon de Valera papers
Richard Mulcahy papers
Ernie O'Malley interview notebooks
Moss Twomey papers

Dundalk
Louth County Archives
Dundalk gaol register

London
National Archives
Boundary Commission papers
Cabinet Office papers
Colonial Office papers
War Office papers

Newry
Newry & Mourne Museum
Éamon Donnelly papers

B. OFFICIAL RECORDS

Census of Ireland 1911.
Dáil Éireann debates.
Department of Agriculture and Technical Instruction for Ireland, *Agricultural Statistics 1913* (Dublin, 1913).
Irish Police Committee, *Royal Irish Constabulary and Dublin Metropolitan Police, Report of the Committee of Enquiry 1914*, Appendix VIII (London, 1914) (Cd. 7421).
Royal Irish Constabulary List and Directory, January 1914 (Dublin, 1914).
General Prisons Board, Ireland Thirty-Fourth report, 1911–1912 (Dublin, 1912).
Commissioners of National Education in Ireland, Seventy-Seventh Report 1910–1911: Section 3 (Dublin, 1912).

C. NEWSPAPERS AND PERIODICALS

Armagh Guardian
Belfast News-Letter
Church of Ireland Gazette
Cork Examiner
Daily Mirror
Daily News
Dundalk Democrat
Éire: the Irish Nation
Freeman's Journal
Frontier Sentinel
Illustrated London News
Iris an Airm
Irish Catholic Directory
Irish Citizen
Irish Independent
Irish News
Irish Times

Irish Worker
Kerry Sentinel
Lurgan Mail
Lurgan Times
Meath Chronicle
Nationality
Newry Reporter
North Down Herald and County Down Independent
Northern Whig
Pall Mall Gazette
Portadown News
Portadown Times
Scotsman
Sunday Mirror
Ulster Gazette

D. CONTEMPORANEOUS MATERIAL

Adgey, R. J., *Arming the Ulster Volunteers 1914* (Belfast, n.d.).

Bateman, John, *Great landowners of Great Britain and Ireland* (1876, reprinted Leicester, 1971).

Collins, Michael, *The path to freedom* (Cork, 2011 [1922]).

County Armagh Grand Orange Lodge, *Annual Report, 1911* (Belfast, 1912).

Hand, Geoffrey, *Report of the Irish Boundary Commission, 1925* (Shannon, 1969).

Keegan, Owen, *Attack on Dundalk, July 1922* (CLAHS, 2022).

Mac Giolla Choille, Breandán (ed.), *Intelligence notes, 1913–16* (Dublin, 1966).

SECONDARY SOURCES

E. PUBLISHED WORKS

Abbott, Richard, *Police casualties in Ireland* (Cork, 2000).

Aiken, Síobhra, Fearghal Mac Bhloscaidh, Liam Ó Duibhir & Diarmuid Ó Tuama (eds), *The men will talk to me: Ernie O'Malley's interviews with the northern divisions* (Newbridge, 2018).

Andrews, T.S., *Dublin made me* (Dublin, 2001 [1979]).

Augusteijn, Joost, *From public defiance to guerrilla warfare: the experience of ordinary Volunteers in the Irish War of Independence, 1916–1921* (Dublin, 1996).

Bardon, Jonathan, '"Grotesque proceedings?": localized responses to the Home Rule question in Ulster' in Gabriel Doherty (ed.), *The home rule crisis, 1912–1914* (Cork, 2014), pp 276–303.

Bartlett, Thomas, 'When histories collide: the third home rule bill for Ireland' in Gabriel Doherty (ed.), *The home rule crisis, 1912–1914* (Cork, 2014), pp 22–35.

Bew, Paul, *Ideology and the Irish question: Ulster unionism and Irish nationalism, 1912–1916* (Oxford, 1994).

——, Peter Gibbon & Henry Patterson, *Northern Ireland, 1921–2001: political forces and social classes* (London, 2002 edn).

Blackstock, Allan & Frank O'Gorman (eds), *Loyalism and the formation of the British world* (Woodbridge, 2014).

Borgonovo, John, '"Army without banners": the Irish Republican Army, 1920–1921' in John Crowley, Donal Ó Drisceoil, Mike Murphy & John Borgonovo (eds), *Atlas of the Irish Revolution* (Cork, 2017), pp 390–9.

Bourke, Cormac, *Patrick: the archaeology of a saint* (Belfast, 1993).

Bowman, John, *De Valera and the Ulster question, 1917–1973* (Oxford, 1982).

Bowman, Timothy, 'The North began … but when?: the formation of the Ulster Volunteer Force', *History Ireland*, 20:2 (Mar./Apr. 2013), 28–31.

——, *Carson's army: the Ulster Volunteer Force, 1910–22* (Manchester, 2017).

——, William Butler & Michael Wheatley, *The disparity of sacrifice: Irish recruitment to the British armed forces* (Manchester, 2020).

Bradley, John, 'The Richardsons of Bessbrook: a Quaker linen family', *Seanchas Ard Mhacha*, 22:2 (2009), 159–91.

Buckland, Patrick, *Irish unionism II: Ulster unionism and the origins of Northern Ireland* (Dublin, 1972).

Burnett, David, 'The modernisation of Ulster unionism, 1892–1914' in Richard English & Graham Walker (eds), *Unionism in modern Ireland* (Houndsmills, 1996), pp 41–63.

Callinan, Elaine, *Electioneering and propaganda in Ireland, 1917–1921* (Dublin, 2020).

Callinan, Frank, *T.M. Healy* (Cork, 1996).

Clarkson, L.A., 'Armagh town in the eighteenth century' in Brenda Collins, Philip Ollerenshaw & Trevor Parkhill (eds), *Industry, trade and people in Ireland, 1650–1950: essays in honour of W.H. Crawford* (Belfast, 2005), pp 51–68.

Coleman, Marie, 'Compensating Irish female revolutionaries, 1916–1923', *Women's History Review*, 26:6 (2016), 915–34.

——, 'Cumann na mBan in the War of Independence' in Crowley et al. (eds), *Atlas of the Irish Revolution* (Cork, 2017), pp 400–8.

Connolly, Linda, 'Towards a further understanding of the sexual and gender-based violence women experienced in the Irish Revolution' in idem (ed.), *Women in the Irish Revolution* (Newbridge, 2020), pp 103–28.

——, 'Sexual violence in the Irish Civil War: a forgotten war crime?', *Women's History Review*, 30:1 (2021), 126–43.

Cousins, Colin, *Armagh and the Great War* (Dublin, 2010).

Cousins, James A., *Without a dog's chance: the nationalists of Northern Ireland and the Irish Boundary Commission, 1920–25* (Newbridge, 2020).

Crawford, W.H., 'Evolution of towns in County Armagh' in A.J. Hughes & William Nolan (eds), *Armagh: history and society. Interdisciplinary essays on the history of an Irish county* (Dublin, 2001), pp 851–80.

Cronin, Maura, *Agrarian protest in Ireland, 1750–1960* (Dundalk, 2012).

de Bromhead, Alan, Alan Fernihough & Enda Hargaden, 'Representation of the people: franchise extension and the "Sinn Fein Election" in 1918', *Journal of Economic History*, 80:3 (2020), 886–925.

Dolan, Anne & William Murphy, *Michael Collins: the man and the revolution* (Cork, 2018).

Dolan, Anne, *Commemorating the Irish Civil War* (Cambridge, 2003).

——, 'The British culture of paramilitary violence in the Irish War of Independence' in Robert Gerwarth & John Horne (eds), *War in peace: paramilitary violence in Europe after the Great War* (Oxford, 2012), pp 200–15.

——, 'Death in the archives: witnessing war in Ireland, 1919–1921', *Past & Present*, 253:1 (2021), 271–300.

Doherty, Erica, '"The party hack, and tool of the British government": T.P. O'Connor, America and Irish Party resilience in the February 1918 South Armagh by-election', *Parliamentary History*, 34:3 (2015), 339–64.

Dooley, Terence, *The plight of Monaghan Protestants, 1912–1926* (Dublin, 2000).

——, *Monaghan: the Irish Revolution, 1912–23* (Dublin, 2016).

Fanning, Ronan, *Fatal path: British government and Irish Revolution, 1910–1922* (London, 2013).

Farrell, Elaine, *Women, crime and punishment in Ireland: life in the nineteenth-century convict prison* (Cambridge, 2020).

Farrell, Michael, *Arming the Protestants: the formation of the Ulster Special Constabulary and the Royal Ulster Constabulary, 1920–27* (London, 1983).

Feeney, Brian, *Antrim: the Irish Revolution, 1912–1923* (Dublin, 2021).

Ferriter, Diarmaid, *A nation and not a rabble: the Irish Revolution, 1912–23* (London, 2015).

——, *Between two hells: the Irish Civil War* (London, 2022).

Fitzgerald, Desmond, 'Michael Collins in Armagh', *History Armagh* (2011), 7–11.

Fitzpatrick, David, *The two Irelands, 1912–1939* (Oxford, 1998).

——, 'The Orange Order and the border', *Irish Historical Studies*, 129 (2002), 52–67.

——, *Harry Boland's Irish Revolution* (Cork, 2004).

——, *Descendancy: Irish Protestant histories since 1795* (Cambridge, 2014).

Follis, Bryan A., *A state under siege: the establishment of Northern Ireland, 1920–1925* (Oxford, 1995).

Fraser, Lovat, *Lovat Fraser's tour of Ireland in 1913: an event within the home rule conflict* (Belfast, 1992).

Garvin, Tom, *The evolution of Irish nationalist politics* (Dublin, 2005 [1981]).

Geraghty, Peter, 'John James O'Hanlon: a forgotten Irish sporting hero', *Seanchas Ard Mhacha*, 26:1 (2016), 168–202.

Greiff, Mats, 'Industrial struggles and trades unions among female linen workers in Belfast and Lurgan, 1872–1910', *Saothar*, 22 (1997), 29–44.

Grob-Fitzgibbon, Benjamin, 'Neglected intelligence: how the British government failed to quell the Ulster Volunteer Force, 1912–1914', *Journal of Intelligence History*, 6:1 (2006), 1–23.

Hall, Donal, 'The Louth Militia mutiny of 1900', *Journal of the County Louth Archaeological and Historical Society*, 24:2 (1998), 281–95.

——, *Louth: the Irish Revolution, 1912–23* (Dublin, 2019).

Hall, Donal & Lorraine McCann, *'Hole in the Wall': Dundalk jail during the Civil War* (Dundalk, 2022).

Hand, Geoffrey, 'MacNeill and the Boundary Commission' in F.X. Martin & F.J. Byrne (eds), *The scholar revolutionary: Eoin MacNeill and the making of the new Ireland, 1867–1945* (Shannon, 1973), pp 199–275.

Hay, Marnie, 'The foundation and development of Na Fianna Éireann, 1909–1916', *Irish Historical Studies*, 136 (2008), 53–71.

Hennessey, Thomas, *Dividing Ireland: World War 1 and partition* (New York, 1998).

Hepburn, A.C., 'Irish nationalism in Ulster, 1885–1921' in D. George Boyce & Alan O'Day (eds), *The Ulster crisis, 1885–1921* (Basingstoke, 2006), pp 151–78.

——, *Catholic Belfast and nationalist Ireland in the era of Joe Devlin, 1871–1934* (Oxford, 2008).

Holmes, Andrew R., 'Presbyterians, loyalty and Orangeism in nineteenth-century Ulster' in Allan Blackstock & Frank O'Gorman (eds), *Loyalism and the formation of the British world* (Woodbridge, 2014), pp 125–44.

Hopkinson, Michael, *Green against green: the Irish Civil War* (Dublin, 2004 [1988]).

——, 'The Collins–Craig pacts of 1922: two attempted reforms of the Northern Ireland government', *Irish Historical Studies*, 106 (1990), 145–58.

——, *The Irish War of Independence* (Dublin, 2002).

Hughes, Brian, *Defying the IRA? intimidation, coercion and communities during the Irish Revolution* (Liverpool, 2016).

Hunt, Tom, 'The diverse origins and activities of early GAA clubs' in Dónal McAnallen, David Hassan & Roddy Hegarty (eds), *The evolution of the GAA: Ulaidh, Éire agus eile* (Belfast, 2009), pp 86–99.

Hunter, R.J., 'County Armagh: a map of plantation, *c.*1610' in A.J. Hughes & William Nolan (eds), *Armagh: history and society. Interdisciplinary essays on the history of an Irish county* (Dublin, 2001), pp 265–94.

Inoue, Keiko, 'Sinn Féin propaganda and the "partition election", 1921', *Studia Hibernica*, 30 (1998/1999), 47–61.

Jackson, Alvin, 'Irish unionism and the Russellite threat, 1894–1906', *Irish Historical Studies*, 100 (1987), 376–404.

——, *The Ulster Party: Irish Unionists in the House of Commons, 1884–1911* (Oxford, 1989).

——, 'Unionist politics and Protestant society in Edwardian Ireland', *Historical Journal*, 33:4 (1990), 839–86.

——, 'The Larne gun running of 1914', *History Ireland*, 1:1 (1993), 28–32.

——, *Colonel Edward Saunderson: land and loyalty in Victorian Ireland* (Oxford, 1995).

——, 'Irish Unionism, 1870–1922' in D. George Boyce & Alan O'Day (eds), *Defenders of the Union* (London, 2001), pp 58–77.

——, *Judging Redmond and Carson* (Dublin, 2017).

——, 'Origins, culture and politics of Irish unionism' in Thomas Bartlett (ed.), *The Cambridge history of Ireland*, iv (Cambridge, 2018), 89–116.

Jefferies, Henry A., *Priests and prelates of Armagh in the age of reformations, 1518–1558* (Dublin, 1997).

Jupp, P.J. & Eoin Magennis (eds), *Crowds in Ireland, 1720–1920* (London, 2000).

Kane, James, 'The arms raid on the Cope family residence at Drumilly, Loughgall in August 1919', *Dúiche Néill*, 23 (2016), 229–40.

Kelly, Matthew J., *The Fenian ideal and Irish nationalists, 1882–1916* (Woodbridge, 2006).

Kleinrichert, Denise, *Republican internment and the prison ship Argenta, 1922* (Dublin, 2001).

Laffan, Michael, *The resurrection of Ireland: the Sinn Féin party, 1916–23* (Cambridge, 1999).

Leary, Peter, *Unapproved routes: histories of the Irish border, 1922–1972* (Oxford, 2016).

Lewis, Geoffrey, *Carson: the man who divided Ireland* (London, 2006).

Lewis, Matthew, 'The Newry Brigade and the War of Independence, 1919–1921', *Irish Sword*, 108 (2010), 225–32.

——, 'The Fourth Northern Division and the joint-IRA offensive, April–July 1922', *War in History*, 21:3 (2013), 1–20.

——, *Frank Aiken's war: the Irish Revolution, 1916–23* (Dublin, 2014).

——, 'Sectarianism and Irish republican violence on the south-east Ulster frontier, 1919–1922', *Contemporary European History*, 26:1 (2017), 1–21.

Loughlin, James, 'The Irish Protestant Home Rule Association and nationalist politics, 1886–1893', *Irish Historical Studies*, 24:95 (1985), 341–60.

——, 'Creating "a social and geographical fact": regional identity and the Ulster question', *Past & Present*, 195 (2007), 159–96.

Lynch, Robert, *The Northern IRA and the early years of partition, 1920–1922* (Dublin, 2006).

——, 'Explaining the Altnaveigh massacre', *Éire–Ireland*, 45:3&4 (2010), 184–210.

——, *The partition of Ireland, 1918–25* (Cambridge, 2019).

Mac Eoin, Uinseann, *Survivors* (Dublin, 1980).

MacMillan, Margaret, *The war that ended peace* (London, 2013).

Magill, Christopher, *Political conflict in east Ulster: revolution and reprisal, 1920–1922* (Woodbridge, 2020).

Maguire, Martin, 'Labour in county Louth, 1912–1923' in Donal Hall & Martin Maguire (eds), *County Louth and the Irish Revolution, 1912–1923* (Newbridge, 2017), pp 59–85.

Magennis, Eoin, 'Sedition in isolation?: Charlie McGleenan and the experience of revolution in north Armagh' in Dónal McAnallen (ed.), *Reflections on the revolution in Ulster: excerpts from Rev. Louis O'Kane's recordings of Irish Volunteers* (Armagh, 2016), pp 52–66.

Martin, F.X. (ed.), *The Irish Volunteers, 1913–1915* (Dublin, 1963).

Matthews, Kevin, *Fatal influence: the impact of Ireland on British politics, 1920–1925* (Dublin, 2004).

Maume, Patrick, *The long gestation: Irish nationalist life, 1891–1918* (London, 1999).

——, 'The *Irish Independent* and the Ulster crisis, 1912–1921' in D. George Boyce & Alan O'Day (eds), *The Ulster crisis, 1885–1921* (Basingstoke, 2006), pp 182–98.

——, Unionists and patriots: James Whiteside and the dilemmas of the Protestant nation in Victorian Ireland' in Allan Blackstock & Frank O'Gorman (eds), *Loyalism and the formation of the British world* (Woodbridge, 2014), pp 145–62.

McAuliffe, Mary, 'Gendered violence against women' in Darragh Gannon & Fearghal McGarry (eds), *Ireland 1922: independence, partition, civil war* (Dublin, 2022), pp 136–41.

McCluskey, Fergal, 'Fenians, ribbonmen and popular ideology's role in nationalist politics: east Tyrone, 1906–9', *Irish Historical Studies*, 145 (2010), 61–82.

——, *Fenians and ribbonmen: the development of republican politics in east Tyrone, 1898–1918* (Manchester, 2011).

——, *Tyrone: the Irish Revolution, 1912–23* (Dublin, 2014).

McConnel, James, *Irish Parliamentary Party and the third home rule crisis* (Dublin, 2013).

McConville, Seán, *Irish political prisoners, 1920–62: pilgrimage of desolation* (London, 2014).

McDowell, R.B., *The Irish Convention, 1917–18* (London, 1970).

McGarry, Fearghal, *Eoin O'Duffy: a self-made hero* (Oxford, 2005)

McGee, Owen, *The Irish Republican Brotherhood from the Land League to Sinn Féin* (Dublin, 2005).

McGinn, Phil, *Armagh Harps GFC: celebrating 120 years* (Armagh, 2008).

McGuinness, Siobhán, 'The February 1918 by-election in South Armagh', *Creggan*, 6 (1992), 59–79.

McIntosh, Gillian, *The force of culture: unionist identities in twentieth-century Ireland* (Cork, 1999).

McMahon, Kevin & Éamonn Ó hUallacháin (eds), *The time of trouble: a chronology of the Anglo-Irish and Civil wars in Armagh, south Down and north Louth* (Dundalk, 2014).

McVeigh, Mary, 'Votes for women: the Armagh campaign', *History Armagh*, 1:2 (2005), 6–10.

Morgan, Austen, *Labour and partition* (London, 1991).

Morrissey, Conor, '"Rotten Protestants": Protestant home rulers and the Ulster Liberal Association, 1910–1918', *Historical Journal*, 81:3 (2018), 743–65.

Mulholland, Ciaran & Anton McCabe, 'Red flag over the asylum: the story of the Monaghan soviet, 1919' in Pauline Prior (ed.), *Asylums, mental health care and the Irish, 1800–2010* (Dublin, 2012), pp 93–114.

Murphy, Kevin, 'Old men were once young: reflections of south Armagh in the O'Kane recordings' in Dónal McAnallen (ed.), *Reflections on the revolution in Ulster: excerpts from Rev. Louis O'Kane's recordings of Irish Volunteers* (Armagh, 2016), pp 101–18.

——, 'Michael Donnelly of Carnally: a revolutionary journey', *Creggan*, 18 (2018), 41–58.

Murray, Paul, *The Irish Boundary Commission and its origins, 1886–1925* (Dublin, 2011).

Nash, Catherine, Lorraine Dennis & Brian Graham, 'Putting the border in place: customs regulation in the making of the Irish border, 1921–1945', *Journal of Historical Geography*, 36:4 (2010), 421–31.

Ní Uallacháin, Pádraigín, *A hidden Ulster: people, songs and traditions of Oriel* (Dublin, 2003).

Nic Dháibhéid, Caoimhe, 'The Irish National Aid Association and the radicalisation of public opinion in Ireland, 1916–1918', *The Historical Journal*, 55:3 (2012), 705–29.

Norton, Christopher, *The politics of constitutional nationalism in Northern Ireland, 1932–1970* (Manchester, 2014).

Ó Caoimh, Pádraig, *Richard Mulcahy: from the politics of war to the politics of peace, 1913–1924* (Newbridge, 2019).

O'Connor, Emmet, *Derry Labour in the age of agitation, 1889–1923: Larkinism and syndicalism* (Dublin, 2016).

Ó Corráin, Daithí, '"A most public-spirited and unselfish man": the career and contribution of Colonel Maurice Moore, 1854–1939', *Studia Hibernica*, 40 (2014), 71–133.

O'Donoghue, Martin, 'Faith and fatherland?: the Ancient Order of Hibernians, northern nationalism and the partition of Ireland', *Irish Historical Studies*, 46:169 (2022), 77–100.

O'Donovan, John, 'The All-for-Ireland League and the home rule debate, 1910–1914' in Gabriel Doherty (ed.), *Home rule crisis, 1912–1914* (Cork, 2014), pp 138–63.

ÓFathartaigh, Mícheál & Liam Weeks, *Birth of a state: the Anglo-Irish Treaty* (Newbridge, 2021).

Ó Gráda, Cormac, 'Economic status, religion and demography in an Ulster town [Lurgan] in the early twentieth century', *Journal of the History of the Family*, 13:4 (2008), 350–9.

O'Halpin, Eunan & Daithí Ó Corráin, *The dead of the Irish Revolution* (New Haven and London, 2020).

Ó hUallacháin, Éamonn, 'Sinn Féin in Cullyhanna (1916–1921)', *Creggan*, 18 (2018), 59–65.

Parkinson, Alan, *Friends in high places* (Belfast, 2012).

——, *A difficult birth: the early years of Northern Ireland, 1920–25* (Dublin, 2020).

Pašeta, Senia, *Irish nationalist women, 1900–1918* (Oxford, 2013).

Phoenix, Eamon, *Northern nationalism, nationalist politics, partition and the Catholic minority in Northern Ireland, 1890–1940* (Belfast, 1994).

——, 'Michael Collins and the Northern question, 1916–22' in Gabriel Doherty & Dermot Keogh (eds), *Michael Collins and the making of the Irish state* (Cork, 1998), pp 92–116.

——, 'Éamon Donnelly (1877–1944): Republican politician and lifelong anti-partitionist' in Newry, Mourne & Down Museum, *The legacy: Newry, 1920–1930* (Newry, 2022).

Privilege, John, *Michael Logue and the Catholic Church in Ireland, 1879–1925* (Manchester, 2009).

Purdue, Olwen, *The MacGeough Bonds of the Argory: an Ulster gentry family, 1850–1950* (Dublin, 2005).

——, *The big house in the north of Ireland, 1878–1960* (Dublin, 2009).

——, '"The price of our loyalty": Ulster landlords, tenants and the Northern Ireland land act of 1925' in Annie Tindley, Shaun Evans & Tony McCarthy (eds), *Land reform in the British and Irish isles since 1800* (Edinburgh, 2022), pp 211–36.

Rafferty, Oliver P., 'Catholic chaplains to the British forces in the First World War' in Oliver P. Rafferty, *Violence, politics and Catholicism in Ireland* (Dublin, 2016), pp 134–62.

——, 'Catholic Church and the Easter Rising', *Studies*, 105:417 (2016), pp 47–57.

Rankin, K.J., 'County Armagh and the Boundary Commission' in A.J. Hughes & William Nolan (eds), *Armagh: history and society. Interdisciplinary essays on the history of an Irish county* (Dublin, 2001), pp 947–90.

Rast, M.C., 'Ulster unionists "on Velvet": home rule and partition in the Lloyd George proposals', *American Journal of Irish Studies*, 14 (2017), 113–38.

Richardson, Neil, *According to their lights: stories of Irishmen in the British army, Easter 1916* (Cork, 2015).

Ryan, Louise 'Splendidly silent: representing Irish republican women, 1919–1923' in Ann-Marie Gallagher, Cathy Lubelska & Louise Ryan (eds), *Re-presenting the past: women in history* (Routledge, 2001), pp 23–43.

Rouse, Paul, *Sport and Ireland: a history* (Oxford, 2015).

Scholes, Andrew, *The Church of Ireland and the third home rule bill* (Dublin, 2010).

Short, Con, Jimmy Smyth & Peter Murray, *Ard Mhacha, 1884–1984: a century of GAA progress* (Armagh, 1985).

Stewart, A.T.Q., *The Ulster crisis, 1912–1914* (London, 1967).

Taaffe, Patrick, 'Richard Mulcahy and the genesis of the Civil War', *Irish Sword*, 118 (2014), 437–58.

Thompson, Frank, 'The Armagh elections of 1885–6', *Seanchas Ard Mhacha*, 8:2 (1977), 360–85.

Townshend, Charles, 'The Irish Republican Army and the development of guerrilla warfare, 1916–21, *English Historical Review*, 94 (1979), 318–45.

——, *Political violence in Ireland: government and resistance since 1848* (Oxford, 1983).

——, *The Republic: the fight for Irish independence* (London, 2013).

——, *The partition: Ireland divided, 1885–1925* (London, 2021).

Travers, Pauric, 'The priests in politics: the case of conscription' in Oliver MacDonagh, W.F. Mandle & Pauric Travers (eds), *Irish culture and nationalism, 1750–1950* (Dublin, 1983), pp 145–63.

——, The conscription crisis and the general election of 1918' in Crowley et al. (eds), *Atlas of the Irish Revolution* (Cork, 2017), pp 323–9.

Urquhart, Diane, *Women in Ulster politics, 1890–1940* (Dublin, 2000).

Valiulis, Maryann Gialanella, *Portrait of a revolutionary: General Richard Mulcahy and the founding of the Irish Free State* (Newbridge, 1992).

Villiers, Eric, 'Commemorative postcards celebrate penalty king', *History Armagh*, 4 (2007), 8–10.

Walker, Brian M., *Parliamentary election results in Ireland, 1801–1922* (Dublin, 1978).

——, 'Actions and views: J.B. Lonsdale, Unionist MP, 1900–1918 and party leader, 1916–1918' in D. George Boyce & Alan O'Day (eds), *The Ulster crisis, 1885–1921* (Basingstoke, 2006), pp 128–45.

Ward, Alan J., 'Lloyd George and the 1918 Irish conscription crisis', *Historical Journal*, 17:1 (1974), 107–29.

Weir, Brian, 'Armagh Cricket Club', *History Armagh*, 4:2 (2018), 31–3.

Wheatley, Michael, *Nationalism and the Irish Party: provincial Ireland, 1900–1916* (Oxford, 2005).

——, '"Ireland is out for Blood and Murder": nationalist opinion and the Ulster crisis in provincial Ireland, 1913–1914' in D. George Boyce & Alan O'Day (eds), *The Ulster crisis, 1885–1921* (Basingstoke, 2006), pp 205–18.

Woods, Damian, 'Dr Patrick McCartan of Carrickmore and Easter 1916 in County Tyrone', *Seanchas Ard Mhacha*, 26: 1 (2016), 1–42.

F. THESES AND UNPUBLISHED WORK

Cosgrove, Patrick Joseph, 'The Wyndham Land Act, 1903: a final solution to the Irish land question?' (PhD, NUI Maynooth, 2008).

Day, Charles, 'Political violence in the Newry/Armagh area, 1912–1925' (PhD, Queen's University, Belfast, 1999).

Evans, Gary, 'The raising of the first internal Dáil Éireann loan and the British responses to it' (MLitt, NUI Maynooth, 2012).

Hall, Donal, 'Violence and political factionalism in north Louth, 1874–1943' (PhD, NUI Maynooth, 2009).

Magennis, Eoin & Lesa Ní Mhunghaile, 'Class and gender in the Irish Revolution in the north east: the case of Nano Aiken' (unpublished conference paper, NUI Galway, 16 Nov. 2019).

McCurdy, Daniel, 'The Ancient Order of Hibernians in Ulster, 1905–1918' (PhD, Ulster University, 2019).

Newman, Seán Bernard, 'For God, Ulster and the "B men": the Ulsterian revolution, the foundation of Northern Ireland and creation of the Ulster Special Constabulary, 1910–1927' (PhD, University of London, 2020).

O'Callaghan, Margaret, 'Democratisation and polarisation in Ireland: the Covenant and the third home rule bill' (unpublished conference paper for Institute of British-Irish Studies, 22 Sept. 2012).

Wilson, Tim, '"The widening gyre": the Altnaveigh killings in context' (unpublished paper delivered to Louth County Council 'Border 100' seminar series, 27 Oct. 2021).

G. INTERNET SOURCES

Dictionary of Irish Biography Online
Irish Historical Mapping Tool for County Armagh at http://airo.maynoothuniversity.ie/
Ulster Covenant online PRONI: https://www.nidirect.gov.uk/services/search-ulster-covenant
Escapees from Dundalk jail, 1922.
https://www.louthcoco.ie/en/services/archives/louth-1916–1923/dundalk-jail-1916–1923.html

H. DOCUMENTARIES

Frank Aiken: From Gunman to Statesman (Mint Productions 'Hidden History' documentary for RTÉ Television, 2006)

Index